D1192227

THE KING'S MESSENGERS, 1199–1377

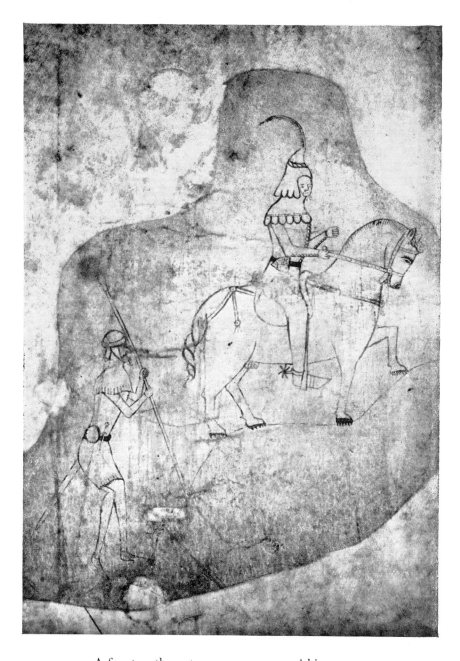

A fourteenth century messenger and his groom

From a drawing on the inside cover of a book of messengers' expenses in 1360 (E.A. 309/11)

THE KING'S MESSENGERS

1199–1377

*A Contribution to the History
of the Royal Household*

By

MARY C. HILL, M.A.
County Archivist, Shropshire

LONDON
EDWARD ARNOLD (PUBLISHERS) LTD

*This book has been published with the help of
a grant from the Isobel Thornley Bequest*

PRINTED IN GREAT BRITAIN
BY W. & J. MACKAY & CO. LTD., CHATHAM

PREFACE

This book is based on a thesis presented for an M.A. degree of the University of London.

A work founded on many brief scraps of information from records as formal as royal orders and accounts cannot hope to be easy reading, however presented, and will not convey to a reader much of the pleasure that discovering and assembling the facts gave the writer. It is offered as a contribution to administrative history, adding detail to a picture already drawn in broad outline by others; and as an account of the social life and status of some of the king's humble but quite indispensable servants.

My grateful thanks are due to the Governors of Royal Holloway College for the post-graduate and Christie studentships which allowed me to do the original research, and to the University for the grant which now makes possible publication of the results.

MARY C. HILL

CONTENTS

THE KING'S MESSENGERS, 1199-1377

INTRODUCTION

Materials and Aims

1

IN spite of the amount of work already done on the administrative development of the royal household, comparatively little has yet been written about its domestic aspects. When Professor Tout in his *Chapters in the Administrative History of Medieval England* described the functions of the wardrobe and the chamber, he discussed very fully the household ordinances of the period; but a complete survey of domestic life in the household was outside the scope of his inquiry. Still less could he deal with any one branch of the household in detail. Introductions to printed household accounts and articles based on this material have scarcely touched the subject except on specific points such as the almoner's activities. Nor have the king's messengers been more fortunate. A little has been written about the delivery of royal letters and writs, and some slight attention has been paid to the messenger on the road, but rather as one among many interesting wayfarers than as a centre of interest in himself. Some light is thrown on the messengers, again, by the fifteenth century writer on heraldry, Nicholas Upton: he saw them as the lowest grade of heraldic messenger, above whom stood the pursuivants and the heralds at arms. No writer, from the fifteenth century to the present day, has concerned himself directly with the medieval king's messengers; and their modern counterparts have fared little better. When a bibliography of works relating to the Foreign Office was prepared by Tilley and Gaselee in 1933, they could find nothing beyond personal memoirs to place under the heading 'king's messengers'. This gap was partly filled in 1935 by the publication of Wheeler-Holohan's *History of the King's Messengers*; but the emphasis was still on feats of travel, and little attention was given to any period before the Restoration. An extensive search through periodicals and bibliographies did not discover any work bearing directly, either upon the messenger service and its relations with other branches of the household, or upon the domestic side of the household generally. The subject seems to have been passed over by historians as needing no explanation. A description of the organization of the messengers and their place in the thirteenth and fourteenth century household must be based entirely upon original sources.

The sources available for this detailed study are, first, wardrobe accounts, summarized and enrolled until 1324 in the pipe roll or chancellor's roll, and thereafter on the rolls of the lord treasurer's remembrancer. These give the bare total of wardrobe expenditure upon messengers during any given year. For details of those expenses, there are the full accounts, listed in the Public Record Office Lists and Indexes No. XXXV under the headings 'Wardrobe and Household', and *Nuncii*. Wardrobe accounts were usually kept by the king's remembrancer's department, but four are among the books of the treasury of receipt; and some odd documents have been placed among bundles 3 and 4 of chancery miscellanea. A few complete wardrobe accounts have escaped from official custody and are now in the British Museum, the John Rylands Library, the Library of the Society of Antiquaries, or the Bodleian. One wardrobe book only has been printed in full. This is the *Liber Quotidianus Gardrobe* for 1299–1300. Selections from others have been published in *Archaeologia* and elsewhere, but these extracts were not chosen to illustrate household organization, and are too slight to have much importance.

In order to present a full account to the exchequer every year, wardrobe clerks kept many subsidiary lists of messengers sent out; they also kept the particulars showing the extra expenditure of messengers who had been abroad. Similar particulars were returned by diplomatic envoys too, and this is why the Rev. Joseph Hunter in 1837, when sorting ancient miscellanea, classified under the misleading heading '*nuncii*' accounts of regular as well as special messengers. His artificial category includes some wardrobe memoranda of messengers dispatched, a few expense claims of regular messengers, and a great many particulars of ambassadors' travelling expenses. A confusion has resulted between the ordinary and the diplomatic messenger which was avoided by medieval clerks.

After the wardrobe, exchequer records prove the most valuable source of material, and especially the issue and receipt rolls. As long as the wardrobe flourished, issue rolls (beginning in 1240) dealt only with extraordinary payments to messengers. The effect of the ordinances of 1317 and 1324 was seen in the increasing bulk of the rolls and the number of relevant entries; and finally in 1342, the exchequer took over from the wardrobe complete control of expenditure on messengers. Thus issue rolls grow in importance precisely as wardrobe books dwindle. One complete roll for 1370 and some miscellaneous extracts have been printed. In contrast to the issue rolls, material supplied by receipt rolls was most valuable for the early part of the thirteenth century, when chancery seems to have paid and dispatched messengers, recouping expenditure by means of writs of *liberate*. Two rolls for the reign of John and ten for Henry III have writs of *liberate* endorsed which include payments to messengers. The practice of enrolling writs of *liberate* on the receipt rolls was given up in 1253; but some time before that date, these enrolments ceased to include messenger expenses. Similar writs of *liberate* were entered on some of the early rolls of writs for issues, and in three surviving exchequer '*liberate*' rolls; a very few of the actual writs survive among warrants for issues.

Pipe rolls and memoranda rolls furnish incidental information only. They show allowance being made to the sheriff for payment of pensions from *elemosina constituta*, and confirm close roll entries authorizing such payments. Omission of a recipient's name or transference of the pension to another, indicate presumably the holder's death; and occasionally the memoranda rolls mention the sheriff's failure to pay the pensioner with proper regularity. Here again, the material is most plentiful during the early thirteenth century. Edward I made fewer grants from the established alms than his father, and found pensions for his aged messengers from other sources. In addition to those pipe rolls already printed by the Pipe Roll Society and other bodies, a few memoranda rolls for Henry III's reign, calendared or in full, may be consulted in typescript at the Public Record Office.

Among chancery enrolments, close and patent rolls provide information about royal gifts, and add materials for the careers of individual men. *Liberate* rolls, like the enrolled writs mentioned before, are a valuable source just as long as the chancery paid messengers directly. From 1226–1233, the *liberate* rolls contain numerous writs for messenger expenses; but as the wardrobe's power grew, detailed writs were superseded by general writs to be spent at the discretion of the keeper of the wardrobe. Thus only Volume I of the printed *Calender of Liberate Rolls* gives much relevant information. For the early period, the close rolls of 1204–1227, printed by the Record Commission, are useful to the same degree because here under John were enrolled those writs of *liberate* which during and after Henry III's minority formed a special roll. Two *misae* rolls of current court expenses give welcome information; the first, 1209–1210, was printed by the Record Commission, and the second, 1213–4, by Cole in *Documents Illustrative of English History*.

Accounts, whether of wardrobe, exchequer, or chancery, present one side only of the picture. Some aspects of the life of the household are described most clearly in the household ordinances. The earliest surviving example, for 1279, was printed by Tout in *Chapters in Medieval Administrative History*; more important, as far as the messenger group is concerned, were the ordinances of 1318 and 1323, both printed in *The Place of Edward II in English History*. The ordinances of the exchequer of 1323, 1324 and 1326, printed in *The Red Book of the Exchequer*, provided regulations to govern the advance of journey money to messengers, and subsequent accounting for their actual expenses. Some further idea of the workings of the household may be gained from 'The Household of King Edward III in Peace and War' edited in *A Collection of Ordinances and Regulations for the Government of the Royal Household* by the Society of Antiquaries, though this was no more than a Tudor antiquarian's extracts from wardrobe accounts.[1] In the same volume was also printed the *Liber Niger* of the household of Edward IV and the regulations for Henry VIII's household made at Eltham in 1526; and both these sources, though later than the period considered here, probably contain much reflecting earlier practice. The royal household, like other institutions, clung tenaciously to its own traditions and traditional rights.

Household discipline was mainly the responsibility of the heads of the wardrobe and of the marshal; and it might be supposed that the marshalsea rolls would throw light on this aspect of life at court. A random sample, however, was found to record nothing but cases happening within the verge of the court and therefore brought into the marshal's jurisdiction; and I discovered nothing here about household discipline in general or the messengers in particular.

2

This detailed examination has two objects, first to describe the means of communication available to medieval English kings, and second, to relate the king's messengers to the household of which they formed a part. The importance of a prompt and reliable system of communication to any government has not been sufficiently realized, yet upon it depended the power to enforce the king's justice, demand the king's revenues, and summon the feudal army or the estates of the realm. But whatever formal organization the messenger service had during the thirteenth and fourteenth centuries depended on the organization of the larger entity, the household. Indeed, for a study of the king's household and the various grades of which it was composed, the messenger group seems of all the most suitable. The messengers were few and easily distinguishable, till it is possible from the accounts to reconstruct their careers and say with some precision when many of them joined or left the king's service. The group was compact enough to acquire some vaguely corporate sense; and sufficiently defined to be regarded by wardrobe clerks as a grade or class among household servants. It is easy to pick out and isolate material relating to messengers, for their expenditure on journeys formed a separate item in every full wardrobe account, and was separately accounted for to the exchequer in the enrolled summary. Their relative position remained roughly the same in household lists covering many years. Such a detailed study of one group is the only means of examining the internal workings of the whole household and seeing it, not from the view-point

[1]Tout *Chapters* I, 37.

of the administrative historian, but of its own members. For them, the household was primarily a domestic organism, existing first to serve the king's personal and domestic needs. It is therefore not unimportant to know the conditions under which one group within that organism functioned. Much has been said here of the messengers' wages and allowances, their perquisites and privileges, their treatment in sickness and old age. Most of these arrangements were not peculiar to the messenger service but were general in the household for men of equivalent professional standing. The messengers' duties show the kind of responsibility given to such men. Travelling conditions too were alike for everyone in a household constantly on the move. Methods of recruitment were unlikely to differ widely as between one branch of the lower household and another. In all these points, the messengers were typical and the messenger service a microcosm of the domestic household.

Questions of fact, as to allowances, wages, pensions, and duties, can be answered with a fair degree of certainty. It is not so easy to speak confidently when one comes to inquire what standing the messenger had outside the household, from what ranks of society he was recruited and whether from one area rather than another. To these questions the evidence only allows tentative answers to be given. Nevertheless, the personal status of the king's servants is worth investigation. Dr. Cuttino some time ago called for 'a detailed investigation of the administrative personnel of the English government. We must know not only the offices they filled but also what previous training they had had, where they came from, their social position, and their actual influence on policy';[1] and this, on a restricted scale, is exactly what I have attempted to do for one section of the household. The messengers were part of the administration, for it could not have functioned without them; they also belonged to the king's domestic staff. This dual role they shared with all medieval civil servants from highest to lowest.

All this assumes the existence by the beginning of the thirteenth century of a professional recognized and self-conscious messenger organization in the household available as an instrument of the administration. When I first began to consider the king's messenger service in the Middle Ages, I saw grave danger of reading into the material more than it would warrant. Kings in all ages have needed messengers, but the messenger carrying any given letter for the king might well be any member of his entourage, any tenant who held estates under him, any villein on any royal manor where the king happened to be. It was necessary to establish, first that the words 'king's messenger' had a meaning beyond the sense 'someone sent with a letter by the king'; second, that the messengers (if themselves

[1] *Bulletin of the Institute of Historical Research* 21 No. 63 (1947).

professionals) were also recognized as such in the household and in some degree organized as a group. Thirdly, a distinction had to be found between the messenger who was simply a letter-carrier and the ambassador or envoy who negotiated or at least had dealings with other potentates on the king's behalf. Until these questions were answered satisfactorily, a further inquiry into the nature of that organization and the position of the messengers within the king's household could have no validity.

The evidence on all three points now appears unmistakable. The accounts prove the long-continued service and constant activity on the king's business of all regular messengers. Though yeomen and grooms might and did take out letters, such men never made an important contribution to the medieval postal service; and still less often were outsiders employed. Of neither was the term *nuncius* used. The additional letter-carrier was said to be *in nuncio mittendo* or *eunti in nuncium*. This distinction was pressed to the point of deleting the word *nuncius* after the name of an auxiliary, Roger of Eswell, in a 1265 roll of messenger expenses.[1] The clerk who wrote this account and the auditor who checked it clearly thought the distinction important. By 1299 there is evidence of formal appointment to the post of messenger, and before that time the messenger had become distinguishable from his fellows by the position in which he wore the royal arms. Henry III's retired messengers were sufficiently conscious of their former position to describe themselves as *quondam nuncii regis*;[2] and a man engaged in a private lawsuit gave 'king's messenger' as his professional description.[3] The further distinction, between the regular messenger of the household and the special envoy, is also fully maintained in wardrobe and exchequer accounts. Their expenses were separately presented to the exchequer auditors in the full wardrobe account, and were separately enrolled on the pipe roll summaries. Envoys were generally spoken of as *nuncii sollempnes*, but occasionally the two types were contrasted in the phrases *in expensis minorum nunciorum* and *in maioribus nunciis*[4] which are very reminiscent of the *pro minutis nunciis* and *pro grossis nunciis* used to differentiate the two in France.[5] The word 'gift', which was never used in connexion with a regular messenger's ordinary expenses, was often employed by the wardrobe when paying out money to envoys, implying that such expenditure was not a normal charge on the department and had to be specially authorized. Before the wardrobe took charge of all such

[1] E.A. 308/2. There are other examples.
[2] e.g. John Chubbe in 1258, after he had left the king's service to become a monk. (*Cal. Ch. R.* 1257–1300 p. 5.)
[3] *C.C.R.* 1272–1279 p. 416.
[4] Chancellor's roll No. 28 (1235–6) and Pipe roll No. 79 (enrolled accounts for 1233–6).
[5] See *Les Journaux de Trésor de Philippe VI de Valois suivis de l'Ordinarium Thesauri de 1338–1339* ed. Jules Viard (1899) p. 51.

payments, the cost of messengers and envoys was entered separately on the *liberate* rolls, the expenses of messengers in batches several times a year, those of envoys individually as they occurred. In no type of document or arrangement of documents were they ever confused until the medieval records were re-sorted in the nineteenth century.

The seemingly arbitrary framework of 1199–1377 has been chosen, partly on account of the material available, but chiefly because the thirteenth and fourteenth centuries do constitute one distinct phase in the history of the king's messenger service. It is true that there is little material for studying the life of the household before John's reign, but the little available seems to show that only with the late twelfth century had the household messenger organization developed. Throughout the thirteenth and fourteenth centuries it remained an organized group within the larger organization, drawn in 1234 into the sphere of wardrobe control and remaining there until messenger expenses were removed to the exchequer in 1342. At first this only meant that the messengers drew their journey money and claimed their allowances from a different department, but by 1377 the real effect of the change was becoming apparent in the decay of the household. When Edward III died, the household phase of the messenger service was virtually at an end.

CHAPTER I

THE ORIGIN AND EARLY DEVELOPMENT OF THE MESSENGER SERVICE

THE origin of a messenger group and the form of letter-carrying organization which preceded it, are matters for speculation. The silence of the *Constitutio Domus Regis* as to household messengers certainly implies that Henry I did not need them;[1] and in the undeveloped state of his administration, there was probably no regular work for more than a single messenger at most. By the beginning of the thirteenth century, a vigorous household group was in existence, although a more primitive kind of organization was still available and still used by the exchequer. Finally by the end of that century, the household messenger had supplanted every other type and was the sole agent employed by the crown for the dispatch of documents from all departments of government. Thus the messenger service grew by stages, and its origin was complex, three distinct elements going to its making.

1. The Serjeanty System and the Exchequer

The first element in the early messenger service was a feudal one, and lay altogether outside the household. In a feudal age, it was natural for the king and his tenants in chief to make letter-carrying an obligation attached to the holding of about a virgate of land. According to Bracton, it was not demanded of tenancies worth more than half a mark, and he therefore classed these as petty serjeanties.[2] For a virgate of land, John Hamond was prepared at his own cost to carry his lord's letters whenever his affairs required it for one day.[3] But like most feudal obligations, messenger duties were severely limited in their scope, either as to area, time, or expense. John Hamond would go for one day at his own expense, but farther only at his lord's. A Leicestershire tenant was bound to carry the king's writs over the whole of England, but only for a period of forty days.[4] A Wiltshire tenant carried the king's writs without limit as to time, but only within his own county.[5] Yet when all these limitations are taken into account,

[1] *Red Book of the Exchequer* III, 807–813.
[2] E. G. Kimball *Serjeanty Tenure in Medieval England* p. 83.
[3] *Rot. Hund.* II, 336.
[4] *Book of Fees* p. 1231. This was the only case noticed by Miss Kimball in which a messenger duty covered more than one or two counties.
[5] Assize roll 1006 m. 67.

the serjeanty system could provide a sufficient messenger service for the exchequer, which wanted its summonses taken out promptly twice a year, but had little business to attend to in between sessions.

The key man in the system was the usher of the exchequer. In return for certain fees and lands, he engaged to find two serjeant ushers, enough green wax for the seals, and the services of sufficient messengers to take exchequer writs and summonses throughout England.[1] This arrangement certainly goes back to the time of Henry I.[2] The hereditary usher was in effect a messenger serjeant whose travelling was done by deputies. The fees received by the usher for hiring messengers were calculated at the rate of 3*d.* a day per man for the outward journey only, and estimated to amount to 20*s.* a year. Some ten or a dozen men working several counties each would have been enough to deliver the bags of writs to sheriffs and other royal officers all over England within fifteen days at most. The local messenger serjeant could then be called in to distribute individual summonses either within the county or the honour or to special persons. In Gloucestershire, a virgate of land at Twigworth was charged with payment of 5*s.* and this duty.[3] In the fee of Peverel, one serjeant took the king's writs in the three counties of Leicestershire, Warwickshire and Nottinghamshire north of the Trent.[4] In Herefordshire, the manor of Marden was responsible for summoning certain lords, as well as distraining for the king's debts and conducting his treasure to London.[5] There was no absolute uniformity, but there seems no doubt that every part of the country was covered by this network of duties. When the usher had hired his men twice a year for the routine summonses he could deal with all the other correspondence issuing from the exchequer with the help of a single messenger, for whom the exchequer bought robes once a year, showing that he was on the permanent staff, though indirectly controlled.

It will be seen that this is less 'an immature expression of the household system possessing the fatal weakness of being hereditary'[6] than a completely different system based on hereditary officialdom at the exchequer and hereditary services in the country at large, perfectly well adapted for a feudal age. Although on one occasion the lands of the usher were seized into the king's hand for a trespass,[7] the business of the exchequer in general with its customary ritual does not seem to have been held up at any time because the necessary writs had not gone out. Hereditary ushers or their deputies, and the serjeant ushers under

[1] *C.I.P.M.* II, 317–8; Madox *Exchequer* II, 271–8.
[2] Henry II gave the office of usher to Roger de Warrenquefort to hold as in the time of the king's grandfather (*ibid*).
[3] *C.C.R.* 1226–1257 p. 357.
[4] *C.I.P.M.* I, 306 (No. 906).
[5] *C.C.R.* 1226–1257 p. 357.
[6] Conway Davies *Baronial Opposition to Edward II* p. 50.
[7] Madox *Exchequer* II, 271–8.

K.M.–B

them seem to have shared the departmental loyalty which is so marked in the *Dialogus de Scaccario*. Possible negligence on the part of the local messenger could be easily checked by the sheriff by threat of fine or forfeiture. For though spring and autumn were difficult seasons for a farmer, the messenger serjeant had the advantage of knowing when his services would become due and how long they were likely to take. The Leicestershire tenant cited above was prepared to do forty days work a year, or twenty days on each half year's summons; and it is doubtful whether he really spent so long away. Perhaps the greatest argument in favour of the efficiency of the serjeanty system under feudal conditions is that nearly a hundred years after the household messenger system had begun, the exchequer was still sending out its summons in the same way. As late as 1284, on the death of the usher Lawrence of the exchequer, his fees and duties were set out in full in the inquisition *post mortem*, as if still in operation. This evidence is accepted by Conway Davies as valid; and though we must always beware of taking inquisitions at their face value, since tenants often acknowledged liabilities which they were seldom asked to meet,[1] the hard-headed exchequer officials were unlikely to pay for messengers and not use them. There is negative confirmation of this, for the duty of finding messengers and the fee for doing so is not mentioned in any later inquisition, either in 1291 on the death of Simon the next holder or in 1308 on the death of a co-successor Maud.[2] Possibly the death of Lawrence in 1284 gave Edward I an opportunity for reviewing the conditions of the serjeanty and so bringing the exchequer into line with the other departments. Indeed, the actual date of the change-over may be somewhat earlier, for we know that at least one local serjeanty, the Gloucestershire one, had been abolished by Henry III in 1251.[3] Some other messenger must have been found to distribute writs in that county instead of Robert le Sauvage. Yet the fact that the duty was formally abrogated and that Robert was willing (presumably) to pay the fee for a letter close to be enrolled, and that this is the only instance of the kind to be found,[4] all add weight to the belief that in general the system was still working in the late thirteenth century.

A question has been asked as to how far serjeanty services 'could have had the same significance in the organization of the king's civil and domestic service as knight service had in the organization of the feudal army.'[5] In the exchequer at least, during the twelfth and most of the thirteenth century, its serjeant ushers and serjeant messengers

---

[1]Kimball *op. cit.*, p. 99.
[2]*C.I.P.M.* II, 501 (No. 820), V, 4 (No. 13) and VIII, 310 (No. 435).
[3]*C.C.R.* 1226–1257 p. 357.
[4]The men of King's Barton got respite from their service of messengers to a tenant-in-chief, the Abbot of Gloucester, in 1240, presumably after a dispute. L.T.R.M.R. 14 m. 12 (P.R.O. typescript abstract p. 73).
[5]Review in *E.H.R.* LIII, 694–696 (October 1938).

were as immediate to its activities as its professional clerks, assayers or tally-cutters. The whole department was not feudal in the same way that the whole army was feudal, but rather a typically English blend of the hereditary and the professional, both being essential to its management. But in the chancery and in the household generally, another solution to the problem of communications had already been found; and to this we must now turn.

2. *The Household System and the Chancery*

The second element in the creation of the messenger service came from the chancery. When letters and writs issued from this department spasmodically, occasional messengers may have been found in the personal servants of chancery officials. There is a hint of this as late as 1210, when Richard, messenger of Peter of the Chancery, was taking out the king's message.[1] At other times, grooms or yeomen of the household were probably sent. But as soon as the development of the chancery had provided enough work for a single regular messenger, the pressure of specialization (the very process which on a larger scale produced in turn exchequer and chancery from the general body of the king's clerks) would be bound to pick on one under-servant of the household and bestow on him by degrees, first the duty and then the title of messenger. A very high degree of functionalization had prevailed in the king's domestic household long before 1200. As the *Constitutio Domus Regis* shows, the household of Henry I was already composed of separate departments, each with its own officer responsible for his expenditure and for the wages or perquisites of his staff. Servants were engaged to serve in one department or another, and like all domestic establishments, we may imagine every branch jealous of its own rights and duties, resenting encroachments on either, and reluctant to do anything but its routine work. As soon as there were letters to take out regularly, professional messengers appeared in the household; and it is impossible to say how far back this happened. If we had more evidence of the work and needs of the pre-conquest secretariat, we might even place the first professional messenger in the service of the Saxon kings. The most that can be said is that at the beginning of the twelfth century, there may have been a single messenger but no more, and certainly no organized group. By 1199, an important date in the history of the chancery, there was one household messenger whose period of service was already behind him, and who was retired on a pension of 60s. and 10d. paid out of the farm of Essex and Hertford annually.[2] In 1202, three other messengers joined him on the retired list.[3] Pensions from the king's established

[1] *R. de Lib.* p. 159.
[2] *Great Roll of the Pipe* 1199 p. 86.
[3] *Great Roll of the Pipe* 1202 pp. 259, 21, 284.

alms would hardly have been given to men who had served the crown
for less than ten or fifteen years; and it may therefore be taken as
certain that Hamelin, Lucas, Walwan, and Roger le Tort, king's
messengers, had been in the household of Richard I, and quite possible
that they had also served his father before him.

The chancery ordinance of 7 June 1199[1] is a landmark to the
historian because the new practice of enrolling out-letters provides
plentiful material for the first time. During John's reign for the first
time household accounts show something of the organization behind
the correspondence. It is tempting to imagine that the messenger
service which handled the letters was started or put on to a business
footing at the same date and by the same hand. But it is more likely
to have grown gradually during the preceding years, as the work of
the chancery grew. The business arising out of Henry II's judicial
innovations can hardly have failed to give it impetus. By 1199, the
department's work had outgrown its office routine, and the accession
of a business-like king gave Hubert Walter an opportunity to press for
reorganization. Chancery was now fully separated from the exchequer,
and its independence was symbolized in a small way by the possession
of its own messenger service, controlled and paid by chancery officials.
The convenience of this is obvious, for the majority of royal letters
were written and sealed in chancery with the great seal, while even
those letters of a more informal kind which were sealed with the privy
seal were sent into the chancery to be enrolled before they were
dispatched.[2]

Evidence for the Chancery messenger service of this period is
abundant in the rolls of current expenses for 1209–10 and 1212–13.
Here chancery clerks accounted regularly for payments to king's
messengers, while a reference to a *nuncius locatus* shows that the title
nuncius regis was already reserved for the king's own regular men and
not used indiscriminately.[3] In the *misae* roll for 1212, the clerk noted
that his department had settled with ('pacavimus') one of these
hired messengers,[4] a small confirmation of the natural assumption that
the chancery was actually the paymaster at this point. A little later, no
doubt on the matter is possible. Numerous writs of *liberate* were drawn
for messengers' expenses between 1219 and 1235.[5] A single writ

[1]Rymer's *Foedera* I, 73. See Galbraith *Studies in the Public Records* p. 66.
[2]Tout *Chapters* I, 154–5.
[3]*R. de Lib.* p. 140.
[4]Cole's *Documents* p. 243.
[5]Originating in chancery, some of these writs are endorsed on receipt rolls,
others appear on the exchequer *liberate* rolls, or on rolls of writs for issues, while
in a few cases the actual writs have been preserved among warrants for payments.
The majority however were entered on the chancery series of liberate rolls from
the beginning of that series in 1226 to 1233. (R.R. 3b, 4, 5, 6, 7, 8, 10b; Exch. Lib.
R. 1202, 1203 and on schedule attached to R.R. 11; rolls of writs for issues 1200,
1201; warrants for issues file 1 nos. 28, 30, 38, which correspond with close roll
entries—see *R.L.Cl.* 1204–1227 I, 411, 413.)

covered a number of journeys by different men and stated their names, destinations and business, showing that these were completed transactions for which the chancery was reimbursing itself, having advanced their travelling expenses according to an accepted scale.[1] The writ authorized the treasurer and chamberlains of the exchequer to pay out of the treasury so much for the services specified, and the expenditure was officially vouched for, so that a warrant for payment of messengers' expenses went through the same office procedure as writs authorizing the payment of large sums into the king's chamber or wardrobe, and was equally subject to investigation in the exchequer audit.

Writs for messenger expenses appear on all *Liberate* rolls till October 1233, after which there is a three-year gap in the series. The rolls recommence in October 1236 but there are no more writs for regular messenger expenses, only occasional emergency payments.[2] Obviously in the interval some other department had become responsible for the payment and therefore the final control of the messenger service, and the chancery's period of responsibility was at an end. This development was connected with the growth in the work of the privy seal. Just as the chancery's increasing business had brought the household messenger group into being in the late twelfth century when the great seal was used for almost all formal correspondence, so the thirteenth-century use of the privy seal as the expression of the king's will and the increasing volume of letters sealed with it, led to the transfer of the main messenger body from the immediate service of the one department to the immediate service of the other. Naturally there were still letters of great seal to be taken out and the household messenger still took them, but they did not fill his bag and he did not regard himself any longer as a 'messenger following chancery.'[3]

The critical date seems to be May 1234, when Kirkham was made keeper of the wardrobe, and the amount of money spent in that department suddenly increased more than four-fold. The total sums authorized by writs of *liberate* and *allocate* for payment to wardrobe officers in 1233 was about £1,210. In 1236 the corresponding figure was £5,684.[4] This is a big difference and was the result of deliberate policy. Everything was to be brought into the closest possible contact

[1]e.g. the roll of writs for issues of Easter 10 Henry III (E. 403/1201) consists of:—

m. 1 writ dated at Westminster 5 May 47 journeys total 50*s*. 10*d*.
m. 2 writ   „   „   „   30 May 13 journeys   13*s*. 6*d*.
    2nd writ „   „   „   3 journeys   4*s*.
m.1d writ   „   „   „   7 July   7 journeys   8*s*.

[2]Seven writs were issued for Adam Haupfield, a chancery clerk who had hired some messengers in 1241–4 (*C.L.R.* II, 136, 139, 141, 147, 169, 177, 189), and on six other occasions messengers sent abroad or hired messengers got their money in this way (*ibid.* I, 383 and III 359; Exch. Lib. R. 1203).
[3]A phrase used in the close roll of 1257 (*C.R.* 1256–1259 p. 166).
[4]*C.L.R.* I (1226–1240).

with the king's will, exercised through the officers of his wardrobe who were less circumscribed by tradition than the officers of either exchequer or chancery. A change in the relationship of chancery to the household must have been going on gradually for some time. Under John, chancery had controlled the household, even to ordering clothing for its members. By 1224–7,[1] the wardrobe had taken over enough of this responsibility to be accounting to the exchequer for most items of household expenditure, but only for household matters. It did not handle the expenses of anything so general as the dispatch of letters. Now in 1234, the wardrobe took over the management of many things which were not 'domestic' at all but 'public', though the distinction between these two aspects of the king's life had not yet been made. The second enrolled wardrobe account to survive[2] shows Kirkham accounting for wardrobe expenditure for one complete financial year and parts of two others. The account runs from his appointment on 19 May 1234 to the end of the year at Michaelmas, from Michaelmas 1234 to the following autumn, and from Michaelmas 1235 to May 1236. In each of these three periods Kirkham accounted for expenditure under the head 'et in expensis nunciorum missorum per diversa loca'—a total of £98 for the two years 1234–1236. For details of the journeys undertaken, he referred the exchequer auditors to the special roll of messengers' expenses 'sicut continetur in rotulo de nunciis', showing that already the wardrobe was keeping its careful record of every messenger sent out, just as chancery had done.[3]

Thus in 1234, the wardrobe assumed control of that small group of between ten and fifteen household messengers which the chancery had first brought into being. These *nuncii regis* were all mounted men, paid for their work at standard rates, and holding a recognized position among other royal servants. It might be supposed that with their transfer to the control of the wardrobe in 1234 the creative period of the messenger service was over, and it had only to expand along the same lines as its work increased. This might well have been the case had an efficient messenger service been the only consideration. But as soon as the number of regular messengers increased to double figures, the king's clerks were forced to consider the increasing cost of communication and to look for a cheaper alternative to the household messenger.

3. The Unmounted Messenger and the Wardrobe

The third source from which the messenger service appears to have derived was the kitchen and the crowd of kitchen knaves and hangers-on who followed the court on its progress. Here the king's clerks could always find someone to send with an urgent letter. This supposition

[1]Tout *Chapters* I, 233–8.   [2]P.R. 79.
[3]The earliest to survive is for 1251–3 (E.A. 308/1).

seems warranted by the name *coquinus* or *cokinus* given to certain unmounted messengers who were not privileged in any way and were not
hired for more than a short time together.[1] *Cokini* were never included
in the lists of household servants receiving robes or shoes, either as
messengers or as *servientes coquine*, for they were attached to no
specific household office. The word *cokinus* was first used about 1251–
3, when fifteen *cokini* were paid for taking out letters[2] and after that
these subsidiary messengers appear frequently in all wardrobe
accounts. It is clear that by mid-thirteenth century the household
messengers were not equal to the work of the administration; but
rather than increase their numbers, the government was turning
more and more to the jack-of-all-trades who had previously helped in
the kitchen or assisted the sumptermen and carters of the wardrobe.
These casual labourers had always been at hand to take out letters in
default of other messengers, but by Edward I's reign, they were used
so extensively for letter-carrying that they ceased to be available for
anything else. Not being mounted and not being eligible for robes or
shoes, these couriers were cheaper to employ than messengers, a great
merit in Edward's eyes. He used them so frequently during his campaigns in Wales and Scotland,[3] that groups of these inferior messengers were regularly 'retained' by the wardrobe, and the relevant
titulus of every wardrobe account was now headed 'de expensis
nunciorum et cokinorum'.

For some reason, the name '*cokini*', though not the men represented
by it, disappeared soon after the accession of Edward II. The very same
men went on taking messages for the wardrobe, but under the new
name '*cursores*'. This word, though used occasionally in *liberate* or
memoranda rolls of Henry III[4] in the general sense of 'messenger',
was not used at all by the wardrobe till after 1300. It crept into favour
first in subsidiary royal households, and was used for some of the
queen's messengers by 1288–90, and for a prince's messenger in 1299.[5]
Then it began to be used in less formal wardrobe accounts for messengers' expenses,[6] while the complete wardrobe books and the enrolled
accounts were still headed 'de expensis nunciorum et cokinorum'. This
suggests that the word *cursor* was current in the king's household before it was used by wardrobe clerks for their formal accounts to the

---

[1]Ducange s.v. *coquinus* 'Homo vilissimus nec nisi infimus coquinae ministeriis
natus, interdum etiam nequam, improbus, ut nostrum Gallicum "coquin".'
Medieval Latin Word List s.v. *cokinus* 'an inferior servant or messenger'.

[2]E.A. 308/1. The word was used at least forty years before the earliest date
(1291) given in the *Medieval Latin Word List*. It is just possible that the William
Cokin, John Cokin, and Geoffrey Cokin, paid by writ of *liberate* in 1229–30, were
cokini also (*C.L.R.* 1226–1240 pp. 163, 164).

[3]e.g. Add MS. 8835 ff. 73, 74, 80, 96 (1303–4).

[4]*C.L.R.* II (1240–1245) pp. 136, 139, 141, 147, 169, 177, 189; L.T.R.M.R. 15,
m. 9d (P.R.O. typescript abstract p. 39).

[5]Add. MSS. 35294; E.A. 358/20 f. 8v.

[6]E.A. 358/27 Nos. 10 and 11; 359/2; 362/17; 364/24; 365/50; 308/19.

exchequer, where conservatism kept the older word alive for some twenty years longer. The use of the new word in wardrobe books for the household of Edward of Caernarvon as prince and its almost immediate adoption in the king's wardrobe when he came to the throne,[1] also indicates that his household officers set the new fashion in names. Messengers may have preferred to forget any early connexion with the kitchen and the secondary implication of rascal attached to the name *cokinus*; while *cursor* implied swiftness of travel which was more flattering. It was also used abroad for royal and papal messengers, and this may have helped to bring the term into favour, though here with a restricted meaning. In any case, the change implied no change in personnel, for the same letter-carriers were called by one title or the other indifferently during the transition period.

On the other hand, the adoption of the new name *cursor* for these messengers may indicate a gradual improvement in their status. Instead of being casual letter-carriers, distinguished only from any hired labourers by being retained in the wardrobe for use when needed and by being in some vague way attached to the court as it travelled, the *cursor* was becoming an integral part of the system. The messenger establishment was becoming a two-level organization. There was the fully privileged and fully trusted mounted messenger who was always used for responsible tasks; and there was the cheaper unmounted unprivileged courier, who would do well enough for taking out routine messages. From this lower grade, the most promising men could be recruited into the permanent service. By 1300 the messenger service regularly included both types; and in the fully developed system which the wardrobe was to pass on to the exchequer in 1342, both mounted and unmounted men had their allotted place.

4. *The Total Messenger Service*

At this point, it seems relevant to ask how many messengers were necessary for the government's routine work from time to time during our period.[2] What proportion of these were members of the established

---

[1]Compare E.A. 365/18 (prince's wardrobe book for 1302–3) with Cotton MS. Nero C VIII f. 99–108 (wardrobe account for 1311–12).

[2]In addition, that is, to men employed exclusively in the subsidiary households of the queen, the prince of Wales, or the king's other children. Each of these minor establishments included two mounted and several unmounted men. Eleanor of Castile, for instance, employed two, sometimes three, *nuncii* and five *cursores* (Add. MSS. 35294, 1288–90.) while Isabella of France during her period of power had two mounted and eleven unmounted messengers in her household, even though she must have been able to command the services of all her son's household group (Society of Antiquaries MSS. 120 p. 32 and 121 p. 60; Nero C VIII ff. 121–153; E.A. 376/7, 20.)

There were one or two messengers attached exclusively to the chancery or exchequer so that they could take immediate messages for the officials of these departments. They did not belong to the regular messenger group and were seldom mentioned in accounts. See Appendix I.

group and how many were only hired for short periods? And of each type, how many made messenger-work their profession and spent their whole working life in the king's service? Both these questions can be answered. There is evidence enough in the records successively of chancery, wardrobe, and exchequer to justify a very definite statement about the number of messengers, superior or inferior, employed by the crown at almost any period during these two centuries. A tabulated summary of this evidence is given in Appendix I. Where household messengers are concerned, the lists of men receiving robes or shoes at Easter or Christmas show conclusively how many were on the establishment. Where unprivileged men are concerned, the figures have to be deduced from the names of those who received payment for taking letters and whose names appear in the accounts with the description *cokinus* or *cursor* added. Occasional payments to men who were neither *nuncii* nor *cursores*, who were paid once only for this service, may be disregarded. They never formed a conspicuous feature of chancery, wardrobe, or exchequer accounts for message-carrying.

The figures in general show that there was no fixed number of messengers in either category. The numbers, both of those receiving household privileges and of those excluded from them, varied from time to time according to the chances of peace or war, and the requirements of the government. John's messenger service was probably composed of about fifteen *nuncii regis* with no second grade of messenger at all, though at times he used odd men about his court who might later have been called *cokini*. During the minority of Henry III, the service was somewhat reduced. Eleven messengers received robes through the sheriff of Oxford in 1220, and the evidence of the *liberate* writs on the receipt roll confirm this figure.[1] By 1236–7, the number had grown to eighteen receiving robes for Christmas.[2] Here the government seems to have decided to call a halt to the expansion of the household messenger group and to use instead *cokini*; only four messengers were paid for journeys in the roll of expenses for 1252–3; but on the same account were entered payments to fifteen *cokini*, making the total number of men employed just under twenty.[3] By 1264–5, eighteen full messengers and nineteen foot messengers were paid for journeys,[4] and this striking increase in the total force was maintained during the following reign, with variations in the proportions of privileged to unprivileged messengers. Edward's wars and frequent absences abroad made messenger service an expensive item in his accounts, and it is easy to pick out these years from the number of messengers he employed. The established service did not vary so much, but the numbers of subordinate messengers rose and fell regularly with the politics of the reign.

---

[1] *R.L.Cl.* 1204–1227 I, 444; Receipt roll No. 4.
[2] Enrolled wardrobe account, Pipe Roll No. 81.
[3] E.A. 308/1.   [4] E.A. 308/2.

In 1288–9 he was using forty-seven messengers altogether, of whom fourteen were privileged and the remainder not.[1] Edward's economical mind saw the advantage of keeping down the numbers of permanent messengers on his staff. His *cokini* were, in fact, nearly as permanent a feature of the court. The same men followed the king from place to place, from England to Wales and from Wales to Scotland if necessary, ready to be called on by the wardrobe clerks whenever there was a press of business. But the king was under no obligation towards them, as towards his own messengers; and he could treat them as casual labour, without any claim on him after wages for their services had been paid. Except when specially retained, they were free to leave whenever they chose, without asking permission from anyone. Yet an analysis of the accounts for the year 1296–7 shows that out of forty-one *cokini* employed at different times, twenty-three were old hands who had served the king many times before and would do so many times again.[2] The rest were temporary additions to meet the sudden pressure of work in the second half of the year.

Edward II employed as a rule rather fewer messengers than his father, for there were no great campaigns abroad to organize. Twelve *nuncii* and twenty-four *cursores* in 1310–11, and eight *nuncii* and twenty-eight *cursores* for 1319–20 were typical figures,[3] the numbers mounting slightly towards the end of the reign. Edward III's French wars and the months of active preparation which preceded the chief campaigns, raised once more the amounts spent on messengers and the numbers of men used by the administration. In 1340–2 and 1350–4, he had as many as twenty-one messengers on his permanent staff, and at the same time about forty couriers.[4] Both groups were reduced later to more ordinary proportions. In the case of couriers, reduction was easy. After a campaign or crisis, extra and unnecessary men could be simply dismisssed. Messengers on the permanent establishment could not be got rid of so easily. They had a claim on the king which he could not disregard, and the only way of reducing numbers was to pension some and appoint no others in their places.

Messengers entered the king's service intending to remain in it for the duration of their working lives. Even couriers attached themselves to the court and worked for the king in their humble capacity for very long periods. One or two examples will suffice here. Roger of Windsor began his career as a king's messenger about 1276 and was still serving Edward I at the end of his reign. Robert of Manfield entered

[1] E.A. 308/10.
[2] Chanc. Misc. 4/6; Add. MS. 7965. Many letters were also taken out by grooms and valets during the rush period.
[3] E.A. 373/30; 374/2; 374/7; 374/8; Nero C VIII f. 30; I.R. 155 (1310–11); E.A. 378/4; Add. MS. 17362; I.R. 189, 191 (1319–20).
[4] E.A. 389/8; I.R. 307, 313 (1339–40); I.R. 317, 320 (1340–1); E.A. 392/13, 326/2 and I.R. 350, 353 (1349–50); 355, 358 (1350–1); 359, 364 (1351–2); 365; 368 (1352–3).

the service of Edward II about 1296 while the latter was Prince of Wales, became *nuncius regis* when Edward became king, and survived him by many years, being still paid for messenger services as late as 1334–5. Jack Faukes, after a preliminary training in two episcopal households, entered the king's household in 1333 and served faithfully for some twenty-six years. For the inferior messengers, Robert of Crowland may be instanced. He was acting as *cokinus* for Edward I in 1289 and was still in service under his successor in 1315 as a courier. Not many of his companions could equal this record, but service of ten or fifteen years was not uncommon.

CHAPTER II

CONDITIONS OF SERVICE

Clothing, Food, Lodging, Equipment, Grooms and Boys

THE position of this messenger group *vis-à-vis* the other groups within the royal household altered very little from the reigns of Edward I to Edward III. It was natural that wardrobe clerks in making up their livery lists should set down the names of members of the household according to their usual status and precedence and from highest to lowest. Thus in a counter-roll of domestic payments for 1284–5,[1] the members of the king's household were grouped as follows:

Milites
Clerici
Servientes hospicii regis
Scutiferi regis

Falconarii et venatores regis
Menestrali regis
Caretarii
Nuncii regis

Vadleti de diversis officiis in hospicio regis
Sometarii, garciones, palfredarii.

Here we have a cross-section of the household from the knights at the top to the grooms and ostlers at the bottom. First the knights; then the clerks, serjeants and squires, the upper levels of society, with whom the less distinguished members of the household had probably little in common. These were the administrators and the clerical staff—the equivalent of the black-coated civil servant of the present day. The next section begins with the introduction of the highly skilled workers, the falconers, huntsmen, and minstrels, each trained in their own craft. With them are classed the head carters, men in charge of the important operation of getting the whole household moved from manor to manor, from London to Edinburgh if need be, with the minimum of trouble and upset. Their task was, in its own way, a skilled one, requiring at the least some organizing capacity. Next come the king's messengers. They were also specialists, trained through years of service for one

[1]E.A. 351/17.

particular type of work. Finally in a third section, are placed the general household servants, the grooms of the offices, the ostlers and stable-boys. The clerks do not trouble to distinguish very minutely here between kitchen or pantry. The main distinction was now between indoor and outdoor servants, between the offices and the stable-yard. If the messengers had little in common with the first section in the household, neither did they share the anonymity of the third.

A second example is taken from a list of 1325–6 'les nomis des genz de Lostel notre seigneur le Roi qui prendront liveree des robes pur le passage de Roi vers les partes de Fraunce lan de son regne xixme'.[1] In this list, written not in formal Latin but in everyday French, we ought to have a slightly different angle on the class-distinctions of the king's household. There were, in fact, omissions and variants, but the three main sections are still there. Here the list runs:

Enfantz en garde (each with a 'master')
Esquiers
Seriantz Hospice
Valletz de la Chambre

Menestraux
Messagers
Vadlets Doffice
Summeters,
Palefreours,
Charetters,

Item Palefreours
Garçens ens Hossice
Venours
Pages de la Chambre

In the first section, the wards, squires, serjeants, and chamber staff; in the second section, the minstrels, messengers, grooms of the offices, head carters, and head grooms; in the third section, grooms again (here clearly the subordinates and assistants), boys, huntsmen and pages. In its main outline, the second list follows the same lines as the first.

Our messengers, therefore, occupied a position of comfortable mediocrity among the king's servants. They were not clerks, and did not belong to the higher administrative grades; neither could they be lumped in with the general run of domestic servants, indoor or outdoor. They provide a more representative group than the minstrels,

[1]Documents subsidiary to the wardrobe account for 1325–6, E.A. 381/11.

whose individual talents might win them special treatment. The messengers belonged to the ranks of the trained or partly skilled men; and investigation into their conditions of service is likely to produce answers valid for other groups on a similar level.[1] I begin, then, with conditions of service general throughout the household.

1. Clothing

One of the privileges claimed by members of the king's household was a yearly allowance of clothes and shoes. It was the king's duty to clothe his retainers, and all who belonged to his permanent establishment, from the highest to the lowest, had the right to receive this livery. The lists of persons taking robes and shoes which have been cited above, show knights and clerks, grooms and palfreymen, receiving alike the allowance appropriate to their station. Among the rest were the king's messengers. It was the most obvious mark of their status as members of the household, and one not shared by *cokini* or *cursores*.

In the partially developed household of John and the minority of Henry III, provision of clothing seems to have been made in two ways —through the chancery, or through the sheriffs of the counties by writs of *computate*. So far as can be discovered, the chamber had no hand in the provision of liveries. A chancery clerk in 1213–4 was ordered to find robes for various members of the queen's household including her messenger Richard,[2] and in November 1214 a writ of *liberate* was issued by the chancery in favour of Laurence the messenger for 10s. to buy him one robe. Presumably this was his allowance for Christmas.[3] Messengers' expenses and household expenditure in general were at that time controlled by chancery, and the department, not yet out of court, was no doubt responsible for seeing that messengers and others were suitably clad. This could most easily be done through the sheriffs, who supplied so many royal needs. A writ of *computate*, giving the name of the messenger and a description of the clothing required, was issued to the sheriff with the assurance that his expenditure would be allowed by the exchequer when he came up to London to make his half-yearly account. There are a number of these writs enrolled on the close rolls for the minority of Henry III. Thus in December 1219, the sheriff of Kent was ordered to provide a robe of

---

[1] An interesting comparison is suggested here between the English king's messenger and the papal courier under the Avignon papacy. The latter was described by Yves Renouard as occupying 'une place bien déterminé dans le hiérachie du personel de la Curie, audessus du groupe de palefreniers pontificaux . . . La fonction de *cursor pape* est une véritable dignité. Qui en est revêtu jouit de grands avantages matériels et moraux, devient un personage.'

This is precisely the position of the king's messenger in the English household.

(Yves Renouard 'Comment les Papes d'Avignon expédiaient leur courriers' *Revue Historique* CLXXX pp. 1–22 (1937) p. 3.)

[2] *R.L.Cl.* 1204–1227 I, 155

[3] *Ibid.*, I, 180.

blue for Robert of Germany (Alemannia) the king's messenger; and in the following year, the sheriff of Oxford found robes for eleven of the king's messengers whose names are given in the writ. Each received a tunic and supertunic of russet or blue, without fur. The same eleven men were clothed by the sheriff of London at Christmas 1221, and nine of them who were still in the king's service a year later took their accustomed robes again from the sheriff of Oxford. The bailiffs of Oxford were likewise called on to supply robes for thirteen messengers in December 1223.[1] These entries suggest that though the king's officials were not obliged to do so, they found it convenient to get clothes for the household regularly from certain localities. Oxford had the duty of finding garments for the messenger section; and similar demands on behalf of other household groups recur each year on the rolls just before Christmas. One tunic and supertunic a year, given just before Christmas in readiness for the feast, was the usual allowance for each member of the household. The recipient's rank was shown, not in the quantity but the quality of the garments.

When writs of this type were issued by chancery to sheriffs, the performance of the command should be traceable on the pipe roll for the following year, and this is certainly the case. Robert's grant in 1219 is duly entered under the account of the sheriff of Kent in 1220, and the bailiffs of Oxford were allowed to claim relief for the thirteen robes supplied by them in December 1223 when they accounted for the firm of Oxford in 1223–4.[2] If a messenger happened to be abroad when the robes were ordered, he was given money instead after he got back safely. Robert le Herberjur, coming from Rome in 1209, was given 10s. with which to buy himself clothing in place of the regular allowance which he had missed. Next year he was again away from court at Christmas, and was allowed 20s. to cover both his tunic and his shoes.[3] Such absences were probably not common at this date, and the messenger's loss was most easily made up to him in cash.

General messenger expenses were included in the wardrobe's account of its expenditure for the first time in 1234, when Kirkham became keeper of the wardrobe and began to extend the scope of its operations. The wardrobe now issued messengers with their journey money and at the same time made itself responsible for providing robes for them and for the whole household. Writs to sheriffs for clothing the household disappeared, and regular entries in wardrobe books for the supply of footwear and garments appeared instead. Soon the great wardrobe developed as a special section of the wardrobe, charged with the duty of supplying all the liveries for the king's officers and servants. Special livery lists[4] were drawn up to indicate,

---

[1] *Ibid.* I, 410, 444, 484, 527, 580.
[2] P.R. 65, 68. [3] *R. de Lib.* pp. 112, 139.
[4] e.g. E.A. 351/17 (1284–5); 351/25 (1286–7); 352/24 (1289–91).

first which offices were privileged to receive clothing and second, which persons were entitled to a particular allocation. The clerk of the great wardrobe accounted to the keeper for all such issues, and the keeper accounted for the sub-department to the exchequer. So from 1234 onwards, provision of clothing was an unquestioned function of the wardrobe and its organization.

The development of the household office may explain an apparent increase in the clothing allowance now made to messengers and others. Instead of the single Christmas issue, messengers began to receive clothes twice a year, in summer and winter. This no doubt reflected one advantage of the new system over the old. The sheriff might provide the garments and be allowed his expenses at the exchequer, but he had yet to convey the clothing to the messengers and they had to arrange to receive it from him. No wonder that an annual issue was as much as could be managed. When the household itself provided its members with clothes and when the great wardrobe was able to buy cloth and leather (or possibly the garments and shoes ready-made) in bulk, these difficulties were halved. A twice-yearly issue became possible. So every year the king's messengers in company with his other servants received a set of winter clothes and a set of summer clothes, with two pairs of shoes; or an allowance of 6s. 8d. each half year for the former and 2s. 4d. each half year for the latter. The wardrobe thus reckoned to spend 18s. a year on clothing for every messenger and for most of the domestic servants in the king's retinue; and more in proportion for the higher grades.

No special writs were needed for the issue of these regular liveries. The great wardrobe had its lists, and each man collected his allowance himself at the appropriate time. Difficulties only arose when messengers happened to be away on business, and on those occasions a senior messenger was deputed to collect the clothes and shoes and distribute them to individual messengers as they returned from their travels. The careful clerks usually made a special note of such issues. In 1301–2, seven messengers took their robes and shoes by the hand of Nicholas Ramage, an old and trusted messenger.[1] In 1313, again, Robert of Newington undertook to collect the garments still in arrears for the year 1310–11 and to distribute them among his companions.[2] No doubt this simplified matters for everyone, clerks and messengers.

Occasionally however, special writs authorizing the issue of clothes to messengers were necessary. This was to provide for men who had been away from court on a long journey and for whom no comrade could be expected to keep the usual allowance. When the messenger returned, he could get a letter close from the chancery or a warrant for robes from the wardrobe and present them to the king's tailor or to the

[1] E.A. 361/14.
[2] Cotton MS. Nero C VIII f. 30v.

officials of the great wardrobe, sure of obtaining his perquisites eventually, though delay might be long. In May 1258, a letter was sent authorizing the issue of a robe to Thomas le Escot, king's messenger, 'who has not yet had his robe for last Christmas because he had set out with haste on the king's message to the court of Rome'.[1] Two years earlier, the same Thomas le Escot and another messenger, John of Lyons (Liuns) were ordered to leave court just before the Christmas issue was made. They seem to have demurred and perhaps threatened not to leave until they had received their due, for a special authorization was sent hastily to the officers concerned to let them have their clothes 'as soon as they come, so that their journey be not retarded for lack of the clothes'.[2] In both these examples from Henry III's time, the method used to authorize a special issue of clothing was the letter close.

Under Edward I or Edward II, a warrant from the wardrobe to its sub-department would have been more likely. The messenger himself could take this warrant to the great wardrobe, and surrender it when his garments had been handed over, so that the officers there might present it with their account to the keeper of the wardrobe. Thus it would be filed with those subsidiary documents which the wardrobe presented with its own account to the exchequer; and in this way, one or two warrants for the issue of clothes to messengers have actually survived. One is dated 1302–3, and is addressed to the head of the great wardrobe, ordering him to find for three messengers, Geoffrey of Bardeney, Simon of Westminster, and William Brehull 'such robes as you have already released to the other messengers'.[3]

There is even one warrant allowing an extraordinary issue of a garment for James Flye, who was only a *cokinus garderobe*, but had presumably merited some special reward.[4] The wardrobe's officials were particularly careful to keep this warrant for presentation to the exchequer because *cokini* or *cursores* never figured on the wardrobe's regular lists for shoes or robes; and if they occasionally received clothing, it was by special gift from the king. John of Carlisle (Karliol) and four other couriers 'following the king's chancery' received robes 'such as the king's messengers receive' in 1257 because they had been in Wales with the king's expedition.[5] A hundred years later, eight couriers attached to the wardrobe received 14*s.* of the king's alms to make them robes of the king's gift.[6] The fact that these robes would cost only 1*s.* 9*d.* apiece, instead of the 6*s.* 8*d.* allowed for a messenger's garments, indicates the difference in status of the two, even though the courier's garment may have been tunic only without the addition of a super-tunic of any kind. So, too, does the word 'alms' used in the order.

[1] *C.R.* 1256–1259 p. 217.   [4] E.A. 366/12.
[2] *Ibid.* p. 14.   [5] *C.R.* 1256–1259 p. 166.
[3] E.A. 363/24 No. 111.   [6] I.R. 386 m. 9.

At no time in their history was the messengers' issue of robes so described.

Messengers who joined the king's household for the first time immediately after one of the half-yearly distributions had to wait until the next allocation before they received any liveries. They might, however, get part of the money allowed for shoes. When Robert Little (Petit or Parvus) and William of Alkham entered the king's service just after Christmas 1296, they lost their right to robes for the year and 2s. 4d. of the shoe allowance, even though Little had previously been messenger in the household of Edmund the king's brother.[1] This seems to have been the general rule in the household, and livery lists often did not mention a messenger's name till he had been working for nearly a year. Stephen of Hamslope, who was called messenger in an account for 1319, received no shoe money in the list for the following year.[2] Other members of the establishment as well as the messengers suffered in this way. Thus an entry in a wardrobe book for 1285–8 explained the omission from a livery list of two of the king's servants, John Barret and Vincent Haggard 'they have no robes for this year because they came too late' for the current issue.[3] Only in one case was unusual consideration shown, and then it was said to be 'of the king's especial grace' that Richard of Malmesbury the king's messenger should receive clothing from the king's tailors 'at the instance of the Countess of Leicester'.[4] The lady being the king's sister had recommended Richard to this favourable notice, and he may have received his preliminary training and experience in her service. Many messengers entered the king's household from that of a magnate or official, or even of another member of the royal family; though, as in the case of Alkham and Little, this might not help them to an allowance of clothing they had not yet earned by service.

The right of messengers and of all other full members of the household to receive liveries was mentioned particularly in the household ordinance of 1318, which defined the rights and duties of all the king's servants. The only point in which the 1318 ordinance varied the traditional distribution was in substituting one garment worth 13s. 4d. for the two half-yearly suits worth 6s. 8d. each. This no doubt reflected the current rise in prices. Cloth was more expensive, and the money value of the issue remained fixed. So the messengers themselves may have preferred 'chescune de eux prendre par an j robe dune seute ou j marc en deniers, et pur chauceure iiij s. viij d.'[5] But payment in cash

[1]Add. MS. 7965 f. 42.
[2]Add. MSS. 17362 and 9931.
[3]Misc. bks. E.T.R. 201 f. 18.
[4]C.R. 1256–1259 p. 61.
[5]Tout *Place of Edward II in English History* 2nd ed. p. 272.
In the next century, one mark and 4s 8d. were still being paid to messengers for liveries, as allowed in the *Liber Niger* of Edward IV.

instead of in kind is clearly envisaged as an alternative, and it is not always possible from the accounts to say which the messengers received. 'Calciatura de sesonis heimali et estivali' was distributed to 329 household servants, valets, messengers, falconers, packhorsemen, and sompterers in 1338,[1] but the entry could apply equally to shoes or shoe-money. It seems probable that soon after the ordinance, if not before, money payments did frequently replace payment in kind. In 1318, the great wardrobe was removed from the competent control of the keeper of the wardrobe, and with that change, the value and convenience of the sub-department must have been much curtailed.

In theory, every member of the king's household received shoes and clothes every year. In practice, the distribution was not nearly so regular. When the king's debts increased after the Scottish and French wars, household liveries fell sadly into arrears. Other claims had to be met first. The messengers, for example, must have money for their journeys; but their clothes and footwear could and did remain overdue for years. Here the inability of the wardrobe to deal effectively with general finance is clearly shown. A proper distribution of liveries was out of the question; and money payments, made in instalments, took the place of any material issue. The great wardrobe must have lost much of its employment by the change. As early as 1297, Simon Lowys (then in the king's service) had received an imprest of 10*s*. towards his robes due the year before; and in 1306 Ralph le Convers and Arnold Bon were receiving instalments of a mark apiece on liveries still unpaid from several years back.[2] Such entries were unusual under Edward I. They became commonplace under his successors, and in the wardrobe books of Edward III, entries referring to imprests abound. An interesting feature of such entries are the notes which in many cases have been added. The debt is cancelled, because the messenger has received his due from the exchequer. In this way debts of £4 and 18*s*. 8*d* to John Wirsop and his fellow messengers for their allowances from 1332 were dealt with at the end of July 1337[3] after they had waited five years for necessary clothing. Such entries show the wardrobe so reduced in scope that it was unable to fulfil even these limited duties. Provision of clothing for the household was precisely the side of wardrobe activity with which the reformers of 1318 did not intend to interfere, yet by reducing wardrobe revenues and removing the great wardrobe from the keeper's control, they had seriously weakened the whole organization. Edward III's attempt to revive the wardrobe's powers only led to greater confusion. The exchequer was paying off

[1] E.A. 388/5 m. 19. There seems no ground for the suggestion that *calciatura* (*Collection of Ordinances* p. 48) might be translated as money for horseshoes (Walker *Haste, Post Haste!* (1938) p. 29). It is not supported by Ducange or the *Medieval Latin Word List s.v. calciamentum.*
[2] Chanc. Misc. 3/48 No. 27; E.A. 368/27 f. 47.
[3] Add. MS. 35181 ff. 12v and 14.

the wardrobe's debts to members of the household for some time before it took upon itself complete responsibility for all non-domestic expenditure in 1343. Wardrobe books are not the only evidence for the breakdown of the household department. On the close rolls for 1339, a writ to the treasurer and chamberlains ordered payment to five messengers of £4 10s. 'in which the king is bound to them for their robes and shoes as may fully appear by a bill in the messengers' possession under the seal of Edmund de la Beche, sometime keeper of the wardrobe'.[1] The exchequer's issue rolls recorded many such payments. In 1351 John Lewer and John Arches received 29s. 4d. and 26s. apiece on account of clothing due;[2] and a number of other messengers found their claims met in this way during 1352.[3] These examples were typical of many.

First chancery, using the power of writs of *liberate*, then the wardrobe, with its own supply department, and finally the exchequer, with the authority of the purse, controlled the issue to members of the king's household of the robes and shoes (or allowances in place of them) which they were all entitled to have. No department questioned their right to the issue, even when money to meet the claim was hard to find. The king's duty of supplying his household with clothes, and the right of all members of the household to receive them, formed part of that complicated pattern of obligation and privilege which characterized medieval life.

Throughout this section, the word 'livery' has been used in its original sense of a general delivery of clothing to members of the household. It was still used with this meaning by the Tudor antiquary who compiled the 'description of the household of Edward III in peace and war' from wardrobe accounts for 1344–7. He employed the term for both clothing and footwear 'Leveryes of men servantes intituled Calciatura—messengers, 20, every man by yere 13s. 4d.' and 'Liveres entitled calciatura, every man at 4s. 8d. by yere.'[4] There is no evidence to show whether the clothing issued was also livery in the modern sense of the word—a distinctive uniform worn by servants with their master's coat of arms or badge. No mention of the royal coat-of-arms on tunics or other garments is made anywhere. The only suggestion of livery as uniform comes from the reign of Henry III, who ordered that the fifty supertunics (*superpellicis*) given out at Christmas 1240 to certain members of his household, should have an R for *Rex* embroidered in red silk below the collar.[5] So far as the accounts show, this

---

[1]*C.C.R.* 1339–1341 p. 7.
[2]I.R. 355 and 358 m. 29.
[3]I.R. 359 m. 15.
[4]*Collection of Ordinances* pp. 10–11.
[5]H. Johnstone 'A Year in the Life of King Henry III' *Church Quarterly Review* XCVII No. CXCIV (1924) p. 323.

experiment was not repeated. At the same time, it was convenient for the sheriff or the king's tailors as the case might be, to provide a batch of similar garments when ordered to clothe a dozen messengers or an entire household. It is not impossible that custom in time assigned a slightly different style of dress to each grade in the king's service. The phrase used in the warrants for clothing, a garment 'as for one of the king's other messengers'[1] suggests that everyone knew pretty well what kind of clothing a messenger ought to wear. Each generation of men had preferences for style and colour, following current fashion, which modified this accepted picture.

The historian can only make a guess at this ordinary set of clothes which were too well known to the clerks to need description. In the close roll for 1220, the sheriff of Oxford was commanded to produce a tunic and supertunic for each of the eleven messengers, and probably with each issue of clothing the messenger received the two garments. In the thirteenth century, blue or russet were the colours mentioned for messengers, and the stipulation 'without fur or lambskin' usually added. The sheriffs receiving writs of *liberate* for clothing in 1220 and 1221 were given a choice of either colour, while garments ordered in 1219 and 1222 were to be of blue[2]. The pipe roll for 1223–4 confirmed a purchase of 78 ells of blue cloth for messengers' clothes, at a cost to the king of 16 pence the ell.[3] Here the price was stipulated in the original letter close to the sheriff: usually price and quality were left to his discretion or to custom. A sheriff who provided poor material would probably be detected by the household officers and find his allowance reduced by the exchequer when he came up to the next account, so it was to his advantage to satisfy the usual requirements when ordered to find cloth or clothes.

By the end of the thirteenth century, striped cloth was coming into favour, though it did not supplant the blue entirely. Generally blue and striped cloths were allotted together if the garments were not given out ready made. When additional robes were given to messengers in place of wages between 1296 and 1299, Robert Manfield and Robert Rideware, the prince's messengers, each received 3½ ells of ray or striped material, and 3½ ells of plain blue. About the same time, Robert Little and nine other messengers in the king's household received 3½ ells of Stamford ray and the same amount of *pounacius* or *pounettus*, a brightly coloured stuff, of which the exact shade is not

[1] e.g. *C.R.* 1251–1253 p. 346.
[2] *R.L.Cl.* 1204–1227 I, 444, 410, 484, 527.
Compare the 'good robe of scarlet' provided through the sheriff of Kent for William, messenger of the Soldan of Babylon, in 1207. (*P.R.* 9 John p. 30); and the red garments with distinguishing fleur de lys worn by French mounted messengers (Vaillé *Histoire Générale des Postes Francaises* p. 154. Red seems to have been the one colour never under any circumstances supplied by the household to the king's servants in this country.
[3] P.R. 68.

known.[1] Striped and plain mixed seem to have been the fourteenth
century fashion too. John Waltham and other messengers in a livery
list for 1337–8 were allotted 1½ ells of 'coloured' and 1½ ells of ray.
This was half the previous allowance and presumably intended as half
a year's issue only; for in an undated account for the same reign, nine
messengers received the full 3½ ells of coloured and 3½ ells of ray as
before.[2] Most of the cloth bought for the use of the king's household
seems to have come from Stamford, and was bought by the king's
buyers at the annual fair. Sometimes it was distributed in lengths, as in
the instances cited above; but more often the great wardrobe appears
to have converted it into garments before issuing it to the household.
Only when cloth was given instead of clothes or in lieu of money payments, did the clerks stop to describe the stuff; and when it became
customary to give the value of the clothes rather than the material or
dresses, evidence for the messengers' appearance grows scanty.

In all the routine issues of clothing, each messenger received tunics
or cloth identical in quality, colour and length. Queen's messengers
were sometimes treated individually. Most queens had only two
established messengers, so they could easily be given something
special. In 1221, Robert the Fleming, queen's messenger, received
through the sheriff of London a garment quite unlike the king's
messengers' clothes, 'unam robam partitam de viridi et burnetta cum
furrure de agnis'.[3] Later in the century, when the king's messengers
were given *pounacius* and ray instead of wages, Simon, the queen's
messenger, had a piece of yellow cloth and a piece of *pounacius* for his
share.[4] Only a narrow cloth could be woven on medieval looms, and so
at least six ells (7½ yards) had to be allowed for each set of clothing.
When Henry III ordered 6 ells of cloth apiece for his messengers, the
price was usually about 16d. an ell, or 8s. a head. For a single garment,
the cost was higher. Laurence the messenger had 10s. to buy his
clothes in 1214[5] and the sheriff of Kent was allowed 12s for the blue
dress bought for Robert of Germany (Alemania) in 1219.[6] Ordering
through the sheriff was not an economical way of clothing the household, and when the wardrobe began to buy cloth in bulk at the cloth
fairs, the cost per head for each set of summer and winter garments
was reduced to half a mark. This remained the standard allowance
even when the amount of stuff provided was slightly more than 6 ells.
The parti-coloured dress fashionable in the fourteenth century took
7 ells of stuff, 3½ of each kind, and this length had to be supplied for the
same sum. The actual cost of these materials was only mentioned if
stuff was being allowed in place of wages, and then prices ranged from
2s. 8d. to 3s. an ell for ray and blue, or 2s. 4½d. an ell for *pounacius* and

[1]E.A. 354/23, 354/27.   [4]E.A. 354/23.
[2]E.A. 388/3, 399/7.   [5]R.L.Cl. I, 180.
[3]R.L.Cl. 1204–1227 I, 450.   [6]P.R. 65.

Stamford ray.[1] Some suspicion must attach to truck valuations, but in any case the price of cloth was rising in the early fourteenth century. When the wardrobe or the exchequer began to pay out a standard 13s. 4d. in cash to each man in the king's service in place of garments, the administration was not the looser; and fixed allowances must have been both simpler and cheaper in the end.

The ordinary yearly clothing issue given to messengers was not trimmed in any way; and in letters close or warrants for such garments, the words 'without fur' are nearly always found. According to the sumptuary laws of the period, the wearing of fur, or even of the humbler lambskin, signified a definite social status. Occasionally, however, a favoured messenger might have a 'good robe' such as the one ordered for Robert Long in 1256 when he brought the king news of his daughter's recovery[2] or the blue tunic with lambskin trimmings ordered for Robert le Herbejur in 1219.[3] Robert Flemming, the queen's messenger, also had lambskin on his particoloured dress of green and burnet in 1221.[4] After that the accounts do not mention such additions to the ordinary clothing of any king's messenger till Edward III allowed nine of his messengers a lambskin apiece,[5] and John Pygot, a king's messenger, drew a miscellaneous lot consisting of three pieces of coloured cloth, three pieces of ray, and one lambskin, in 1363.[6] Gilbert, messenger of Queen Philippa, had lambskin on his Easter suit in 1332,[7] and a lambskin worth 2s. was provided for a messenger of the dowager Queen Isabella in 1358–9 by her special command.[8] It seems likely for a number of reasons that the status of the king's messenger within the household was improving slightly all through our period, and quite definitely towards the latter half of the fourteenth century. These gifts of lambskins by Edward III are one small indication of this; though even then messengers did not expect to wear such trimmings regularly, much less any other sort of fur.

Probably the most accurate idea of the dress of a fourteenth century king's messenger is to be had from a drawing on the inside cover of a book of expenses for 1360[9]. This drawing is reproduced here as a frontispiece. The only accounts in this roughly kept wardrobe book were those of messengers sent out with writs for summoning parliament and with routine dispatches for the sheriffs; so there seems no reason to doubt that the picture shows a messenger and his groom setting out on their travels. The messenger, as depicted here, wore a short tunic, buttoning down the front to the waist and up the sleeves to the elbow. A cape with scalloped edge covered his shoulders, and over this he set a hood, ornamented with a band and

[1] E.A. 354/23; Add. MS. 7966 ff. 165 and 165v.
[2] *C.R.* 1254–1256 p. 288.
[3] *R.L.Cl.* 1204–1227 I, 409.
[4] *Ibid.* p. 450.
[5] E.A. 399/7.
[6] E.A. 394/16 m. 6.
[7] Cotton MS. Galba E III f. 188.
[8] Cotton MS. Galba E XIV f. 45v.
[9] E.A. 309/11.

tall feather. His shoes were provided with exaggeratedly large spurs, symbols of the speed at which he could travel on the king's errands, such spurs as were bought in London by Jack Faukes and his companion when they set out for Avignon post haste in 1343.[1] A courier's dress was probably less elaborate than a messenger's. Faukes, when he started off for Avignon with the courier Robert of Arden, may have been accompanied by a runner clad in a long tunic of the same type as the groom wore here, or as the running messenger wore in the fifteenth century illustration reproduced by Jusserand.[2] Characteristically, the messenger in the 1360 drawing had at his belt the shield-shaped pouch with the king's arms on it, in which he carried important letters, while the later drawing of a courier showed him with a plain pouch only, befitting his less exalted station. Nicholas Upton, writing in the fifteenth century, declared that the pouch was the only place in which an inferior messenger was allowed to wear his master's arms, though he might carry them there; and that a mounted messenger could bear the royal arms on his left shoulder as well.[3] In these assertions, Upton seems to be making a rule out of common practice; but illustrations and references alike show that the pouch with arms was generally taken as the messenger's distinctive badge.

2. Food

Though the right to receive livery from the king was the outstanding mark of a servant in the royal household, the right to receive meals in the king's hall came second in importance. The established messengers had always taken their food with the rest of the household, and the privilege was so well known to wardrobe clerks that they found no reason to mention messengers' meals till 1300. The household ordinance of 1279[4] dealt specifically with the rights and duties of a few important officials, but did not set out to be a complete description of the household on its different levels. An organization which distributed meals daily to several hundred poor, with additions up to a thousand on the greater feasts of the church[5] was not likely to refuse a bite to any man working for the king, and even couriers may have received their food while they were 'retained' by the wardrobe and waited for messages.

The expenses of the Scottish war and the noticeable increase in wardrobe personnel during the 1300 campaign, were the reasons for Edward I's decision to reduce the number of persons allowed to eat in hall. At St. Albans, when the court was on its way north, a statute

[1] E.A. 312/4.
[2] Jusserand *English Wayfaring Life* p. 224.
[3] Upton *De Studio Militari* cap. IX p. 18.
[4] Tout *Chapters* II, 158–163.
[5] H. Johnstone 'Poor relief in the royal households of thirteenth-century England' *Speculum* IV 149–167 (1929).

was promulgated dividing the household into two classes, servants who had the right to food in court, servants who had no such privilege. By a fortunate chance, the title of the statute *De Aula non tenenda in Hospicio Regis* and the date on which it came into force, 13 April 1300, have been preserved through a memorandum drawn up in the ward-robe, though the actual provisions of the statute have been lost.[1] The main intention of the new order was without question to effect economy in household management by paying money in lieu of meals to all king's servants genuinely entitled to be maintained by him, thus eliminating the hanger-on and the casual labourer who scrounged a living for himself out of the king's hospitality.[2] The new allowances were to be paid through the marshal's department.

The king's messengers were among those household groups affected by the order. Esquires downwards, most of the domestic servants found themselves receiving wages instead of board, according to this list drawn up to guide the marshal during the first months of the new experiment. The list is in two parts: the first recorded the wages of the more or less static members of the household, important officers and domestic servants; the second dealt with general household expenses, and gave in the margin the names of messengers who came and went from day to day. To the official mind drawing up a scheme of this sort, the messengers must have been a great embarrassment. Names of twelve king's messengers appear in the margin of this roll, with dates showing how long they were in court between journeys, from 13 April (when the order was put into force) till 7 October following. The list shows that the ordinary messenger was kept per-petually on the move, and this must have been awkward for the clerks who had to calculate the days spent in court and the amount of money due to each man individually.

Most of the messengers' names in this wage list are those of men on the regular establishment, but besides the twelve king's messen-gers, and one messenger attached to the prince's service, six couriers also received allowances in lieu of food during the period. It seems as though a few, but by no means the majority of the couriers employed by the wardrobe had had meals in hall while retained for the king's service; but only two inferior messengers had any money allowance before July 1300. These were Richard of Warrington and John Whiting, who were both allowed wages for food on 5 June. It happens

---

[1]E.A. 357/28 'Rotulus de vadiis scutiferorum et aliorum diversorum existen-cium ad vadia in rotulo marescalli, tam pro expensis equorum et garcionum suorum quam in orum suorum incipiens die xiij Aprilis quo die aula vacauit ex toto per statutum factum apud sanctum Albanum de aula non tenenda in hospicio regis.' Tout *op. cit.* ii, 49–51.

[2]French messengers in the royal household, both mounted and unmounted, received their meals in court; but in France too a reduction was found necessary. From 1360, only thirteen foot-messengers and six mounted men were allowed food in court (Vaillé *Histoire Générale des Postes Françaises* p. 164).

that there is an account for the ordinary wages of the household covering June 1300, which shows that Richard and John were only two out
of ten couriers in court on that date.[1] The ten names are given with the
marginal note 'cokini venientes post statutum, v die Junii', so the clerks
evidently knew that the statute had deprived the inferior messengers
of any claim to board, except in some special cases. John Whiting, at
any rate, was an old hand. Probably most of the inferior messengers
had never had any right to take meals at the common tables, whatever
they may have done in practice; and had therefore no claim to compensation even if they waited in court to be at hand when the wardrobe
needed them.

The position of the messengers belonging to other royal households seems to have raised some questions in the official mind. It was
not made clear in the statute whether the prince's servants were to be
included in the order if they came to the king with messages from their
master or on his business. A messenger of Edward of Caernarvon,
happening to be in court on 13 April, was paid his wages by the
marshal with the rest till 22 April, when he presumably rejoined the
prince. But Robert of Manfield, another of Edward's messengers,
received wages at court till 30 April, when his position was reviewed
and he 'vacated' the marshal's list for the future 'because he eats in
hall', though arrears at 3*d.* a day were made up to him.[2] Perhaps there
was some extraordinary reason for this, for in July 1303, Adam
Belesey the prince's courier, took 2*d.* a day from the prince's officials
as wages for the fifteen days during which he remained in court and
outside the prince's 'hall.'[3] Within the prince's household, of course,
the statute of St. Albans was applied just as in the king's household.

Another man whose position did not square with the new regulations was Simon, the queen's messenger, who had a pension of 4½*d.* a
day granted in 1296 for his past services to Eleanor the king's mother.
In addition to the pension, he continued to work for the king, receiving
the money whenever he remained in court and his expenses while
away on business. The wardrobe clerks paid his 4½*d.* as usual up to
13 April, and then in doubt entered a note in the account, that he
'vacated' their lists on that day 'until the wishes of the king himself
should be known.'[4] The king must have decided that Simon's case was
an exception, for he never received any allowance from the marshal
and presumably continued to draw his wardrobe pension, and to eat
in hall as well.

The St. Albans limitation on the number of those eating in hall
seems to have been rigidly enforced till the end of 1300, and to have

[1] E.A. 365/22.   [2] E.A. 359/14.
[3] E.A. 363/18 Account of the household of the Prince of Wales.
[4] *L.Q.G.* p. 101. For his usual alternation of pension and salary, see Add. MS.
7965 f. 40 (1296).

been relaxed thereafter for some household groups. The marshal's roll for the first months of 1301[1] gives the names of knights and valets of various offices to whom wages in lieu of food were paid according to rank. Messengers, however, were not included. No further record was kept of the days they spent in court and the days they were away; and it seems as though from Christmas 1300 they took their meals once more at the common tables. Probably the clerks found their comings and goings too complicated for the wage system, and in consequence they were among the first for whom the rule was relaxed. Some groups never till the end of the reign recovered their right to meals; but when money grew scarce and the wardrobe much in debt, it became simpler to find food than to pay wages, and the Statute of St. Albans, never revoked, was conveniently forgotten.

No reference at all to the statute of 1300 was made in the household ordinances of 1318 and 1323.[2] But among those who ate in hall were the established messengers, to whom the phrase '*messagers qi mangeront en sale*' was applied to distinguish them from the couriers who did not share the privilege. It is possible that the limitation on the number of household servants, started in 1300 and continuing under the influence of the Ordainers and of reforming clerks, prevented the inferior messengers from becoming a subsidiary group within the establishment as soon as they might otherwise have done.

Motives of economy, jealousy of wardrobe activity, and the desire for an exact definition of everyone's rights and duties, were all tending to prevent household expansion, and make its organization rigid. The sixteenth century author of the *Liber Niger* might praise Edward III as the 'furst setter of certeynties among his domestycall meyne uppon a grounded rule' and as one who 'appointed diverse duties unto his offices and officers, by a formal and convenient custume, more certayne than was vsed byfore his tyme, that is to say, of all wages within court and without; all manner of lyveres of wynter and somer; the fees of all estates and of officers and housholde and degrees . . . within the court'.[3] The framers of the household ordinances of 1318 and 1323 might have smiled a little at this tribute. Yet it is true to say that the early fourteenth century found a flexible household organization, which had in the past supplied the king with first one instrument and then another through which to act; the end of the century left a rigid household, in which every man knew his place and none could overstep it, and in which the only development possible for a department was to 'void' itself from the household altogether. The author of the *Liber Niger* was aware of this when he compared Edward III's household

[1]E.A. 359/14 'Visus vadiorum tam militum quam valletorum de officiis et aliorum de hospicio regis nomine comedencium in aula factus apud Northampton. . . .'

[2]Tout *Place of Edward II* (2nd ed.) pp. 241–284.

[3]*Collection of Ordinances*, pp. 18–19.

with the one he knew intimately. A new regulation, he tells us, was necessary for this very reason, that since the earlier customs were set out, the privy seal, the marshal's department, the great wardrobe and household treasurer, had all been 'discharged', and with their going, the number of serjeants at arms, messengers, and archers accompanying the king had been much reduced. The messengers naturally went with the sealing departments which gave them their work, the artificers of the great wardrobe went with it; it became possible to unite the offices of clerk of the kitchen and buttery. All the changes which the fifteenth century regulator found were changes caused by decay, not development. No new household department had expanded into a department of state; old organizations had left the household to continue their work outside it; the rest remained as the rules prescribed.

The fifteenth century household was already tradition-bound, and the messengers' position is proof of this. Under Edward IV there were still established messengers eating in hall, but there were only four of them. The name 'messengers of the household' survived, and they still claimed the right to 'sitt togeder in the halle at theyre meles'.[1] There was also one 'messager of the countyng-house, etyng in hall'.[2] But five messengers did not constitute the sum of the king's messenger service in the mid-fifteenth century. It is clear that, as household development became static, messengers outside the household took over the main letter-carrying duties. The four household messengers of the *Liber Niger* were a survival from an earlier stage in the household's life. This is confirmed by later ordinances and descriptions of the household which show them still provided for among members of the Tudor court 'which have no Bouche of Court but . . . dine and sup at the tables hereafter appointed'.[3] The Elizabethan establishment also included four 'currors', but the messengers' work was done by thirty 'standing posts appoynted by the Master'[4]. Yet since nothing in the king's household was ever altered because it had outlived its usefulness, it is not surprising to find that in the nineteenth century, four messengers in ordinary were detailed in turn to wait upon the king, and were fed and lodged at the palace during their period of duty.[5]

The kind of food provided for messengers and other like members of the household may be gauged from the regulations laid down in the *Liber Niger* for anyone who happened to fall sick or who perhaps had been bled. Then his food might be collected for him and was to consist of 'one loffe, one messe of grete mete, dim' gallon ale'. This was the

---

[1] *Ibid.* p.49.   [2] *Ibid.* p. 64.

[3] *Ibid.* p. 169 'Ordinances made at Eltham in the xvii year of King Henry VIII' (1506). A single queen's messenger had neither 'meate, board-wages, nor bouche of court within the household, but wages only'. p. 170 (*bis*).

[4] 'A general collection of all offices in England with theire Fees in the Queen's gifte'. MS. in the possession of Col. Orlebar.

[5] Wheeler-Holohan *op. cit.* p. 49.

customary allowance for the yeomen of the household, though serjeants received double. In Henry VIII's establishment, bread, ale and
meat (of several varieties) or fish for fast days, were specified as the
diet suitable for grooms, porters, yeomen and so forth; eggs, butter,
and fruit seem to have been reserved for their superiors.[1] Two meals a
day was the regular medieval practice, and if we imagine the messenger
eating his portion of meat with bread and ale to his dinner, and more
bread and ale to his supper, we shall probably not be far out.

The almoner provided bread and fish or bread and meat to feed
the poor, and the king's servants are not likely to have done worse.
It may be worth noting that when abroad, a messenger of Edward III
charged daily for two substantial meals, dinner and supper, with a
morning drink when his journey became urgent.[2] The food allowance
given to papal couriers seems to have been superior to that of English
messengers. The pope's household also contained established messengers who had the privilege of eating in hall, and a regulation of
Clement V for his staff provided that each courier should receive
'unum vivandum de pane, cum carnibus, piscibus, ovis, ficubus'.[3]
Bread, meat, fish, eggs and fruit would seem to medieval eyes a
liberal diet for any below the ranks of knights and esquires. Though the
king's messenger here did not get eggs or fruit, nor, so far as we can
tell, any kind of vegetable, he did not fare ill with wholemeal bread and
an ample helping for his 'messe of grete mete'.[4] Meat was comparatively cheap, and was provided on what sounds now a lavish scale in
most large houses.[5] As the day began early, the two meals were spaced
to leave about six hours between them. In 1526, dinner and supper
times were said to be at ten o'clock and four o'clock on working days
when the king's hall was kept, or at 11 and 6 if it was not; and on holy
days according to the time of service.[6]

3. Lodging

All the king's established servants received livery; most of them
received food or wages in lieu of it; very few of them had any right to
lodging in or near the court.[7] This seems odd at first sight, but it is

[1] *Collection of Ordinances* p. 191.
[2] E.A. 312/4. Expenses of Jacke Faukes, 1343.
[3] Baumgarten *Auz Kanzlei und Kammer Erörterungen zur Kurialen Hof-und-
Verwaltingsgeschichte in xiii, xiv, und xv Jahrhundert* (1907) p. 221.
[4] The regulations in force at the French court do not appear to mention in detail
the allowance given to messengers or couriers.
[5] cf. the quantity of meat provided at Bishop's Castle for the visit of Bishop
Swinford in 1290 (1½ carcasses of beef, 2 calves, 2 pigs, 11 kids, a quantity of
venison, 19 geese and 64 fowls for a single day's meals)—*Roll of the Household
Expenses of R. de Swinford during part of the years 1289–1290* ed. Webb, Camden
Society LIX and LXII (1854–5).
[6] Collection of Ordinances p. 151
[7] Tout *Chapters* II, 49.

explained by the peripatetic habit of the court. Clothing could easily be provided, food with rather more difficulty, lodging only with certainty for the highest wardrobe clerks. The chancery alone, having settled down at Westminster, could provide lodgings for its clerks in addition to their robes and food; yet by the end of the fourteenth century, this privilege had fallen into abeyance.[1] As far as the king's messengers were concerned, no mention of them is made in any household ordinance when it comes to speak of lodging; and it is clear that messengers, and the vallets of the household generally, were left to fend for themselves in the wild rush for accommodation, described in an earlier reign by Peter of Blois.[2]

The ordinance of 1318, amongst its regulations for the king's *familia*, laid down expressly that no member of the household 'de quele condicioun qil soit' should bring his wife to court,[3] a rule designed to restrict the number of those travelling in the king's train. The ordinance also laid down some general principles to guide the herbergers in their allocation of lodgings. Those members of the household 'qi ne purra estre herbergez dedeinz lostell en la ville ou le roy, serra herbergez par lez herbergers dedeinz le verge, solonqe soun estate . . . Et qi les officers dostell soient herbergez a pluis apres la court qils purrount estre prestez affaire lour office toutz les foitz qi bosoigne serre: toutz lez autrez de le dit mesnee a pluis pres qi la pays purra bonement suffrer'.[4] Admirable in intention, this ruling can have done little to help the herbergers in their difficult and delicate task of assigning precedence to officials and to their duties.

Even in the fifteenth century, the *Liber Niger* had little to say about lodging for messengers or others; and since the court still moved frequently, the four messengers attached to the household were probably provided for by the herbergers or found their own accommodation. The only exception mentioned is the single counting-house messenger, who must be 'redy horsed and lodged nyghe to serve suche erraundes as the countyng house woll send hym on'.[5] Yet one sort of accommodation had to be found for all messengers: they could claim the right to 'logginge for their horses nygh to the courte'.[6] This would tally with the 1318 rule that duty gave priority. Grooms certainly and perhaps even messengers could sleep in the loft above the stables (as was the practice on farms till a much later date), and be ready to rouse and saddle should an important letter require instant dispatch. Riding 'night and day' with dispatches is occasionally

---

[1] B. Wilkinson *The Chancery under Edward III*, p. 87.
[2] Quoted by Stretton 'The Travelling Household of the Middle Ages' *Journal of the Brit. Arch. Ass.* new series XL, 75–103 (1935) pp. 94–5.
[3] Tout *Place of Edward II*, 2nd ed. p. 280.
[4] *Ibid.* p. 273.
[5] *Collection of Ordinances*, p. 64.
[6] *Ibid.* p. 49.

mentioned in accounts, though time was not so great a factor in the life of a medieval messenger as of his successors.

4. *Equipment*

Stabling was as great a problem as lodging for a travelling household, and messengers were exceptional only in having it found for them conveniently near the court. Important personages in the king's service would not journey with a single horse, and each official had his personal servants, also mounted, for whom accommodation must be found near his. Even if the king's serjeants, yeomen, falconers, minstrels, and messengers had but one apiece, the number of horses to be stabled on their account must have been considerable.

A mount was an essential part of the equipment of every member of a mobile household above the very lowest ranks; and even more so for the riding messenger who could not function without it. But it was equipment which he must provide for himself, just as the feudal army was expected to meet the king prepared for battle. The office of messenger did not carry with it either the use of a horse or an allowance towards the expense of buying one, and not till Elizabethan times did the words 'riding horse by discretion of the Court' appear in a description of the establishment.[1] If a messenger or any other member of the household lost his horse in the king's service, that was his misfortune, and no concern of anyone's. Only in time of war, involving abnormal risks, were horses valued for compensation in case of injury; and even then, the valuation did not cover any but the higher grades of the household. It might be extended as far down the lists as the serjeants. Simon Atteleigh, messenger of Eleanor of Provence, was promoted after her death to be one of the king's serjeants at a wage of 12*d.* a day, four times as great as his allowance while messenger. His privileges were correspondingly enlarged. The 12*d.* was paid from 17 August 1297 'on which day his horse was valued',[2] a remark which shows that, as messenger, his beast had had no official existence. To provide his whole train with horses or to replace all horses injured on his account, would have involved a medieval king in endless trouble and prohibitive expense.

Practice, however, was not as stern as theory. If the messenger lost his horse through carelessness, he alone suffered; but if through accident or zeal, the king's generosity might be invoked. The accounts show that compensation for lost horses was frequently paid to members of the household, but it was as a gift and of the king's especial grace, not as a right. Such payments were made, either in time of war,

[1]Col. Orlebar's MS. description of the Elizabethan establishment. The words relate to a messenger from the Court of Wards and Liveries only. The 'messenger redy horsed' spoken of in the *Liber Niger* had no such allowance.
[2]Add. MS. 7965 f. 40.

or for the loss of horses abroad, or when the king had ordered a journey to be made with all possible speed, a command which may have implied promise of compensation. Even the niggardly Edward I allowed 30s. to his messenger Brehull 'for the replacement of his black horse, dead in parts beyond the sea',[1] and 40s. to the prince's messenger Robert of Newington for the detriment which he suffered by the death of his rouncey while serving the king in Scotland in 1301.[2] A journey to Vienne and back was accomplished in thirty-nine days by two of Edward II's messengers, but at the cost of two hackneys lost 'on account of the very great haste to which they were enjoined by the king'; for these, they were allowed to claim 60s. when presenting their account to the wardrobe.[3] At least nothing was lost for the asking, and Thomas Wynebaud, the treasurer's messenger, ended his particular of expenses for three journeys (one to the Marches of Wales, another to Gascony, and a third to meet the Cardinal at Stamford) with the words 'E vous pri lavaunt dit Thomas restoraunce de ij hakeneys perduz en lavaunt dit chemin'.[4]

Probably these gifts fell short of the market value of a horse strong enough to be useful to a messenger. The amounts given vary from 6s. 8d. to 40s. for each horse, and the second figure is more likely to represent the cost of a good beast, though a serviceable one might be purchased for less.[5] This is the impression given by a chancellor's messenger temporarily in the king's service in 1331. He claimed compensation to the tune of £24 4s. for horses lost on two journeys abroad 'as he has shown the king that he went by the king's orders upon two occasions from the city of York to Gascony upon certain of his affairs and expended the aforesaid sum in horses lost on the journey and in other expenses'.[6] The difficulty here is to know what other expenses were included and how many horses the messenger expected to have replaced. Issue rolls prove that the sum was allowed and duly paid in instalments.

Payment of compensation for horses was becoming more common under Edward III, though still with the words 'of the king's gift' or 'of the king's special grace' to show that it was not a privilege. Richard Hert, for instance, was given 6s. 8d. towards the purchase of a mount in August 1357, and was allowed 20s. in April 1362 when he

[1] E.A. 355/10.
[2] E.A. 359/6 f. 21.
[3] Cotton MS. Nero C VIII f. 55.
[4] E.A. 371/8 No. 35A.
[5] *C.C.R.* 1330–1333 p. 386; I.R. 276/mm 3, 14.
[6] This seems to agree with the theory that the ratio between money values in the fourteenth and twentieth centuries pre. 1939 is approximately 1:40. The same difficulty over comparative price of horses has been found by Miss Putnam in assessing the values set on horses in assize rolls (B. H. Putnam 'Records of Courts of Common Law, especially the sessions of the Justices of the Peace' *Proceedings of the American Philosophical Society* vol. 91 No. 3 (1947) pp. 258–273).

had the misfortune to lose it while taking letters under the privy seal to
the north 'pro arduis negotiis dominum regem tangentibus ibidem
expediendo'. In January 1367, armed with a writ of privy seal, Richard
was able to demand part payment from the exchequer of six marks
'which the lord king ordered for him of his gift in recompense of two
horses lost by him in the northern parts in the king's service'; and
during the following month, the exchequer paid another 20s. on the
same writ.[1] Messengers of the queen or the prince were treated in
much the same way. Gilbert, messenger of Queen Philippa, received a
mark for his expenses with a sick horse in May 1332, and a further 40s.
to replace it when it died in August.[2] The *Black Prince's Register*
noted 20s. paid as compensation to John Wetherherde the messenger
in 1359.[3] Similar payments, it is interesting to discover, were made by
the Pope's officials to his couriers when they lost horses by accident
on the road.[4]

The rest of the messenger's special equipment, his spurs, letter
pouch, and basket, were provided for him. Presumably other members
of the household received appropriate equipment also. Faukes was
allowed to claim 6s. 8d. for two pairs of boots and two pairs of spurs
in 1343, as necessary for his journey to Avignon with a courier companion. A letter pouch was so important to a messenger that the issue
of one for the first time was spoken of as equivalent to a formal appointment. A stock of these leather pouches was kept by the wardrobe for
issue to new messengers and replacements. The supply was temporarily exhausted in 1297, however, for the sum of 2s. was given instead
to Robinet Little 'to buy him a pouch at the time when he was first
made a messenger, because there was no pouch found in the wardrobe
at that time.'[5] Three types of pouch were used. The first, for hanging
on the messenger's belt, was strong and serviceable but had the king's
arms marked on it. This cost between 1s. and 2s. For ceremonial
occasions, a more expensive article might be used, elaborately painted
with the royal arms and other decoration. Such was the pouch bought
by John of Bristol, messenger to Elianor the king's sister in May
1332 on the occasion of her marriage, when he was given 13s. 4d. at
Dover 'of the lady's own gift to buy him a pouch with the arms of
England and Guelders'.[6] Even more sumptuous was the silver-gilt box
enamelled with the prince's arms, with a silver-gilt garnished girdle
enamelled with the ribbon, which was presented by the Black Prince
to his favourite messenger in 1355. This was no ordinary pouch and

---

[1] I.R. 387 m. 26; 410 m. 2; 429 mm. 23, 26.
[2] John Rylands' Library Latin MS. 235 ff. 17v, 19.
[3] *Black Prince's Register* IV, 321.
[4] Rodocanachi *Revue d'Histoire Diplomatique XXVI* p. 395.
[5] Add. MS. 7965 f. 108 v.
[6] Add. MS. 38006 f. 8 and E.A. 386/7.

belt intended for daily wear and tear, but one for special occasions.[1] The third type was much cheaper and smaller than either of the others. It was the equivalent of the modern correspondence file, and was used in the wardrobe as a container for small documents, and by the messenger to separate or to protect letters within his main bag. Such a pouch enclosing its warrants can still be seen at the Public Record Office.[2] A strip of leather was doubled and thonged together to make a bag about six to eight inches square, and then provided with a drawstring at the top. The cost, to judge from entries in two sets of accounts for 1276–7, was 1*d*.[3] When intended for letters going abroad, to separate one batch from another within the messenger's pouch or basket, it might cost a little more. One for letters to the court of Rome in 1276–8 cost 2½*d*., and while John Piacle was abroad about the same time, he found it necessary to purchase a pouch of this sort which cost him 9*d*.[4]

Some entries speak also of the messenger's hanaper or basket, a large container into which bulky objects or bundles of letters went. Men who set out with summons addressed to the sheriffs of several counties needed something larger than a pouch which could be hung at the belt. So William Alkham,[5] who entered the king's service in 1297, received dispatches and journey money for one of his first trips, together with 12*d*. 'to buy him a hanaper to put the letters in'. Four years later, when he needed another, he was allowed only 1*d*. for it. Many entries speak of baskets for letters, but include their cost with the rest of the messenger's expenses, so that comparison of prices is impossible.

The bag for letters with the king's arms on the outside became a familiar sight all over the country; and references to it even got into the sermons of the day. Dr. Owst, as an illustration of the fourteenth century preacher's fondness for homely comparisons has quoted a sermon of Master Rypon of Durham, in which the clergy were compared to couriers travelling swiftly for the king. 'Again, it is the courier's duty to carry a box painted with the arms and insignia of his lord, containing his lord's letters sealed and enclosed in it. He has, moreover, his special credentials to deliver by word of mouth'. Rypon then enlarged on the comparison. 'The box of morality is the priest's mind, on which box are painted the arms and insignia of Jesus Christ, viz. the theological virtues; in which box ought to be inclosed letters sent of Christ, to wit, knowledge of the letters of the Old and New

[1] *Black Prince's Register* IV, 150.
[2] e.g. E.A. 311/14.
[3] E.A. 350/26 m. 1 and Add. MS. 36762 m. 6. Almost every issue roll for the reigns of Edward I and II contains an entry relating to the purchase of pouches. e.g. I.R. 85.
[4] E.A. 350/26; Chanc. Misc. 47/4/4 f. 17.
[5] Add. MS. 7965 f. 113; E.A. 364/2 No. 2.

Testaments, sealed with the seal of Christ. . . .'[1] The comparison was not completely original when Master Rypon delivered it in his sermon, for similar illustrations were used by other preachers of his day. 'Currours and eke messangers with boistes'[2] must have been well known to everyone if such a detailed comparison could be drawn in a popular talk. Obviously the things about the messenger which impressed the ordinary man were his celerity and his pouch, with the king's arms blazoned upon it, hanging conspicuously at his belt.[3]

5. Grooms and Boys

The servant's servant had also to be considered and regulated by the household officers. The messenger and his fellows might provide their own horses, but they expected the king to pay and clothe the grooms who looked after them. The poorest student at the medieval university, the most needy parish priest, found it necessary to have a page to wait on them; and the king's messenger, though humble in status compared with the knights, squires, and serjeants of the household, had his own little position to keep up. He did not expect to attend to his horse himself, though if he were a wise and experienced messenger, he probably supervised the operation. In 1278, when there were twelve riding messengers attached to the household, seven grooms, distinguished as *'garciones de nuncii regis'* received their shoe allocation at Windsor on 17 July.[4] The ratio of seven grooms to twelve messengers seems much the same as that contemplated in the *Liber Niger*, 'one clene childe' to each pair of household messengers,[5] though fourteenth century household regulations did not set a definite limit. The ordinance of 1318 merely acknowledged that grooms working for the king's principal household officials, or for his Welshmen, archers or messengers, were entitled to receive clothes and food.[6]

When six or seven grooms had to be shared between a dozen messengers, it seems likely that their services were monopolized by the senior men; and that newly-joined messengers had to wait their turn for the boys or look after their own beasts when, as occasionally

[1]G. R. Owst *Literature and Pulpit in Medieval England* (1933) p. 30 and note 3.
[2]Chaucer *Hous of Fame* Bk. II, ll. 2128–9.
[3]The royal arms continued to be the insignia of the king's messengers till Edward VII replaced them with his monogram, breaking a tradition of at least 600 years (Wheeler-Holohan *History of the King's Messengers* p. 240).
Can the girdle of silver-gilt 'enamelled with the ribbon', which the Black Prince's messenger received in 1355 (*Black Prince's Register* IV, 150) be a reference to the garter ribbon, which has always been associated with the messengers' greyhound badge? The greyhound appears to date from the seventeenth century only.
[4]Add. MS. 36762 m. 4.
[5]Collection of Ordinances p. 49.
[6]Tout *Place of Edward II* p. 275.

happened, all the king's messengers were in court together. At any rate, the illustration in the wardrobe book of 1360[1] shows a messenger setting out accompanied by his groom; and a number of entries refer to messengers taking their grooms with them. Nicholas Ramage (certainly one of the senior messengers under Edward I) had his groom with him when he made a round of the Gascon towns in 1288–9; and in the same year his colleague William of Dogmersfield delivering a letter to the Senechal of Gascony, was accompanied by a groom. Ralph Laundeles also took his groom to Gascony when, like Ramage, he visited the Gascon towns.[2] The king's messenger did, in some degree, represent the king, and his prestige abroad must be upheld. When Robert of Newington and William Loughborough were sent with the king's letters to the Council of Vienne in 1310, each messenger was supported by his groom to emphasize the importance of the mission.[3]

At home, the messenger did not take his groom on routine journeys (unless he paid for him out of the expenses allowed for himself, in which case no mention of the groom would be made in the accounts). The single exception mentions William of Ledbury's groom going with him to the Bishop of Chester 'by the king's order,' which supports the view that a messenger had to get special permission if he wanted to take a groom on an English journey.[4] Occasionally an entry in the account refers to a groom who, in the absence of other messengers, had been entrusted with urgent letters. Such were the letters of secret seal with which John le Taillour, groom to Ralph Say, was sent off hastily on business described as secret in October 1326.[5]

In a few of these entries, it is made quite clear that the connexion between senior messengers and their grooms was a personal and lasting one. William Ledbury was still a newcomer to the service in 1288–9 when he was sent with letters which for some reason were important enough to require a groom as well as a messenger. Not having one of his own, William borrowed a groom for the occasion, and Richard, groom of the messenger Adam of Bayworth, was sent with him.[6] Adam's groom is mentioned in another account for the same period as journeying to Ireland with his messenger;[7] and in several other cases, the senior messengers' grooms are named. John Pyacle had a servant called Robert of Lincoln, John le Taillour was attached to the messenger Ralph Say. So close was the connexion between groom and messenger that in some instances, the king in demanding a corrody for his retiring servant, stipulated that the groom should be provided for too. The abbot and convent of Middleton were ordered 'to admit Gervase the king's messenger and his

[1]E.A. 309/11.
[2]E.A. 308/10.
[3]Cotton MS. Nero C VIII f. 55.
[4]Add. MS 7966 f. 126 v.
[5]E.A. 382/6.
[6]E.A. 308/10.
[7]E.A. 305/12 m. 1.

groom to their house and minister necessaries to them' in 1285,[1] and William of Alkham was given a corrody for himself and his groom at Vaudey in 1310.[2]

Many of these grooms, especially the men who by habit or preference attached themselves to some one messenger, remained in the household all their working lives without changing their occupation. They probably entered the king's service young, justifying the *Liber Niger's* description of them; but the groom who followed his messenger in the wardrobe account illustration was no longer a boy, for the draughtsman has clearly indicated a rough pointed beard. The groom wore a tunic reaching nearly to his knees, a caped hood and a hat of twisted cloth on his head, a formidable sword and a knife at his side, together with his pouch which did not bear the royal arms. His whole dress was less fashionable than that of the messenger, and as he went on foot, running behind his master's horse (like the page boys in ballads) he was equipped with a huge staff, an aid to walking and a useful weapon at a pinch. Such a man received 2*d.* a day for his expenses out of court[3] and shared many of the household privileges, so that his position was not one to be altogether despised. An ambitious boy, however, might make it the stepping-stone to something better. Such a boy was Thomas Wynebaud, who started as a groom, then served for a while as courier, gained some valuable experience as messenger of the treasurer, and finally undertook many commissions for the king, to whose service he seems to have been transferrred. He was probably not the only groom to work his way up to a more respected position. Some advancement of this kind seems to be contemplated by fifteenth century officials. 'It is here enacted by the kinge, that every man of this courte, whych shall drawe furthe any servaunt in it, that such younge servaunt be commyn of clene bloode, goode of condytions, vertiouse, and of person lykely; that if it fortune theym to growe to the King's service, the worshipp of the courte continue by suche chosen people.'[4] That not all grooms lived up to this description, and that some messengers were not content to share a servant, may be guessed from the remarks made by the framers of Henry VIII's ordinances at Eltham, who insisted that no serjeant, herald, pursuivant, messenger, minstrel, falconer, huntsman, or footman, might bring into Court 'any boyes or rascalls nor also other of their servants but such as accordeth to the ordinarie allowance of the King's household'.[5]

[1] *C.Ch.W.* I, 28.   [2] *C.C.R.* 1307–1313 p. 248.

[3] e.g. Richard (Adam Bayworth's groom) in 1288–9 (E.A. 308/10).

[4] *Collection of Ordinances* p. 67.

[5] *Ibid.* p. 147.

It is to be hoped that the state of additional and unauthorized servants was not like that of the wretched scullions serving under the master cooks in the king's kitchen, who were no longer to 'goe naked or in garments of such vileness as they now doe and have been accustomed to doe, nor lie in the nights and dayes in the kitchen or ground by the fireside' (*Ibid.* p. 148).

CHAPTER III

CONDITIONS OF SERVICE

Wages, Gifts, Discipline and Seniority

1. Wages

A LL members of the king's messenger service, whether *nuncii* or *cursores*, were entitled to wages in court while they waited to be sent on the king's business, provided that they had been formally appointed or retained for this duty. Such wages were quite distinct from travelling expenses out of court, and were calculated on a different scale. Out of his English travelling expenses the messenger was at liberty to save what he could; in court he usually received less but had no expenses to meet out of it, except the cost of his lodgings. 'Wages' and 'expenses' were never paid concurrently. The earliest description of the household speaks of Marshalsea serjeants who received 3*d.* a day if sent out on the king's business, but not in court 'sin autem in domo Regis commedant'.[1] The same principle was still enforced in 1321, when Donald of Athol took letters of privy seal to seven persons but received nothing for the work 'because they were all in court' and he had delivered the letters without leaving court himself.[2]

Under Edward I, the messengers' wages in court were reckoned at $\frac{1}{2}d$ a day. On this basis the wardrobe paid five of them who were left behind when the king went abroad in May 1286. One hundred and fifty-three days passed before the king's return, and for each day's waiting the messenger drew his $\frac{1}{2}d.$ 'a halfpenny a day while he is in court and outside the court nothing'. Thus Roger of Windsor, in court for 142 of the 153 days, was paid his 5*s.* 11*d.*; and the others similarly. The entry recording these payments definitely states that this sum was to cover lodgings 'pro conductione lecti et pro gentaculo suo'.[3] There does not seem to have been much work for the messengers to do in the king's absence; four of them had each spent a few days out of court on business, for which they received the usual expenses; but the fifth, Richard of Norwich, seems to have taken himself off for something like sixty days holiday without pay. For, as the household ordinance

---

[1]*Red Book of the Exchequer* III, 812.
[2]Add. MS. 9931 f. 38.
[3]Chanc. Misc. 4/3 ff. 20 v, 21 v.
Two other entries suggest a $\frac{1}{2}d.$ wage; the imprest of 10*s.* 7$\frac{1}{2}d.$ paid to ten *nuncii* on their wages in 1301, and the 9*s.* 7$\frac{1}{2}d.$ received by Nicholas Ramage as wages in the same year. (E.A. 360/25 m. 2 and 359/4).

of 1318 stated plainly, messengers who shared in the common meals
'ne aillont nulle part hors del hostell sils nessoient en messages'.[1]

Wages were paid on a more generous scale towards the end of
Edward's reign. Eight messengers enjoyed a wage of 3*d.* a day in
1303–4, according to a schedule of wages paid to officers of the household,[2] and about the same time other sums which imply a 3*d.* rate were
paid under this heading. Arnold Bon, for instance was the senior
messenger who collected wages for himself and eight comrades in
1300: the amount paid was 3*s* each, representing twelve days spent in
court at 3*d.* a day. Later in the same month he again distributed 3*s.*
wages to himself and six other messengers; and a very short time
afterwards received an additional 3*s.* for himself only.[3] These payments
cannot conceivably have been made on the old basis of ½*d.* a day. Even
the couriers retained in Edward's service were being paid at a higher
rate, as the *Liber cotidianus* for 1297 plainly states. 'To Gilbert of
Ludgershale for his wages and those of 15 of his courier companions
from the 26th of September until the 26th day of October, both counted,
for 31 days; to the said Gilbert 3*d.* a day and to each of the other
couriers 2*d.* a day, subtracting 4*s.* 6*d.* in all' for wages already entered
under another heading and 'because some of them were out of court
for 2 days and others for 3 days'.[4] A number of similar entries confirm
the statement that couriers were being paid wages at 2*d.* a day while
retained,[5] though a senior man might be rated for the time as a privileged messenger. In no case did these wages become anything like a
regular salary. It is significant of the basis on which these men were
engaged that couriers' wages cease each year with the approach of
winter and the end of the campaigning season.

Needless to say, wages in court were not paid promptly either to
messengers or couriers. Imprests on debts frequently appeared in
wardrobe accounts, and were sometimes paid off in money, sometimes
in cloth. Edmund Moses and ten other messengers received extra
garments as an imprest on wages owing to them for the period 1296–
99,[6] and in 1300–1, nearly every messenger received cloth or robes
instead of money due to him.[7] The practice cannot have had much to
recommend it from the messenger's point of view, for if he had had to
find himself lodgings, he could hardly pay for them in clothing three
or four years afterwards. But when money was scarce and cloth to
hand, harassed wardrobe officials resorted to these truck payments
again and again.

[1]Tout *Place of Edward II* p. 272.
[2]E.A. 365/22.
[3]E.A. 357/21 mm. 7d, 8, 8d.
[4]Add. MS. 7965 f. 84 v. *et seq.*
[5]E.A. 357/23; 357/21 mm. 7d, 8; 363/18; 360/24 No. 4; Add. MS. 35292;
E.A. 364/13 f. 101 v; Add. MS. 8835 ff. 73 v, 80, 96.
[6]E.A. 354/23.
[7]E.A. 359/4; Add. MS. 7966.

The reformers of 1323 knew well enough that household wages had fallen into arrears and that confusion over their payment delayed the presentation of every wardrobe account at the exchequer. The York Ordinance[1] appointed a special clerk under the Marshal to keep an account of the money due to each member of the household and make out a bill in his own hand at the end of each half year for every payment due, so that the wardrobe could collect these slips by way of receipt from each man paid. This regulation may have done a little to straighten out the accounts, but it did not solve the major problem, how to find the ready cash to pay anyone.[2] Messengers after 1323 may have received their bills half yearly, but they were no nearer to getting their wages, and in many cases wardrobe bills were still unpaid two or three years after issue. Nor did the exchequer ordinance of 1324[4] solve the difficulty. This forbade imprests altogether and ordered the payment of wages at fixed intervals, but never in advance. The payee must account for the money owing to him before he received anything, and take no part payments. But the fact remained that the wardrobe could not produce the sums needed to clear off old debts and start afresh. Lacking this, it could hardly refuse small advances to members of the household whose wages were several years in arrears. Thus the ordinances of 1323 and 1324 failed of their immediate purpose.

Indirectly, however, the introduction of bills did ease the difficulty. A bill was made out for the sum due and was cashed, not by any household department, but by the exchequer. Several messengers were able by this means to claim wages long owing to them,[3] and the payment was recorded on the issue rolls. The word 'imprest' did not entirely disappear but it was now the exchequer, not the wardrobe, which paid out household wages in driblets, and the delays were less. A messenger who wanted his money more speedily might persuade some obliging Chamber officer to cash his warrant for him, as a private transaction and personal favour, paying him, no doubt, commission on it.[4]

When wages were much in arrears, the messenger might be pacified for the time by a gift 'for his wages and regards, to help out his livelihood' as one entry had it.[5] Another expedient was to grant the impatient servant a pension, either temporarily or permanently. Gilbert, messenger of Queen Philippa, had a grant of this kind in 1331 soon after he entered her service. This was intended to last only until the king could provide him with an equivalent in land or rents, but in

[1]Tout *Place of Edward II* pp. 281–4; Johnson 'The system of account in the wardrobe of Edward II' *Trans. Royal Hist. Soc.* 4th series XII 75–104.
[2]*Red Book of the Exchequer* III, 848–969.
[3]See for instance the account of imprests made at the exchequer of receipt during the Easter term of 1350 (E.A. 326/2).
[4]Tout *Chapters* IV 317 note 4.
[5]I.R. 400 mm. 15, 21.

fact he held it throughout his long career in the queen's household.[1] In 1376, most of the messengers then in the king's service received a pension of $4\frac{1}{2}d$. a day as long as they should be 'in the office of messenger, not labouring at the king's wages among the king's messengers'.[2] This ambiguous phrase can only mean, I think, that the pension was to be paid instead of wages, unless the recipient were out of court on the king's business and receiving ordinary expenses for his labour. In one case, the grant was renewed for life.

Up to this point, wages had only been paid for days spent in court, waiting for work. Gradually during the fourteenth century, there seems to have been a change, and by the end of Edward III's reign, messengers and other members of the household appear to receive something more like a modern salary. Regular wages were undoubtedly paid to messengers and others during war time: such wages of war for the siege of Calais were being paid off to messengers during 1350, when a number of them received the amounts set out in a certain wardrobe bill, for wages, robes and shoes.[3] Soon the practice was extended to cover times of peace as well as times of war. The indiscriminate use of the phrase *pro vadiis et expensis* indicates this. Hitherto the words had represented distinct payments, now they were becoming merged. In the next century, the *Liber Niger* of Edward IV's household speaks of messengers receiving 'oute of courte, wages and all, v d. by day as other yomen of houshold',[4] suggesting a payment which was not solely intended to cover travelling expenses. The entry describing the counting house and its servants confirms this. Here was to be kept 'one yoman also in thys offyce called Messager of the countynghouse, etyng in the hall; he shold be redy horsed and lodged nyghe, to serve suche erraundes as the Countyng-house woll send hym on, takynge for hys wages dayly, being present in courte in the chekker-rolle, iii d, and for bouche oute of courte in message ii d more dayly'—that is, 5d. altogether, the sum paid to the other messengers out of court. By the time that Henry VIII's officers were revising his first set of household ordinances, an allowance of 53s. 4d. 'for his yearly wages' was being paid to William Johnson, messenger of the household; while ordinary messengers had wages within the household of £5 17s. 4d. per annum. Elizabeth's messengers also received yearly salaries.[5]

Some such development, from wages paid under special circumstances to regular salaries, is found at the papal court among the pope's messengers; and is worth citing for comparison. From 1351, if not before, papal couriers were accustomed to have 2 *gros tournois* a day

[1]*C.P.R.* 1330–1334 p. 159; *C.C.R.* 1337–1339 p. 64.
[2]*C.P.R.* 1374–1377 pp. 351, 397; I.R. 462 mm. 5, 9.
[3]*Collection of ordinances* p. 9; I.R. 354 mm. 7, 8, 10, 19. See too, accounts of imprests on these wages recorded in E.A. 326/2 m. 6.
[4]*Collection of Ordinances* p. 49.
[5]*Ibid.* pp. 64, 169, 213; Col. Orlebar's MS.

for wages, plus an allowance for lodgings; while at the same time they received food and probably clothing on much the same terms as king's messengers in England.[1] The middle of the fourteenth century, therefore, saw a change from irregular to regular wages which affected messengers in more than one large establishment. Since English messengers often travelled with letters to Avignon and papal couriers brought their master's letters to England, it is possible that these developments were interrelated.

2. *Gifts*

Messengers and others in the household received special gifts from time to time, either as members of the king's establishment or as individuals.

It was customary for the king and the heads of the lesser royal households to provide New Year presents for all their servants; and though the accounts say little about the nature of the gifts, it is clear that messengers shared in the general distribution. The *Liber Niger* mentions this privilege specifically. 'They have part of the gyftes geyven to the houshold, if they or any of them, be present when it is geven, but none aprons'.[2] The gift often took the form of clothing or cloth, or such articles as the belt worth 5s. which Queen Isabella gave her messenger William in 1330.[3] They were seldom as extravagant as the silver-gilt box enamelled with the ribbon, which the Black Prince gave to a favourite messenger John Dagonet in 1355. Two ells of striped cloth were bought as a New Year's gift to the prince's runner Clays d'Espagne (de Ispannia) in 1347, and this was probably thought quite good enough for a courier. Another useful gift for a mounted messenger was a horse; and the *Black Prince's Register* mentions two such presents. A hackney bought at Tichfield was given on 31 May 1346 to John Dagonet the messenger; and in January 1349 he received a grey sumpter horse in the distribution of gifts for that New Year.[4] It is significant that in two of these instances, the New Year's gift was some four months late; and by the time they arrived, presents may frequently have been out of season. In such difficulties, a present of money may sometimes have been substituted, and perhaps the 'rewards' which were paid to messengers with their wages in 1359 should properly come under this heading.[5]

Besides New Year presents, all important occasions were marked by gifts, and members of the household expected to receive extra clothing whenever the court went abroad. Such distributions accom-

[1]Yves Renouard *Revue Hist.* CLXX p. 3.
[2]*Collection of Ordinances* p. 49.
[3]E.A. 384/18.
[4]*Black Prince's Register* IV pp. 68, 70, 150.
[5]I.R. 400 mm. 15, 21.

panied the transfer of the wardrobe to Gascony, and a list still remains showing which of the king's servants were to have had robes if the king had actually gone abroad, as he planned, in 1326.[1] In the same way, the household of the king's sister was provided with wedding garments in preparation for her marriage to the Duke of Guelders and her progress abroad.[2]

An individual present to a messenger was usually a reward for bringing good news or for valued service; but sometimes merely an expression of the king's favour. Clothing was most often given, money occasionally. Robert Long, the queen's messenger, received 'one good robe' for the good news which he brought Henry III of the recovery of his daughter Katherine in 1256,[3] and several king's messengers received gifts of clothes in 1257.[4] Edward I ordered the issue of cloth to his son's messenger, Robert of Ridware for the robe 'which the king promised him when he went to France'.[5]

Though Henry III gave Alberic his messenger a mark in 1223,[6] money gifts were not usual till the fourteenth century. Then John Faukes received £1 of the king's gift in 1355 and in 1357 eight couriers were given 14s. each to make them clothes;[7] other instances could be cited in plenty.

3. Discipline

The messengers, like other members of the household, worked under the authority and discipline of the household officers,[8] obeying their commands 'for the honour and profit of the household' as the *Liber Niger* put it. During the period of the wardrobe's supremacy, the authorities with whom all the king's servants had principally to deal were the keeper and treasurer of the wardrobe and their subordinates. By the middle of Edward III's reign, the chamber had become the only effective household department; and consequently it was the commandment of the chamberlain, the steward, or the treasurer of the household whom Edward IV's messengers were adjured to obey. The chamberlain 'hath the puniton of all them that are longing to the Chaumber for any offence or outrage: savynge the right of the Countyngehouse in chekking them for their vacations or for lak of recordes' or for losing household stuff, which would be the treasurer's concern.

---

[1] *E.A.* 381/11.   [2] *E.A.* 386/20.
[3] *C.R.* 1254–1256 p. 288.
[4] *Ibid.* 1256–1259 p. 160
[5] *E.A.* 363/25 No. 14.
[6] *R.L.C.* 1204–1227, I, 542.
[7] *I.R.* 376 m. 32; 368 m. 9.
[8] *Collection of Ordinances* pp. 31, 48, 57. French messengers in the fourteenth century were under the Grand Ecuyer de France. (Vaillé *Histoire des Postes Françaises*, p. 17.)

All three of the principal household officers had the power to 'punyshe offences unto the stockkes by theyre discretion' if necessary. No doubt the appointment of most of the king's staff lay in the thirteenth century with the wardrobe officers, as it was to lie during the fifteenth with the chamberlain. To cite the *Liber Niger* again, 'the chamberlain presenteth, chargeth, and dischargeth all such persons as be of the kinges chaumbre; except all suche officers of houshold as ministre for any vytayle for the kinges mouthe or for his chambre'.[1] This threat of being discharged was probably the strongest disciplinary hold which the authorities had over the king's messengers, though it was naturally much disliked. Edward I in 1303 attributed the great unpopularity of his treasurer Walter Langton to his removal of certain 'useless' servants.[2] Some messengers, as for instance John Stygan[3] were appointed during good behaviour only, and this may really have been the common practice. Temporary suspension from office was the usual penalty for seventeenth century messengers who misbehaved;[4] and was a punishment in use also in the papal court in the fourteenth century.

Within the household, it was the marshal's department which drew up the lists of those receiving wages in lieu of board in 1300 and regulated the common tables. Serious offences, and all disputes between members of the household, as well as those between the king's servants and the world outside the verge, came before the marshal and were dealt with by his authority. In his court, too, were tried cases between private citizens who happened for the time to be within the limits of the court as it moved from place to place. The marshal was the keeper of the debtor's prison, in which defaulters could be confined by the sheriff: even sheriffs might find themselves in the marshal's custody if they could not account satisfactorily for the farm of their counties. If a messenger made off with money allowed for his travelling expenses abroad without producing a convincing explanation to the wardrobe or exchequer, or behaved indiscreetly, he too might find himself handed over to the marshal. For, as the *Liber Niger* puts it, any officer of the household known for a 'commyn dayly drunkyn man' was to be given no responsibility until he reformed, while 'if any offycer or minister longing to this court be noysed, or by suspicion, be a theefe or outrageous roystour, in muche hauntyng sclaunderous places, companyes, and other, then he to be rehersed hereof afore the Soveraynes, and to be sent by the Stewarde's power to the Marshalcye Prison, there to abyde untyll he be declared, and as

---

[1]*Collection of Ordinances* pp. 48, 31. The appointment of messengers is dealt with more fully in Chapter VII.

[2]Johnstone *Edward of Caernarvon* p. 70.

[3]*Issue Roll of Thomas de Brantingham* ed. Devon p. 8.

[4]Wheeler-Holohan pp. 16–17, 37–8. This penalty was in such frequent use that set forms were employed for the suspension and reinstatement of messengers.

the lawe wolle awarde'.[1] There is no record, however, of messengers
being concerned with either debts or trespasses within the verge, perhaps because they were so frequently out of court. If any trouble did
arise, it may have been dealt with summarily and not recorded.

The cases of which the marshal's clerks kept full details were those
between the king's servants and others. Typical of such actions is the
plea of contempt and trespass brought by Thomas Cokerel, serjeant of
the king's household, who had borrowed from the mayor and bailiffs of
Lincoln a pair of cart horses to carry the king's victuals, money, and
private belongings to Clipstone. He complained that on the way the
carters, John Scarlet and others, overturned the carts, tipped the
king's victuals into the ditches, and carried off what they wanted, after
assaulting the unfortunate Thomas, who took proceedings against
them and against the bailiffs of Lincoln in the belief that they had
plotted the accident. In another instance, Thomas Bedford, the butler's
servant, brought an action against the mayor and three citizens of
Oxford, for not reserving some wine which Thomas had selected for
the use of the household and asked them to keep till the morrow.[2]

Messengers too might have been involved in cases like these; but
I have not found evidence of it. The only action recorded here which
might concern a messenger is a plea of trespass brought by Adam le
Coreour against William le Taverner living near St. Mary Arches.
But the name is ambiguous, for 'le Coreour' may stand for 'the
courier' or 'the currier', and in any case the suit was not prosecuted.[3]

The most serious household restriction, as far as the messengers
were concerned, was the rule which forbade them to leave court without permission. This permission could be got, according to the
ordinance of 1318, from the steward or treasurer of the household;
later the steward, treasurer, or chamberlain could give leave to
depart from court.[4] That such a rule was in force earlier is plain from
wardrobe accounts. In 1299, Edmund Moses was given permission to
leave the king's service entirely; he was said to be *licenciatus totaliter a
servicio ipsius regis* and 13*s.* was given to him for wages due. John
Somer, another of Edward I's messengers, was also given this permanent leave of absence. Robert Manfield, the prince's messenger,
had to ask leave to return to his master after he had been for a while
attending the household of the king's other children on the prince's
business, and he also received a present 'taking his permission to return to his said lord'. John Piacle, after his illness in 1299, was sent
to his own home.[5] Such licences to depart from court must have been

[1]*Collection of Ordinances* p. 67. See also *Memoranda Roll of the King's Remembrancer 1230–1231* ed. Chalfont p. xxx.
[2]Marshalsea Roll 10 Edward II. E37/2.
[3]Adam may, of course, have been one of the London couriers. See Appendix 3.
[4]Tout *Place of Edward II* p. 272: *Collection of Ordinances* p. 49.
[5]E.A. 357/21; 371/8 m. 129; 366/15; 356/8 m. 12.

granted fairly often, for the wardrobe clerks abbreviate the entries as if common form, though leave of absence unaccompanied by a gift would not be recorded.

Even couriers had to ask for permission to leave the king's service, if they had been formally retained. Richard Trokesford and Adam Cressenhale, wardrobe couriers, were allowed to visit their own part of the country in 1334 and to stay away from court till the king's return from Scotland; the meagre sum of *3s. 4d.* apiece was given them for their expenses.[1] That permission was necessary shows how the fourteenth century courier was winning a position for himself in the establishment. Grooms, on the other hand, had always belonged to the household and been subject to its rules. The twenty-five grooms left in charge of some horses in February 1277 were said to be *licenciati* because they were not with the court and yet were to receive their clothing allowance as usual.[2]

4. *The Senior Messenger*

Messengers of long standing and experience naturally made for themselves a special position among their fellows. The old hand had his personal servant to wait upon him while in court and to accompany him when he went abroad, and foreign commissions were entrusted most frequently to the older messengers. Gifts from the king probably came his way more often too, and if he had the misfortune to lose his horse, the faithful old servant could tell his pitiful tale to the authorities with better assurance of being heard. But besides these advantages, or perhaps in consequence of them, the senior messenger seems to have been given a special degree of respect and responsibility by the messengers themselves.

Something like the modern practice of choosing the senior member of the service as the doyen of the corps, seems to have been in existence during the Middle Ages. The advantages were obvious in having a leader to speak for them, collect their money, receive gifts and clothing for those away from court, and see that anyone sick in court got his food allowance sent out to him. How far the position of the senior messenger was recognized, how far unofficial, it is impossible to be certain; or even whether one messenger or more acted in this capacity during the same year. Probably two or three men would be qualified by age and long service to act for the rest, and would take it in turns to do so whenever they were in court.[3]

[1] Cotton MS Nero C VIII f. 202 v.
[2] E.A. 350/26 m. 2.
[3] My publishers inform me that today (1961) their senior educational representative in Great Britain has achieved by virtue of long service a kind of unofficial command over the others. On the other hand in West Africa the senior representative has been formally instructed to carry out certain supervisory duties in respect of his colleague.

Many examples of the practice can be quoted. When Robert Little
entered the king's service, he came too late to receive his Christmas
clothing allowance, and when Easter came he happened to be out of
court, but his summer shoes had been kept safe for him by Nicholas
Ramage, who performed the same service again in 1302 for seven of
the messengers who might otherwise have lost their allocation.[1] Twice
during 1300 the wages of the messenger group were paid out to a
senior messenger and distributed by him; this time it was Arnold Bon,
who paid the ordinary messengers their due and also paid the wages
of Simon Lowis, a former queen's messenger.[2] Robert Little in his
turn acted as senior and collected money for the messenger Brehul
during his illness.[3]

Under Edward II, his well-tried messenger Robert of Newington
was the one most often responsible for collecting and distributing the
messengers' clothing. The sums allowed instead of the long overdue
clothes for 1310 were paid at last to Robert, who not only received the
money, but accounted with the wardrobe officials on 9 November for
the payment.[4] Under Edward III, a senior messenger, Robert of
London, was acting as intermediary for the messenger John Arches in
1351, collecting for him at the exchequer all the clothing allowances
which the wardrobe had been unable to pay.[5] At a later date in the
history of the service, the king's messengers found it worth while to
pay an agent to negotiate for them with the government officials and
see that they got their correct pay and that their service rota was kept
up to date. The medieval messengers relied on one of their own number to do all this for them. It is worth noting that papal messengers
also formed some such 'association' with a leader who could speak for
them, though the voluntary organization there soon hardened into
something different.[6] The oddest task performed by any senior
messenger, was that given to Alan Barley in 1375, when he superin-
tended the funeral arrangements of his fellow messenger Andrew of
Retford, who had been one of the older members of Edward III's
service.[7]

Among the couriers, a leader was also indispensable. Indeed, the
couriers needed someone to speak for them more than the established
messengers, for they had fewer privileges and were less sure of their
status. Gilbert of Ludgarshall collected wages for the couriers
'retained' in the king's service in 1297, and Adam Abel did the same

[1]Add. MS. 7965 f. 42; E.A. 361/14.
[2]E.A. 357/21 mm. 7d and 8: E.A. 372/14.
[3]E.A. 356/9 m. 3d.
[4]Cotton MS. Nero C VIII f. 30 v.
[5]I.R. 358 m. 29.
[6]Wheeler Holohan *op. cit.* 219–220, 105; Rodocanachi *Revue d'Histoire Diplo-matique* XXVI pp. 395–6.
[7]I.R. 456 m. 21.

for seven inferior messengers in 1300, though he was paid no more than the others.[1] But Gilbert's position was indeed superior, for he was paid 'for his wages and those of 15 companion couriers - -, to the said Gilbert 3*d.* a day, and to every other courier 2*d.* a day'. This additional 1*d.* a day, making Gilbert's wages equivalent to the expenses allowed to mounted messengers, and very considerably more than the meagre ½*d.* a day allowed by Edward I to his messengers during his absence abroad, suggests that Gilbert was perhaps more than a doyen of the couriers; that he had in fact collected and organized his little band of fifteen and was more like the messenger-master abroad, who organized a group of messengers and hired out their services to princes and prelates. No payment of the kind was ever made again, so far as the accounts show. The phrase 'senior courier' is actually used once, but not of any man in the king's own service. John Faukes, while gaining experience in the household of the bishop of Winchester that was to serve him in good stead later in the king's household, was lent by the bishop to the king on four occasions, and took letters to Paris via Whitsand, his expenses being entered as those of John, the bishop's senior courier.[2]

Whatever tacit authority might be allowed to the leader of the messenger group, either by the king's officials or by his fellows, it is clear that his was no government appointment. If chosen, he was chosen by the other messengers. The senior messenger was very far from being a messenger-master of the type found in Avignon by the fourteenth century. Such a man had complete control over the messengers under him, he received money from the pope's officers and paid it out to couriers at his own discretion, he was responsible for their good behaviour, and in default of it had disciplinary powers.[3] Something faintly like this messenger-master was introduced later under the Tudors, who appointed a '*magister nunciorum cursorum sive postarum tam infra regnum nostrum Angliae quam in aliis partibus transmarinis in nostro dominio existentibus.*'[4] This was an experiment, to see whether the employment of standing posts on some principal routes would expedite the conveyance of letters, but the idea was not developed, probably on account of the expense involved.

[1]Add. MS. 7965 f. 84 v; E.A. 357/21 mm. 7d, 8.
[2]E.A. 309/21 m. 1.
[3]Baumgarten *Aus Kanzlei und Kammer erorterungen zur Kurialen Hof-und-Verwaltungsgeschichte in xii, xiv, und xv Jahrhundert* (1907).
[4]J. A. J. Housden 'Early Posts in England'. *E.H.R.* XVIII 713–718.

CHAPTER IV

PROVISION FOR SICKNESS AND AGE

T HE medieval king acknowledged an obligation to his servants, over and above that of paying, feeding, and clothing them. The head of every household was bound by a personal tie to those who served him, similar to that which the feudal system created between lord and tenant. The lord must protect the interests of those who held their land from him, the head of a household must look after the interests of his servants. A good example of this is provided by the action of John, Earl of Richmond, who maintained a number of his household servants, including William Burdaunt his messenger, because they had the misfortune to be born 'of the power of France'.[1] From this tie and duty the king was not exempt.

In addition to the personal obligation, medieval society recognized a religious one. Almsgiving was 'as much a part of the daily ceremonial as sleeping or eating'[2]; and though the king's almsgiving was chiefly directed to feeding the poor, it included gifts to suppliants of all sorts and conditions. As head of his *familia*, the king was expected to maintain his servants as long as they remained with him; as a Christian, he was expected to see that they were not turned away destitute when they could no longer work. Though they could claim neither as a right, the messengers and their fellows in the household could feel pretty sure of help should they fall ill, and of sufficient provision for old age.

1. *Provision During Illness*

Illness was not uncommon among messengers, for their life was hard. Major Wheeler-Holohan remarked of the later king's messengers that scarcely a year passed without an application for sick leave, as a result of riding or carriage accidents or of illnesses brought on by hardship. Similarly, of the medieval messengers known to us by name, few escaped without one serious illness at least. How much was due to accident, how much to disease, it is impossible to judge. Peter of Blois complained that, thanks to Henry II's uncertain movements, members of his household suffered indigestion from eating 'bread hastily made, without leaven, from the dregs of the ale-tub, leaden bread, bread of

---

[1]*C.P.R.* 1324–1327, p. 57.
[2]H. Johnstone 'Poor relief in the royal households of thirteenth century England' *Speculum* IV (1929) 150.

tares, bread unbaken', with sour wine, diseased meat and putrid fish.[1]
It may be that later messengers, with little comfort or stability in their
lives even when in court, were similarly afflicted.

If the messenger were not seriously ill, he might be able to remain
'in court', receiving his ordinary allowance of food by the hand of
another messenger or his own groom. The court sometimes rested for
several weeks at one of the favourite royal manors, and during these
periods, a messenger might be unable to work without any entry to that
effect appearing in the accounts. According to the *Liber Niger*, if any
messenger fell 'sicke in courte, he taketh one loffe, one messe of grete
mete, dim. gallon ale' for his sustenance.[2] He would not need to claim
any special allowance.

A prolonged illness, however, always involved absence from court.
The household seldom stayed long in one place, and when it moved on,
the sick had to be left behind and an allowance, in lieu of the food they
should have received in court, was paid to them later, generally on the
same basis as their expenses. Several messengers fell ill when the king
was in Gascony in 1286; two were left behind at Cognac because they
were too ill to proceed with the king, and another was three days out
of court for the same reason. Two of the patients recovered quickly
and were soon at work again, but the third, Adam of Bayworth, was
unfit to work from September 1287 till the end of March 1288, during
which time he stayed at Bordeaux supported by a sick allowance of 3*d.*
a day. His recovery in the spring seems to have been only partial, for
he was ill again for thirty-five days during June and July.[3] This instance
shows how long the king's officers would continue to pay allowances
without diminution to a member of the household in distress. Not all
messengers received 3*d.* a day for sick pay. The same accounts mention
a fifteen days' absence from court for which Jonyn the Burgundian,
another messenger, received 2*d.* a day. Paris was the scene of his
unwelcome holiday.[4]

The money seems as a rule to have been paid after the messenger
returned to duty. At least this was the case when John Piacle fell ill
at Huntingdon in 1296 and was seventy-seven days before he was fit
for work again. At Nayland in December, he received by his own
hand from the wardrobe 26*s.* 8*d.* 'of the king's gift and alms on
account of the expenses he had during his illness, and for the money he
spent on the salary of the doctor assisting the cure of the same John,
and for divers medicines bought for him in his said illness'.[5] As he
collected the money himself, he must have been considered well
enough to return to work by that date. John had a second illness,

---

[1]The whole passage is quoted in Coulton *Medieval Panorama* (1943) p. 233.
[2]*Collection of Ordinances* p. 49.
[3]Chanc. Misc. 4/3 ff. 21, 21 v; Misc. Bks Exch. T. of R. 201 ff. 21, 29, 29 v.
[4]Chanc. Misc. 4/3 f. 16 v; Misc. Bks Exch. T. of R. 261 f. 26.
[5]Add. MS. 7965 f. 10.

however, in 1299, when on his way home with good news. At Canterbury he received a gift of a mark from the king, and was sent to his own home to recuperate.[1] But his recovery was not permanent, for in July of the same year he was ill at Ware and receiving 5s. for his expenses on that account.[2] John may have been unlucky, but his record supports Wheeler-Holohan's contention that the messenger paid dearly for his advantages.

Though the sick allowance of 2d. or 3d. a day was fairest to the messenger and the most economical to the wardrobe, the almoner's clerks found such calculations troublesome. They tended to substitute for a daily allowance, a lump sum of 13s. 4d. for a long illness or 6s 8d. for a short one. Nicholas Ramage, having been ill in London in 1297, received half a mark of the king's alms on account of his expenses[3] and Robin Little, who was taken ill on his way to Germany in 1298, was given a mark at Westminster on 15 April, after his return to England.[4] By this method, sometimes the wardrobe, sometimes the messenger, scored. Repayment after the man had returned to work was preferred by the wardrobe, because then he could collect his money himself, and there was no question of accounting afterwards for sums advanced. There were however, times when a sick man must be helped at once. Thus when the messenger Brehull lay ill at Leeds in September 1299, he was given a mark for his expenses 'remaining behind the court at Leeds on account of the infirmity which was detaining him, of the king's alms, . . . until he should recover'; and since he was unable to collect the gift himself, it was paid to him 'by the hand of Robin Little, his companion'.[5] Similar consideration was shown by the prince's officers to his messengers. When Edward of Caernarvon passed through Northampton on his way to Langley to attend the funeral of the Earl of Cornwall, his messenger Robert Rideware fell ill and had to be left behind. The prince's wardrobe gave him half a mark for his immediate expenses on 11 January 1301, and when he had sufficiently recovered to join the prince at Lincoln on 19 February, he was allowed a further 7s. for the cost of medicines during his illness so much more serious than they had anticipated, and the expenses of his prolonged stay at Northampton.[6]

It was well for the messenger that the duty of helping the sick was regarded so seriously. Otherwise the king's charity might have suffered as many delays as did wages and clothing allowances; and even with the obligation of almsgiving unquestioned, household payments on account of sickness sometimes fell into arrears. The messenger Roger Windsor found himself obliged to accept a tardy imprest of half a mark in payment of part of his expenses incurred while he lay ill

[1]E.A. 356/8 m. 12.   [4]E.A. 354/5 and 356/2 m. 2.
[2]E.A. 355/27 m. 1d.   [5]E.A. 356/9 m. 3d.
[3]Add. MS. 7965 f. 9.   [6]Add. MS. 7966 ff. 66 v and 67.

at Winchelsea.[1] Imprests on alms were not common, however, either in accounts of the wardrobe, or later in accounts of the exchequer, when that department took over the duty of providing for the king's servants during sickness. Money 'from the king's alms' to help him meet the expenses of illness was paid by the exchequer in 1351 and again in 1356 to the messenger Merlin.[2]

If a messenger fell ill while carrying urgent dispatches, he was expected to send them on by another hand. If the matter were less immediate, he might wait until he could bring them himself. Some rule of this kind guided the messengers who, on falling ill, found another messenger to take their dispatches. Usually these were letters sent abroad. John (or Jack) Faukes, a messenger of Edward III, was on his way to Avignon with letters to the king's ambassador there, when he was taken ill at Paris. The affair was urgent, so a courier was hired at once, even though it cost John 6 florins, worth 3s. 4d. each, to do it.[3] On the other hand, John Piacle, on his way home with good news for the king, was detained by illness, but waited till he could bring the message on himself.[4] The prospect of receiving a reward for the news may have influenced him; and perhaps too, the fact that it was an inward not outward bound letter. In England, routine dispatches were not considered important enough to justify hiring special couriers.

In all the instances cited so far, the messenger did eventually return to work, even though his illness had lasted for several months, and had included a short convalescence at his own home. There is only one entry telling of a man so badly injured that he was unfit for any future service. John Taverner, either in the wars or as the result of an accident, was maimed in the king's service, and the injury proved so serious that he was retired on a pension from the king's alms.[5]

These instances of assistance given to messengers during illness might be paralleled for any of the other household grades. There are fewer instances of the same treatment for wardrobe couriers, because they did not belong to the king's *familia*. He had no duty towards them, as towards his household, though they might be relieved by his charity as any other mendicants. There are only two instances of Edward I making any sort of allowance to a courier who fell ill. John Whiting was left behind when the court left Milton in 1297, and the king's almoner gave him a small sum in aid of his living expenses.[6] A courier happened to be returning with another man to the king in Scotland in 1304, when they were both set upon and wounded by the Scots.[7] Such a tale could not fail to rouse sympathy, and on this occasion, the courier was given something for his expenses

[1] Misc. Bks. Exch. T. of R. 202.
[2] I.R. 359 m. 13; 378 m. 27.
[3] E.A. 386/11.
[4] E.A. 356/8 m. 12.
[5] *C.P.R.* 1348–1350 p. 146.
[6] Add. MS. 7965 f. 6 v.
[7] Add. MS. 8835 f. 104 v.

and as compensation. Normally the unmounted messenger was hired for a particular campaign or a particular task only; and that done, the king had no more interest in him. He had no right to eat in court, and therefore could claim no money allowance in lieu of food if he were out of court. Perhaps he suffered fewer mishaps than the mounted messenger, for a number of illnesses must have been the result of riding accidents.

Edward of Caernarvon, on becoming king, took into his new household all the messengers, mounted or unmounted, who had served him as prince. Among them was Warin his courier, and in the first month after this promotion, he fell ill at Carlisle, when the court was moving northwards to the Scottish campaign. The connexion between the inferior messenger and the rest of the establishment seems to have been rather closer in the smaller royal households. Warin at least received 4s. to pay for his illness,[1] less than a messenger would have received, no doubt, but still enough to keep the unmounted man for many days.

Under Edward III, the status of a courier was improving, and one sign of this is the increase in the number of payments to sick couriers. William London, the queen's courier, was given 1s. when ill at Clipstone in 1331;[2] John Pynchon had 2s. of the king's alms in 1351[3] and John Blakerl, being seriously ill, was allowed the astonishingly large sum of 40s. in 1352.[4] John Twycros received 5s. during an illness in 1354,[5] and William Burton was twice helped during illnesses while in the king's service.[6] The entries are more frequent towards the middle of Edward III's reign, suggesting that more notice was being taken of couriers' ailments. Whether as an act of mercy to the sick or as an obligation due from the head of a *familia* to a member of it, the king through his almoner did provide for his household in sickness and health; and into that household, the courier was slowly making his way during the fourteenth century.

2. *Provision for Old Age*

As in sickness, so in old age, the king was morally responsible for the welfare of his immediate servants. Men of all ranks in the household might expect to receive some form of pension after long service, either in the form of a direct money grant or of a sinecure post outside the court, or of a corrody, a charitable grant of food and shelter at a religious house. By one or other of these means, the king strove to

[1]E.A. 373/15 f. 20.
[2]John Rylands' Lib. Lat. MS. 235 f. 9.
[3]I.R. 358 m. 27.
[4]I.R. 359 m. 13.
[5]I.R. 373 m. 19.
[6]I.R. 400 m. 21; Roll of writs 1303 m. 12 d.

provide for his old servants so that they might receive the greatest benefit with the least trouble and expense.

The grant of a pension was usually made a little before the messenger actually retired. In some instances they are hard to distinguish from the pension in support of wages which has been mentioned already, though the allowance intended to console the messenger for delays at the exchequer was seldom made for life. Pensions granted for faithful service were always for the life of the recipient, and the grant was usually marked by some special phrase, 'for very long and praiseworthy service'; 'for good service done to the king himself'; 'for long service and because he is now too old and infirm to labour in the office'; 'because he is so feeble that he cannot well work in attendance on the king', and the like. The phrases read like official citations of more recent date, in the variety of the explanations concealed under the clerks' formula; yet clearly it was not mere common form to say that a man had served the king well, and was now 'broken with age'.

(a) *The Direct Pension*

The simplest type of pension was the direct payment to be made daily by the wardrobe or the exchequer. Henry III granted several pensions of this kind towards the end of his reign, perhaps anticipating changes among the household staff after his own death. At any rate, grants of $2d.$ or $3\frac{1}{2}d.$ a day for life were made to the messengers Roger Stanleigh, Philip Escoville or Schocchevill, and Colin le Waleys, who were to receive them from the exchequer in addition to any other wages or allowances they might be paid for their services to the king. The three of them drew their pensions for 178 days from 9 October 1259 to 4 April 1260 while continuing in the king's service;[1] and similar pensions were granted to Nicholas le Waleys, Roger the messenger of Edmund the king's son,[2] and John of Rothby who 'for his very long service' drew an allowance of three half-pence a day,[3] and yet continued to hang about the court, doing little work, so far as the accounts indicate, but a member of the household whenever there were clothes or shoes to be distributed.

All these pensions were in arrears at the end of the reign. One of the first steps taken by the officials of the new king, while Edward himself was still abroad, was to order payment of arrears up to date; and these were duly made. Nicholas le Waleys received half a mark 'on the arrears of $2d.$ which he receives at the king's exchequer during his life', and a further $30s.$ $6d.$ for the first 189 days of the new reign.[4] John of Rothby and Roger Stanleigh also received arrears and 189 days pension at the rate of $1d.$ a day. Colin and Philip may have been dead

---

[1] Roll of writs for issues, No. 1307 dorse; I.R. 18.
[2] I.R. 28, 33.
[3] *C.P.R.* 1258-1266, 241; Roll of writs for issues No. 1307.
[4] I.R. 21.

by this time, for they fade out of the picture; apparently no arrears were due to Roger the messenger.

The experiment had lasted long enough to prove that under a medieval government, the simplest method might not be the most satisfactory, either to messengers who had to wait for their money, or to the king. When Edward I arrived in England, the machinery of government was ovehauled, and the question of pensions came under revision also. The daily pension paid by the exchequer was given up. No more were granted. Those already in existence were all commuted within two years of the king's arrival. Lump sums were paid to cover arrears and future claims; and though Henry III's old messengers may have considered a lump sum better than a daily pension in arrears, it was certainly the king who benefited most from the remission. The exchequer's work was no longer hindered by petty payments, and the king's liability ended. Even the messenger may have been glad to be relieved of the bother of applying for his allowance.

The amount of compensation varied according to the value of the pension but amounted to roughly two years' purchase. Nicholas le Waleys, formerly messenger of king Henry, received 10 marks in 1275 instead of his daily 2*d*. and two years arrears, for he had not received anything since the payment of arrears in 1273.[1] Roger Stanley, formerly messenger of the present king's father, received £10 instead of a daily 3*d*. and arrears.[2] John Rothby received £5 and Roger the messenger 5 marks in place of their 1½*d*. pensions. The new king might be more hard-headed than his father, but according to his lights he was not unjust.

Edward I's dislike of the direct pension is seen all through his reign. He granted none to his own messengers, though to his mother's messenger Simon Atte Leigh, he gave a pension of 4½*d*. a day from the wardrobe; and to Simon Lowys, messenger of Eleanor of Castile, a pension of 3½*d*. a day from the exchequer.[3] The grant to Lowys was made 'for the very long service which he did to the queen, the king's late consort', and in both cases the circumstances were exceptional. I have not found any other direct pension from wardrobe or exchequer being granted by Edward I, or by his son.

The direct pension was only revived by Edward III towards the end of his reign, when all other expedients had failed. Messengers and couriers benefited equally from his generosity, which indicates the changed position of the unmounted man. John Pynchoun one of the king's couriers, was in 1353 granted 2*d*. daily at the exchequer of receipt, as reward for his long service 'and because he is so broken with age that he can labour no longer'. From that date he drew the allowance regularly month by month, and the exchequer accounted for it; during the first part of 1356, for instance, he was paid his pension in

[1] I.R. 28 m. 2.   [2] I.R. 30, 33.   [3] *L.Q.G.* p. 101; I.R. 90, 91.

January, March and April.[1] Philip Langdon, another courier, whose work had mainly been connected with the dispatch of exchequer writs and summons, received a daily allowance of 3*d*.[2]

Until the middle of Edward III's reign, direct pensions payable by either wardrobe or exchequer, had been calculated on a daily allowance. But just as the almoner preferred to pay half a mark or a mark instead of so many days' expenses to the sick messenger, so exchequer clerks began to realize the convenience of a pension payable only at the two half-yearly exchequer sessions. The first experiment of this kind was made in 1364, when John Pygot was granted a pension of £10 a year 'for good service performed by him for the king, or until some other provision shall be made for his estate'.[3] The wording of the grant suggests that the arrangement was tentative, to be stopped if it proved inconvenient; but in effect the temporary grant was permanent, and Pygot continued to receive his annuity for some years afterwards. Under Richard II, the clause *quous que pro statu suo aliter duxerimus ordinandum* became obligatory if the pension were to be valid, and all grants made for life were rendered void; this must have affected many of Edward's old messengers, if they were still alive in 1387.[4]

(*b*) *The Grant of Established Alms*

The second method by which the king could provide for his household was by a grant from the established alms. In many counties, sums of money had by custom been set aside as *elemosina constituta,* from which the king could grant a daily allowance to religious houses or to his old servants. All that was needed was a letter to the sheriff ordering the payment to commence, and another to the treasurer and barons of the exchequer ordering them to 'compute' the same to the sheriff when he made his account with them. Any grant of established alms should therefore be recorded on the close rolls, with a corresponding allowance in the pipe or chancellor's roll for the following year; and in some cases a note to that effect on the memoranda roll also.

This method of providing for old servants was the one favoured by John and Henry III. Possibly when the messenger left the king's service and no longer followed the court, he found it inconvenient to draw his pension from an itinerant wardrobe or an exchequer settled at Westminster, and may have preferred an allowance which he could collect from the sheriff of his own county. Certainly the pension given to Walter le Grant the king's messenger in 1205 was intended to supply his needs after retirement to the country, for the letter close

[1]*C.P.R.* 1350–1354, 488; I.R. 378 mm. 22, 32, 34.
[2]Roll of writs for issues No. 1303 m. 7d.
[3]*C.P.R.* 1361–1364, 504; I.R. 423 mm. 9 and 14.
[4]11 Richard II c. 8, an Act for making void annuities granted by the king, his father, or grandfather, unless with clause *quousque pro statu suo aliter duxerimus ordinandum.*

which authorized it clearly stated that his $3\frac{1}{2}d$. a day, formerly paid to William le Lommer, was given 'so that he shall hold that allowance and shall no longer follow our court.'[1]

Since these payments from the established alms were customary they could only be re-allotted on the death or resignation of a former holder. This limited the usefulness of the grants as a means of retiring worn-out members of the household. If they went on working in hopes of a pension falling vacant, this may explain why many pensioners lived so short a time after retirement. Yet annuitants proverbially live long. Hamelin the king's messenger, whose working days had been spent under Richard I and his father, was already receiving 60s. 10d. a year, or 2d. a day, from the farm of Essex and Hertford in 1199. The following pipe rolls regularly record the payment of this pension,[2] and in the memoranda roll of the first year of Henry III, in a list of pensioners paid through the sheriffs[3] comes the name of Hamelin the messenger, together with those of two colleagues Walwan and Lucas. These two messengers had shared with a third, Roger le Tort, an allowance of 22s. 10d. a year during the first three-quarters of the exchequer year 1202–3. Then Roger dropped out, Lucas was given the whole of that pension and Walwan provided with another of 37s. $5\frac{1}{2}d$. a year, which materially improved his prospects.[4] These were the pensions which Lucas and Walwan, like Hamelin, were still receiving in 1217.

Because the total number of pensions was limited by custom, clerks who drafted grants of alms were careful to mention the name of the previous holder as well as the name of the new beneficiary. The same information was usually repeated by the sheriff when he came to make his account with the exchequer. From these two sources, the names of the pensioners who held in succession the king's established alms can be traced over a number of years. In spite of a tendency to replace a messenger by another messenger, a serjeant by another serjeant, and so on, there was no fixed rule that it should be so, and all the household benefited in turn as pensions fell vacant. Thus the $1\frac{1}{2}d$. a day out of the issues of Essex, which had been held in turn by William le Charetter and Roger Passavant, both messengers, was granted after Roger's death to Luke, *sometarius* of the wardrobe.[5] Yet in most instances, alms which had supported a retired messenger were regranted after his death to another retiring colleague. Walter Cornwaleis succeeded to William le Engleis' allowance out of the issues of Herefordshire.[6]

[1] *R.L.Cl.* 1204–1227, I, 54.
[2] *P.R.* 1199 p. 86; 1200 p. 37; 1201 p. 58; 1202 p. 259; 1203 p. 123; 1204 pp. 23, 24; 1205 p. 183; 1206 p. 227; 1207 p. 90; *Rot. Canc.* 1201–2, p. 144.
[3] L.T.R.M.R. No. 1 m. 5 (P.R.O. typescript transcript p. 188).
[4] *P.R.* 1202–3 pp. 284, 259; 1203–4 p. 123.
[5] *C.R.* 1227–1231 pp. 477, 512.
[6] L.T.R.M.R. No. 15 m. 9d (P.R.O. abstract p. 39); *Ibid* No. 27 m. 3 (P.R.O. abstract p. 262); *C.R.* 1237–1242 p. 34 and 1242–1247 p. 17.

John of Wallingford, a former messenger of Henry III, was given in 1273 the $1\frac{1}{2}d$. alms paid by the bailiffs of London, which had been held for sixteen years by Guy the king's messenger.[1] It happens so often that contrary instances might look like exceptions to a rule, if there were no letters authorizing the barons of the exchequer to allot the next vacant pension without discrimination to some member of the household. An instance of this, which also illustrates the succession of pensioners to one established grant, is the gift of $2\frac{1}{2}d$. a day paid by the sheriff of Hereford which was allotted to Simon the queen's messenger in 1248, on such a recommendation. This was probably the pension which had earlier been drawn by William le Engleis and Walter Cornwaleis. Simon held it till 1254, when the money was divided between two needy messengers, Roger Stanlegh and William Sholls. The latter died about 1267, and his share was regranted to yet another messenger, Alan Lindesey, who shared the allocation with Stanlegh until the accession of Edward I.[2] Since Stanlegh was also the holder of a pension from the exchequer, his half was probably provision enough, if regularly paid.

Henry III had granted pensions from the king's established alms' freely, even in some instances exceeding the customary allotments. Edward I reversed his father's practice. Alms paid through the sheriff were open to all the criticisms which could be made of the direct pension paid by a government department. They reduced the king's revenue, by deducting from the farm of the county sums which ought to have been paid into the exchequer; and sheriffs, like other officers, fell into arrears in their payments. When Henry died, the king's ministers in England ordered the payment of all overdue pensions,[3] and as soon as Edward returned home, he took steps to end the system altogether. A number of grants to messengers and other members of the household were in force at the time, and these, like the exchequer pensions, were commuted.[4] William le Burguillon, who had held a pension of $1d$. a day from the firm of Buckingham, received 5 marks compensation; Alan Lindesey, who still drew his $1\frac{1}{2}d$. alms out of the issues of Hereford, received 6 marks 3 shillings and 4 pence. Roger le Messager who had served the king's brother Edmund, and Thomas of Oxford, the queen mother's messenger, also lost their daily pence. Even John of Wallingford, whose grant had been given in Edward's name for his good services to King Henry, the king's father, was obliged to be content with 100 shillings. The result of these changes was to remove the item *In elemosina constituta* from the pipe rolls of Edward I after 1275, except for a few allowances paid to religious

[1] *C.R.* 1256–1259 p. 54; *C.C.R.* 1272–1279 p. 13.
[2] *C.R.* 1247–1251 p. 93; 1253–1254 p. 101; 1264–1268 p. 30.
[3] *C.C.R.* 1272–1279 p. 23.
[4] I.R. 28 mm. 1, 2.

houses. For the rest of Edward's reign and that of his successor, the grant of established alms was no longer used to provide for old household servants.

It was left to Edward III to renew the old practice, as he also renewed the direct pension. In 1343, John Russel received 2*d.* a day for his good services from the issues of the county of Nottingham; and the original grant was later enlarged by 10*s.* yearly for life from the same county to provide him with clothes.[1] Nicholas of Ufton, another messenger, secured a grant of 4½*d.* a day in 1346 'in consideration of good services to Edward II and the present king', which was to be paid out of the firm of Northumberland; and when a new sheriff was appointed in the following year, he received instructions to continue the allowance for life.[2] John Taverner, the messenger who was maimed while in the king's service, was pensioned from the issues of Lincoln.[3] Even couriers were eligible for these grants. Robert Blakherl 'for long service and because he is now so feeble that he cannot well work in attendance on' the king, was given 3*d.* a day 'in aid of his sustenance' out of the issues of Oxfordshire.[4] Henry, courier of the king's chamber, received a similar allowance in 1357.[5] Towards the end of the reign, as one might expect, the number of pensions granted became greater. Men who had joined the household when Edward was first king were now past work and had to be retired. Others, though with less service to their credit, pressed for grants in case a new king or his guardians, might prove less generous. John Faukes in 1355, Richard Hert in 1360, Henry Croft, John Taylfer, Andrew Retford, Robert London, William Clerk, Alan Berle and Walter Cardinal in 1362, all had letters patent granting them pensions of 4½*d.* a day out of the issues of various counties.[6] Thus Henry Croft 'for long service and because he is now too old and infirm to labour in the office' of messenger, was to have 4*d.* from the firm of the City of London, and John Taylfer 4½*d.* from the Sheriff of Kent, who was to take his acquittance for every payment 'as the king of his favour and for John's good services has granted him by letters patent 4½*d.* a day . . . for life, or until other order be taken for his estate'. A chamber messenger, John Typet, received an annual payment of £10 from 1356 onwards out of the issues of Kent.[7] By 1377, nearly all Edward's principal messengers were receiving these alms, and most of the older men had left the household for good.

One entry suggests that the fourteenth century pensioner found the

[1]*C.C.R.* 1343–1346 p. 200; *C.P.R.* 1345–1348 p. 16.
[2]*C.P.R.* 1345–1348 p. 56; *C.C.R.* 1346–1349 p. 334.
[3]*Ibid.* 1350–1354 p. 366.
[4]*Ibid.* p. 356.
[5]*Ibid.* 1354–1358 p. 564.
[6]*Ibid.* p. 245; 1358–1361 p. 479; 1361–4 pp. 174 and 195; *C.C.R.* 1360–4 p. 318.
[7]*C.P.R.* 1354–8 p. 365.

same difficulties in getting his pension paid to time by the sheriff as the thirteenth century ones had done. Cecilia the wife of Walter Cardynall, late one of the king's messengers, had to collect 66*s.* 8*d.* due to her husband on his 4½*d.* pension, from the exchequer of account in 1374.[1] It ought to have been paid to him by the sheriff out of the issues of Somerset and Dorset; and if either of those counties were Walter's native place, his wife had had a long journey to Westminster to extort the money from the exchequer. That the wife came, rather than the pensioner himself, suggests that Walter (who retired in 1362) was by 1374 too old or too ill to do any more travelling.

It is interesting to see that in two instances, Edward III was obliged to revert to the practices of the early thirteenth century. Edward I had abolished both the exchequer pension and the established alms; Edward III restored both. The alternatives employed to meet the same need and the reason for their failure by the middle of the fourteenth century, will be discussed in the next two sections.

(c) *The Grant of other Offices, Houses, or Land*

The third method by which the king could provide for his old servants was by the gift, permanent or temporary, of some sinecure post or income in the form of houses and land. If the office were one in the king's own service, it was generally bestowed for life. If however, it were attached to a wardship in the king's hand, or to a bishopric during a vacancy, the grant was temporary and served only to support the pensioner until a permanent post became available. The king made full use of his powers over property of minors and revenues of vacant sees, and from the incomes made frequent grants to members of his household.

The posts most commonly given to support an aged servant were those belonging to the king's castles, forests or parks. The introduction to the *Liber Niger* praised earlier kings for generosity in granting 'outward offices' to 'household men', and mentioned particularly appointments as parkers, foresters, warreners, keepers of manors or bailiwicks, constables, porters and receivers; adding as other rewards the gift of corrodies, wardships, and marriages.[2] To all these advantages, the messenger and his fellows in the household might aspire. To be keeper of a park or porter of a castle did not involve as much strain as riding with the king's dispatches. Most of the offices granted to former messengers were supervisory ones, for which a messenger with his long experience of the world might be very suitable. Positions in the household, which would involve travelling with the court, were seldom given as rewards for service. The one exception was the appointment of John Messager 'to lodge the cart-horses and sumpter

[1]I.R. 451 m. 19.
[2]*Collection of Ordinances* p. 19.

horses of the household, and purvey hay, oats, litter and other necessaries for them', in March 1347, an appointment which was repeated
for two months in July and again in September of that year.[1] The fact
that the post was for such a limited period shows that it was not intended for John's permanent enjoyment.

Henry III seldom or never gave positions of this kind to his messengers. The duties attached to them may still have been connected
with sergeanties. Edward I, on the other hand, frequently did, for such
gifts were a useful alternative to a money pension. He provided in this
way for some of the messengers who had served his father or his
mother Eleanor of Provence, and had so far received no acknowledge-
ment of their good services. In 1272 his government in England
granted in his name the post of gatekeeper of Windsor to Robert
Lightfoot, a wardrobe courier,[2] and he held it for many years. After the
death of the queen mother, her messenger William Crisp was provided
for by the king, who made him custodian of the warren of Pevensey,
with $1\frac{1}{2}d$. a day for wages which he was to receive from the bailiff.[3]
In place of the ten acres of purpresture within the manor of Havering,
which the queen had given him and which now escheated to the king,
William was allowed, after nine years' delay, the custody of the park
of the manor of Stoke by Nayland for life at $2d$. a day.[4] Eleanor's other
messenger Simon Atteleigh, has been mentioned before as one of two
exceptions allowed by Edward I to his policy of no money pensions;
the second was his wife's messenger Simon Lowis, who was also given
custody of the manor and park of Guildford for life in 1298.[5]

To his own messengers from time to time, Edward made similar
grants. William of Dogmersfield was made steward of Sherwood
Forest in 1298 and Roger of Windsor became very appropriately
viewer of the works at Windsor Castle during the king's pleasure,
with wages of $2d$. a day for his maintenance.[6] John Pyacle 'in consideration of his long service and especially for the news he brought to the
king of the birth of Edmund the king's son' was given custody of the
pessage of the town of Southampton, for which he was to answer at the
exchequer; and a mandate to this effect was sent to the sheriff in 1302.[7]
Even a messenger serving principally in the chancery or exchequer and
so outside the usual scope of household rewards, might be provided for
in this way. John le Messager 'by reason of his long service to Robert
late Bishop of Bath and Wells, the chancellor' was recommended to
the king for a lighter post and was given custody of Kennington Park,

---

[1] *C.P.R.* 1345–1348 pp. 294, 353, 406.
[2] *C.C.R.* 1272–1279 pp. 34, 393; 1279–1288, p. 447.
[3] *C.P.R.* 1281–1292 p. 467.
[4] *Ibid.* 1292–1301 p. 522.
[5] *Ibid.* pp. 81, 372.
[6] *Ibid.* pp. 323, 407
[7] *Ibid.* 1301–1307 p. 7.

with wages to be paid to him by the keeper of the manor. He was still parker when Edward II became king, and continued in the office several years after.[1]

Edward II, for some reason, made very few grants of this kind. Robert of Hoton was made gaol keeper at Stafford in 1315.[2] Robert Rideware, who had been in the household of Edward as Prince of Wales, was bailiff of Dartford soon after his accession, and answered for the farm of that place in 1311 and 1312, though no formal letter of appointment was enrolled by chancery.[3] Apart from these two instances no messengers received sinecure offices under Edward II. It is difficult to say whether this was the result of accident or design.

Sinecure rewards were freely granted again by Edward III. Among the messengers who benefited were John Paris and Nicholas Ufton, who became porters at the royal castles of Hereford and Newcastle.[4] Nicholas held his post from 1336 to 1352, when it passed to another messenger, William Fox, who was made at the same time gaol keeper within the castle.[5] The messenger Nicholas Maol was given custody of the meadows at Woodstock Park in reward for services to the late king,[6] and the courier William Hanworth was made parker of Ayleshamburgh for the same reason.[7] Though messengers had the advantage of closer contact with the king and the household officers and were more likely to be chosen for a sinecure post, couriers under Edward III were sometimes pensioned in this way, and three are mentioned on the patent rolls in this connexion. In addition to William Hanworth's appointment, Adam Leonard became bailiff of 'the park of Wrichewode' by Bamburgh during good behaviour, and a certain Adam le Corour received the humble post of chief swineherd to the town of Nottingham for life, a grant which he afterwards surrendered, perhaps on receiving a more lucrative position.[8] A rather different type of appointment went to Adam Merlin, one of the messengers, who was made portejoie in the chancery, and petitioned the king in 1354 complaining of the insufficiency of the wages attached to the office.[9] His petition was favourably received and an additional $1\frac{1}{2}d.$ a day was allowed to him, to be paid out of the issues of the hanaper of the chancery. The general rise in the cost of living during the fourteenth century made necessary such readjustments of the wages

---

[1] *Ibid.* p. 56; *C.C.R.* 1307–1313 pp. 11, 22, 87.
[2] *C.P.R.* 1313–1317 p. 366.
[3] I.R. 159, 164. In his capacity of bailiff, Robert was later in trouble over the wrongful seizure of a cow; and the sub-bailiff of his native village of Newington became surety for his appearance to answer the charge (K.R. writs bundle 10).
[4] *C.P.R.* 1330–1334 p. 52; 1334–1338 p. 263.
[5] *Ibid.* 1350–1354 p. 295.
[6] *Ibid.* 1330–1334 p. 219.
[7] *Ibid.* 1330–1334 p. 35.
[8] *Ibid.* 1330–1334 p. 54; 1327–1330 pp. 169, 185.
[9] *Ibid.* 1354–1358 p. 148.

customarily paid in many offices, whether the duties performed were real or nominal. These instances show the kind of post which the king might grant by way of pension to deserving members of his household.

The pensionary character of some of the appointments given to servants in the Black Prince's household is emphasized by the words 'for past and future services' used in a grant to John Bolton his messenger, of a position and wage in the castle, lordship, and honour of Wallingford in 1365.[1] The gift would provide for the messenger as long as he remained in the household and would also be a support for him afterwards, for it was to be held for life. Had the duties of the office been real instead of nominal, the appointment would have been during good behaviour only. Such was the position of bailiff of Wallingford, which was given to the prince's messenger Roger Pope, and which was taken away from him in 1359 on account of the misconduct of his underbailiff.[2] Though not a good administrator, Roger had been quite satisfactory as a messenger, and when the prince seized the bailiwick again, he compensated Roger with £4 because of his former good services.

In addition to these permanent posts, there were the temporary appointments which the king could make while he held the lands of a vacant bishopric or a tenant-in-chief. Walter Cardinal the king's messenger was put into possession of the bailiwick of hayward at Alresford 'now in the king's hands by reason of the voidance of the see of Winchester, for such time as it shall remain in his hands'.[3] A companion, John Typet, benefited twice from these temporary grants, for he was given the position of lathe reeve of St. Augustine's, Canterbury, in 1354, with the accustomed fees, and in 1366 was put in charge of the bailiwick of the liberty of Southwark while the archbishopric remained vacant.[4] Thomas Kendal, messenger of the Black Prince, was actually given the wardship of the lands of a small tenant in chief, John Atte Hill of Wamplingham, with the marriage of the heir, and an exemption from all rent to the king. This was for his past good services both to the prince his master and to the king.[5] A more lucrative grant of the same type was made by Edward III to his chamber messenger, John Stygan, in 1374. John was to have the keeping of eighty acres of land, seven acres of meadow and 53s 8d. of rent in the County of Derby, together with the marriage of the heir. His position was confirmed in 1376, and like many other guardians, he no doubt profited from the minor's estates.[6]

When houses or lands escheated to the king, there was another opportunity to provide for his household. Henry III made a number

[1] *Black Prince's Register* IV, 549.   [2] *Ibid.* IV, 292.
[3] *C.P.R.* 1343–1345 p. 562.
[4] *Ibid.* 1354–1358 p. 10; 1364–1367 p. 235.
[5] *Ibid.* 1354–1358 pp. 511, 515.
[6] *C.P.R.* 1370–1374 p. 456; 1374–1377 p. 469.

of gifts from such escheats. John Chubbe, one of his messengers, was given a house in Bridport, which he held till 1257 when the property reverted to the king's hand because John 'had taken the religious dress'. The inquisition taken at the time showed the house to be worth one mark annually, and Henry promptly regranted it to another deserving member of his household, the king's mason.[1] Less valuable, but still worth accepting, was the house in Shrewsbury given by Henry to Robert Blund his messenger in 1231. The rent was 12*d*. a year, to be paid by Robert and his heirs to the bailiffs of the town in perpetuity,[2] and having paid this small sum every year, Robert enjoyed the income of the property (which no doubt he let) even though he did not retire till just before 1250. Then the king ordered all arrears of pension to be paid up to him, and he left court for good, perhaps to live in Shrewsbury for the rest of his days. He was certainly alive in 1253, when a false report of his death nearly lost him his allowance; but two years later, a long and useful career in the king's service was brought at last to a close.[3] Another messenger to profit from Henry's kindness was Nicholas le Messager, who was to have seizin from the sheriff of all the king's right in a messuage in Stamford 'until the king should order otherwise',[4] and to this gift a virgate of land was later added.

Even if the king could not find a complete house for his servant, he might give him the timber to build one. This may have been the object of two grants of Windsor oaks which Henry made to Walter of Marden or Mawordyn in 1261 and 1266.[5] The same intention may be read in Edward I's gift of chestnut trees to Robert Rideware, his son's messenger. Robert came from Newington in Kent, and may have been building himself a house in his native village with the idea of retiring there in due course. Chestnut wood was largely used for roof beams, and the order for Robert to have 'in the king's wood of Castaveis of Middelton four of the best chestnut trees near the king's highway from Newenton to Sidingburn, to wit, two on one side of the street and two on the other, of the king's gift,'[6] may have been intended to complete the work. Robert did in fact retire from service a few years later, in 1307. He may have thought himself lucky to get such a grant, for Edward I did not give presents lightly; and very few grants of property of any sort were made to members of the household in his time. Nor did Edward II choose this method of rewarding his faithful servants. It was left to Edward III to imitate his great-grandfather in this respect and to resume the practice of giving away houses and land as fast as they escheated to the crown.

[1]*C.Ch.R.* 1257–1300 p. 5; *C.I. Misc.* I, no 2045.
[2]*C.Ch.R.* 1226–1257 p. 134; *Cl.R.* 1227–1231 p. 519.
[3]*Ibid.* 1253–1254 p. 3; 1254–1256 p. 35; *C.P.R.* 1247–1258 p. 179.
[4]*Ibid.* 1247–1258 p. 179; *Cl.R.* 1253–1254 p. 19.
[5]*Ibid.* 1261–1264 p. 36; 1264–1268 p. 279.
[6]*C.C.R.* 1296–1302 p. 263.

A great many grants of different sorts were made by Edward III to his chamber messengers, John Stygan and John Currour. In 1373, Stygan was allowed to accept a grant from another of the king's pensioners of a messuage 'in Grublane without Crepulgate in the suburb of London' and to retain it for life.[1] He later got direct from Edward a messuage and four shops in Cornhill which the king had recovered in a lawsuit.[2] His profitable wardship has been mentioned already; and he had as well £10 a year from a Yorkshire manor in the king's hands,[3] not to mention his pension at the exchequer, which continued whether other temporary grants were received or not. The pension at the exchequer he finally exchanged for a corrody at Christ Church Priory, London.[4] These gifts suggest that Stygan was a favoured member of Edward's staff, perhaps a Londoner, certainly a man who knew how to turn his services to good account. His companion, John Currour, was nearly as successful. In 1374 he was given a messuage in Northampton 'which is in the king's hands on account of an outlawry on a plea of trespass, and is extended at 20s. yearly, to be held as long as it shall be in the king's hand for that cause.'[5] Again in 1375, he received two shops in Barking 'which pertain to the king because they were built by Thomas Samkyn of Berking without licence on the king's highway, and are arrented at 10s. yearly at the exchequer.'[6] Finally, in the same year, John received for life the office of porter in the abbey of Eynsham with the fees and profits, as previously held by another royal nominee. This last grant is marked as 'vacated because surrendered and nothing thereof was done', probably because a letter close dated the day following had recommended him to the same abbey for a corrody.[7]

The multiplicity of gifts made to messengers by the late fourteenth century, in contrast to the single grant of an earlier period, illustrate both the decreasing value of money and the increasing importance of the messenger. It was not to the king's financial advantage to give away escheats as fast as they came in, and Edward I might have said much on this head to his impecunious grandson. Yet a good messenger was worth encouraging, and loyal service, past or present, demanded adequate recognition.

(d) *The Grant of a Corrody*

The fourth and last way in which the king could help his old servants was by requesting or demanding a corrody for them at some monastery or hospital.

[1] *C.P.R.* 1370–1374 p. 289
[2] *Ibid.* 1374–1377 p. 84.
[3] *Ibid.* 1374–1377 p. 381; *C.C.R.* 1374–1377 p. 398.
[4] *C.P.R.* 1370–1374 p. 170.
[5] *Ibid.* 1370–1374 p. 420.
[6] *Ibid.* 1374–1377 p. 83.
[7] *Ibid.* 1374–1377 p. 204; *C.C.R.* 1374–1377 p. 288.

The corrody was a grant of food, necessaries and lodging at a religious house, and in this context, a grant to a layman. Private individuals paid a lump sum down as consideration for their maintenance until death. But founders and benefactors were regarded as entitled to claim free maintenance for themselves or their nominees; and of all benefactors, the king had the largest and least well-defined rights.

Houses of royal foundation or those which held part of their lands in frank almoign were obliged to grant certain customary allowances to the king for the support of his former servants, and in addition he claimed the right to present corrodies in any house during a vacancy. Even monasteries where the king had no rights found it hard to resist. Larger foundations and alien priories suffered most, the former because they might be presumed to be able to afford more, the latter because they were so frequently in the king's hand.[1]

The practice of giving corrodies at all has been frequently denounced, both in medieval and modern times, and as often defended. As a simple grant of food and shelter to aged persons (whether private individuals or royal nominees) it was an act of charity which satisfied a real need of society. Laymen were eager to buy such provision against old age. But their presence in any community, other than a hospital, raised problems not easily solved. The whole idea of inclosure was violated. A pensioner could not be restricted to his own chamber, and yet his conversation and manners were not those of a religious, he was not under obedience to any rule, he could not help bringing a flavour of the world, unfavourable to good discipline, with him. Episcopal visitors made rules against monks playing games of chess or draughts with pensioners, but they were really attacking something more subtle than time-wasting recreation. Any teacher knows what a disproportionate amount of trouble a small distraction can cause in a class.

Again, the sale of corrodies for money was the only way a religious house could raise cash without pawning or mortgaging its property, and as such the corrody was welcome. In any agrarian economy, ready money is a problem. A well-endowed and well-managed house might still have difficulty in meeting sudden demands, because so much of its assets and profits were not convertible. The corrody could be said to be a necessity if estates were to be kept clear of debt. And yet, once the premium had been spent, the house was burdened with the maintenance of the private corrodian for an indefinite term. A royal nominee was a greater grievance because here nothing could be entered on the credit side but some long past benefaction.

Records of corrodies given to messengers show how long a house might have to provide for the king's retired servants. Robert Rideware

---

[1]Morgan, M. *The English Lands of the Abbey of Bec* pp. 130–1. Corrodies in alien houses were sometimes granted to the king's servants in return for remission of debts.

held his corrody for twenty-three years, from 1307–30;[1] Peter le Messager, who died at Muchelney in 1317, had served Edward I;[2] and William le Messager, who was given a place at the Augustinian priory of Launde (Leicestershire) by request of Edward II, actually lived on till 1366.[3]

Finally, the corrody demanded by the king did not end as a simple grant of food and shelter. It became a money payment to a non-resident and not necessarily an aged man, though it is true that a grant to a man still in active service might become a pension for him in course of time. We often hear of these non-resident *corrodarii* only by accident. The preceptor of the hospital of St. Nicholas, Carlisle, told his bishop that he had provided corrodies for two men on letters patent of the king commanding him to receive them as brethren for life, yet neither 'have made or are making stay in the hospital, nor observing the rules at all'[4] and this remark was only recorded because St Nicholas' hospital was in financial difficulties. On the other hand, when Edward II asked the prior and convent of Holy Trinity, London, for suitable maintenance for his messenger Simon 'who long served the late king and is now blind', he added the express stipulation 'whether staying within or without their said house.'[5]

The cost of living was rising in the fourteenth century, and if corrodies could be given instead of increased wages, the king did not have to find the extra amount. He had an inducement, therefore, to give a corrody long before the messenger was ready to retire. Robert of Newington had served Edward of Caernarvon since about 1300 and after he came to the throne was one of his principal messengers. Twice Robert was protected while on the king's business, he travelled widely, and remained with the court, collecting shoes and clothes for himself and occasionally for his companions till 1320. Then his name disappears from the accounts and we may presume he retired. But he had been sent to St. Augustine's, Canterbury, to receive a corrody there in 1310.[6]

By the date of Robert's death in 1330, it was not uncommon for a messenger to have two corrodies simultaneously. Donald or Douenald of Athol, a king's messenger, was sent to take a corrody at the abbey of St. Thomas the Martyr in Dublin in 1319 and a second at the hospital of Kilmainham in 1331. This last was undoubtedly supplementary to the other, which Donald drew till his death in 1344. Meanwhile, he remained active till about 1330, received two years' protection in 1324

---

[1]*C.P.R.* 1307–1313 p. 9; 1327–1330 p. 494.
[2]*C.C.R.* 1313–1318 p. 452.   [3]*Ibid.* 1364–1368 p. 267.
[4]*C.P.R.* 1340–1342 p. 123.
[5]*C.C.R.* 1313–1318 p. 69.
[6]Robert accounted for all the messengers' clothing for the year 1310–11 on 9 November 1314 (Nero C VIII f. 30 v). Protection given (*C.P.R.* 1313–1317 p. 374; 1317–1323 p. 420). Corrody granted (*C.C.R.* 1307–1313 p. 341.)

and 1328, was one of the messengers who were to have gone abroad with the king in 1325–6 and often took letters to France.[1]

In these cases, the king was bestowing corrodies by way of reward for past service and encouragement for the future, just as he would have given a benefice in his gift to a clerk. Such corrodies to men still active and unlikely ever to want to reside, could scarcely be regarded as charitable.

How great a strain did royal corrodies impose on religious houses? There can be no simple answer to the question because the number demanded varied so widely, and probably their value also. It has been stated that at Glastonbury, there were at one time as many as six royal nominees, the average value of their maintenance being £4 6s. a year.[2] This may be reckoned (on the 1:40 basis) as equal to about £172 a year each in pre-1939 currency, and perhaps twice as much in 1960. If all were paid in cash, Glastonbury would be compelled to find something like £2,064 a year in modern terms; if only one of the six were actually non-resident at any time, the house might still and with reason begrudge an outlay to the value of £344 a year for no tangible return.

There is a very definite pattern to be observed in the grants made to king's messengers during our period. Henry III, a good son of the church, was chary of making too many demands. Few if any messengers received corrodies at his request. When the abbess and convent of Barking had given one to a royal servant, Henry undertook not to charge the nuns 'with lay-brethren, messengers, or other persons against their will', so long, that is as the present holder of the corrody should live and the house not be in the king's hand by voidance.[3]

Edward I, on the other hand, virtually abolished pensions from the exchequer and the sheriff's firm, and made the corrody the commonest form of superannuation. No doubt it seemed a simple and economical way of meeting his obligations. Thus in 1285, chancery warrants included an order 'to write under the great seal to the abbot and convent of Middleton in Dorset, to admit Gervase, king's messenger, bearer of these, who is broken with age, and his groom, to their house, and minister necessaries to him; and write back to the king what they have done in this.'[4] Here residence, both for messenger and groom, was clearly intended; and indeed all Edward I's grants seem to have been pensionary. The final clause, to 'write back to the king what they have done' is common form. Not every request was granted immediately and this was one way of ensuring that none were refused without good reason.

[1]*C.C.R.* 1318–1323 p. 117; 1330–1333 p. 319; 1342–1346 p. 481; *C.P.R.* 1331–1334 p. 410; 1337–1330 p. 309; E.A. 381/11.
[2]Coulton *Five Centuries of Religion* III 245.
[3]*C.P.R.* 1247–1258 p. 180.
[4]*C.Ch.W.* I, 28.

The king's persistence in making and the growing reluctance of religious in granting these requests, is plain. Several attempts were made to find a corrody for Geoffrey le Waleys, a messenger who had been in Edward's service since about 1283. The abbots of Burton-on-Trent, Tavistock and Gloucester were approached with requests for 'victuals and vesture for life for him in the abbey' and these were probably meant as alternative not concurrent pensions. All appear to have been refused, and it seems likely that Geoffrey was eventually accommodated at Prittlewell priory, where Geoffrey le Messager died in 1341, possessed of a corrody granted by request of Edward I.[1] A difficulty in dealing with this subject is that usually we have one side of the correspondence only, and sometimes not always that; some letters were undoubtedly sent out which have not been enrolled at all. Geoffrey le Messager's corrody at Prittlewell must have been given him as a result of a letter which does not appear on the rolls. So too the corrody at Leominster priory, a cell of Reading abbey, which William of Ledbury held at his death in 1325, said to have been given at the late king's request.[2]

In every case it was the privileged messenger and not the courier who profited from Edward I's importunity.

Edward II extended the corrody system still further. He did not confine his demands to houses of royal foundation, but appointed corrodians where he had no possible right. Hospitals suffered, because according to Edward, all 'the hospitals in the realm were founded by the king's progenitors for the admission of poor and weak persons and especially those in the king's service who were unable to work'.[3] With this excuse, he appointed corrodians to the episcopal hospital at Worcester over which he could have no authority. In houses where the right to one corrody was undisputed, he demanded more.

Edward II's abuse of the practice naturally led to more refusals and evasions. This opposition is well illustrated by the story of his dealings with St. Andrew's priory, Northampton and what followed. Here there was one established corrody, held by a former servant of Edward I. On the holder's death in 1325, the corrody was demanded for a messenger Richard Swyn, but the prior and convent refused on the grounds that they were maintaining several royal nominees whose corrodies were not customary. The king retorted with further demands and eventually Richard Swyn was accepted. In 1335 Edward III re-allotted his pension to John Swyn, one of the chancery staff, but according to the prior he had been premature, for Richard Swyn was still alive. For some reason, the house did not protest at once. But when Edward tried to appoint yet another person to the same allowance,

[1] *Ibid.* I, 175; *C.C.R.* 1302–1307 pp. 91, 104; 1339–1341 p. 657.
[2] *Ibid.* 1323–1327 p. 354.
[3] *Ibid.* 1323–1327 p. 358. See Clay *Medieval Hospitals of England* p. 213.

they refused it because the only 'established' corrody, Richard Swyn's, had already been disposed of in anticipation. The third corrodian, Robert de la Chapele, 'sued before them for such maintenance' and was refused admittance. The king wrote again, reaffirming his order, and the sequel is unknown.[1]

Against stubborn passive resistance, the king could do little to enforce his demands. This is clear from the case of William of Loughborough, a messenger for whom Edward II demanded a corrody from the prior and convent of Holy Trinity, London, in 1323. It is not clear whether this was the corrody bestowed a few years earlier on the non-resident, blind Simon, or a second unprecedented one; but in any event the demand was refused and the refusal maintained. Ten years later, Edward III sent the same William 'who long served both the king and his father, and for whose maintenance no provision has yet been made' to Battle Abbey, where a corrody was then vacant. The king's right to this could not be disputed, but the abbot delayed complying until the unfortunate messenger died without receiving anything from the house.[2]

In fact, by arousing opposition, the attempt to claim extra corrodies defeated itself and led to condemnation of the system in general. Corrodies for royal nominees were condemned by statute in 1314–5; in *Articuli Cleri* the king was especially petitioned not to abuse his powers; and on Edward III's accession he was obliged to promise the clergy that he would 'no more such things desire but where he ought' and that 'there shall be no more grants of corrodies at the king's requests'.

A more conciliatory tone is certainly observable in Edward III's letters. A request for 'competent maintenance' from the abbot and convent of Thornton concluded with the plea that 'the king will be specially bound to them' should they agree.[3] In some instances, the king agreed to give up well-established corrodies. In response to an appeal from the master and brethren of the royal hospital at Ospringe in 1330, Edward promised 'that they shall be free from providing sustenance out of their house, such as, at the late king's request, they provided for Robert le Messager of Newenton now deceased', and he renewed this promise in 1334.[4] This was the messenger usually called Robert of Rideware, whose grant of a corrody at Ospringe in 1307 was made by Edward I and confirmed by the new king. He had held another corrody at Leeds priory since 1304, but was probably resident at neither house. He had a grant of timber in the king's wood on the Newington–

---

[1]*C.C.R.* 1323–1327 pp. 515, 532; 1337–1339 p. 624; 1339–1341 pp. 112, 455; *C.Ch.W.* I, 571.

[2]*C.C.R.* 1318–1323 p. 694; 1333–1337 pp. 128, 538

[3]*Ibid.* 1339–1341 p. 275.

[4]*Ibid.* 1307–1313 p. 3; *C.P.R.* 1307–1313 p. 9; 1327–1330 p. 494; 1334–1338 p. 30.

Sittingbourne road in 1299 and this fact, coupled with the description 'of Newington' given here, suggests that he had settled down in the village, supported by two money pensions.[1] As he lived till 1330 and had held the Ospringe pension for twenty-three years, Edward's promise of future exemption for the hospital may be explained by the financial strain such long tenure had imposed on master and brethren, especially since Robert was not the only royal corrodian there.[2] Yet this was a royal hospital, peculiarly subject to demands, and Robert's pension was no innovation but had been held by another before him, so that the promise meant one regular pension the fewer from outside sources, one more to find from the king's revenue.

Where corrodies had been illegally demanded, the king was often compelled to retract. At Fountains, for example, the community had granted 'maintenance befitting his estate' to Patrick the messenger, on condition that it should not be made a precedent since they already supported another messenger, John of Waltham. At the time Edward was prepared to agree that John's corrody was not 'established' either. In 1353 a letter was enrolled, stating the facts. 'Whereas the king lately granted for the security of the abbot and convent of Fountains (who, at his request, had granted for life to John of Waltham, late his messenger, now deceased, sustenance from their house) that such grant should not prejudice the house as a precedent, and afterwards, notwithstanding the same letters, commanded the abbot and convent to grant to John of Cherteseye his servant, such sustenance in their house as John of Waltham had had at his request; and whereas on search of the rolls of the chancery and the exchequer, it is not found that the abbot and convent hold any lands in chief or that the abbey is of royal foundation whereby they should be held to grant such sustenance, the king, for the tranquility of them and their successors, by these presents, discharges the abbot and convent of the grant of the said sustenance to the said John of Cherteseye or any other person at the king's command'.[3] To obtain two immediate corrodies, Edward had promised future immunity, only to go back on his assurance; but Fountains won its case on the evidence of the rolls, which recorded the promise and also proved that he had never had any right to claim anything.

Edward III's difficulties were greater than his predecessors because by the mid-fourteenth century, the king was providing pensions for couriers as well as messengers. Edward II had done this only in

[1]*C.C.R.* 1307–1313 p. 3; *C.P.R.* 1307–1313 p. 9; *C.C.R.* 1302–1307 p. 222; *Ibid* 1296–1302 p. 263.
[2]Gilbert of Sheffield in 1335 was sent to Ospringe 'to receive such maintenance in that house for life as John Toght deceased had there at the request of Edward I' (*C.C.R.* 1333–1337 p. 506).
[3]*Ibid.* 1340–1343 p. 504; *C.C.R.* 1341–1343 p. 653; *C.P.R.* 1350–1354 p. 479.

exceptional cases;[1] thirty years later, entries on behalf of couriers are quite common.

Richard of Trokesford or Troxford was given letters, asking for maintenance at Byland in 1329, at St. Leonard's hospital, York, in 1332, and finally at Whitby in 1338.[2] Two couriers, John Pynchon and Adam Danark, were sent off together in August 1334, with 6s. 8d. for their expenses and letters to two priories, in either of which they might find shelter.[3] Other couriers for whom Edward III provided corrodies were Adam Leonard, Richard Frere, Gilbert Sheffield, Richard Fox, and William atte Halle.[4] At the same time, he did not neglect his household messengers, and letters were sent asking for corrodies for John Lewer at Darley, for Adam Merlin at Kirkstall, for William Harding at Dunstaple.[5]

One special type of corrody remains to be mentioned, the grant for a limited period during the king's absence abroad. From December 1324 to June 1325, John of Noyon the queen's messenger was boarded at a religious house and was given an allowance to pay for his keep.[6] But when Edward went abroad in 1339, he left behind three couriers unfit for strenuous travel though not yet completely retired from work. For them the king asked for temporary places until his return. Richard Frere 'who had long served the king and his father' and Robert of Chester 'who is so broken by age that he cannot travail in the king's company beyond the seas' were lodged at Trentham and Leicester respectively with 'suitable maintenance', but it was more difficult to find accommodation for Brice of Corbridge, and application on his behalf was made first to the prior of Barnwell and then to the abbot of Eynsham.[7] Wardrobe expenditure in 1339 had reached a very high level and this is no doubt why Edward was trying to get places for them without offering even a token payment. It is in sharp contrast to the arrangements made by Edward I when he left five messengers behind in England in 1286, for they were given wages as in court for the whole period of his absence,[8] and less generous than the allowance paid for John of Noyon's keep.

By 1360 or thereabouts, the number of permanent corrodies avail-

[1]He sent Robert Ryburgh to Guisburgh, and Robert Crowland in turn to Reading, Burton-on-Trent and Revesby. Presumably he meant these three letters to offer alternative rather than three-fold maintenance. Neither courier resided. Both remained in the king's regular service till November 1320 when they died in York and were buried at the king's expense. (*C.C.R.* 1313–1318 pp. 599, 463, 610; 1318–1323 p. 117; Add. MS. 17362 f. 3).

[2]*C.C.R.* 1327–1330 p. 587; 1330–1333 p. 581; 1337–1339 p. 512.

[3]Cotton MS. Nero C VIII f. 202 v.

[4]*C.C.R.* 1337–1339 p. 411; 1339–1341 p. 107; 1333–1337 p. 506; 1346–1349 p. 610; 1330–1333 p. 135.

[5]*Ibid* 1333–1337 p. 515; 1354–1360 pp. 74, 389; 1374–1377 p. 63

[6]I.R. nos 211, 213.

[7]*C.C.R.* 1339–1341 pp. 107, 219; 222, 241.

[8]Chanc. misc. 4/3.

able was so much reduced that Edward III was forced back upon his great-grandfather's use of direct pensions and county alms. Edward I had deliberately rejected both, preferring to spare the royal purse and secure pensions from charity, but that vein was worked out and of the many pensions given by the old king in the last years of his reign, only three came from religious houses. One of these was granted by an abbey as substitute for the office of porter bestowed during a vacancy on a chamber courier.[1] When Edward III died, it was plain that future kings would never find maintenance for retired servants unless they were prepared to pay for it.[2]

3. *The Value of Pensions and Corrodies*

The usefulness of a pensions system, whatever form it might take, depended on the relation between the income provided and the cost of living. Were the sums paid or the maintenance provided adequate to support the retired messenger? The question is difficult to answer in the absence of a detailed study of the cost of living during this period, but some comparison can be made with wages and prices which is worth consideration.

In the early thirteenth century, John had given $3\frac{1}{2}d$. a day to the messenger who was to live on his pension and nothing else.[3] During his reign, the rate of expenses allowed for a messenger on horseback or an accountant coming up to the sessions of the exchequer was $3d$., and by this standard $3\frac{1}{2}d$. was probably sufficient to keep the retired servant in some comfort. The usual rate of $1d$., $1\frac{1}{2}d$. or $2d$. a day, was the same as a labourer's wage; and bore rather better comparison with the cost of living than an old age pension today, even with supplementary allowances. We know that bed and breakfast could be had for $\frac{1}{2}d$. a night[4] and a substantial meal with meat or fish would not cost more than the $1\frac{1}{2}d$. or $1\frac{1}{4}d$. which the king's almoner was allowed per head when he fed the poor on feast days. A penny would buy a less generous meal, of the kind provided when the almoner was ordered to fill the great hall as full as it would hold with poor.[5] Still, there would be little margin on the daily pension of $2d$. and none at all on $1d$. or

---

[1]*C.P.R.* 1374–1337 p. 204; *C.C.R.* 1374–1377 p. 288.

[2]There was a general reduction in the number of corrodies after the early fifteenth century (Dom David Knowles *The Religious Orders in England* III 267) and the virtual disappearance of the royal corrodian was one contributing factor. If fewer private corrodies were sold, this was no doubt partly because, once monastic estates were not worked directly, an alternative method of raising cash became available. Granges were leased to lay tenants for long terms of lives or years at a nominal yearly rent, which must mean that a substantial consideration was paid at the time of the grant, though it is not as a rule mentioned in the lease itself.

[3]*R.L.Cl.* 1204–1227 I, 54.

[4]Chanc. misc. 4/3 ff. 20 v. 21 v.

[5]H. Johnstone 'Poor relief in the Royal Households of Thirteenth Century England' *Speculum* IV, 149–167.

$1\frac{1}{2}d$. for buying the clothes and shoes hitherto provided for the messenger by the king. This inadequacy was recognized, for men who had deserved well of the king were allowed to accumulate grants from different sources until they amounted to a living rate. Robert Blund had two pensions of $1\frac{1}{2}d$. each out of the issues of Gloucestershire, and the gift of a house at Shrewsbury.[1] The messenger Walwan had two pensions of $2d$. each,[2] and Roger le Messager (messenger of Edmund the king's son) had a pension of $1d$. a day from the Sheriff of Kent, two grants of $2\frac{1}{2}d$. and $1\frac{1}{2}d$. from the king's alms, and an exchequer pension as well.[3] Since the messenger was paid his expenses only while he travelled for the king, and an irregular wage in court, he was unlikely to have saved a great deal towards his old age. It may be that the $1d$. or $1\frac{1}{2}d$. pension had been adequate when first established as a regular payment out of the issues of a county. By Henry III's reign the allowance was insufficient to support the king's old servant in comfort and yet the amount was fixed too rigidly to be increased by a simple order to the sheriff. The insufficiency of the smaller pensions is proved by the two grants of $4\frac{1}{2}d$. and $3\frac{1}{2}d$. made by Edward I to mark his appreciation of the services of two queen's messengers, Simon Lowys and Simon Atteleigh.[4] Edward, in contrast to his father, was as business-like in almsgiving as in anything else. If a lesser sum would have provided satisfactorily for these two messengers, he would have allowed them less.

By the reign of Edward III, the cost of living had risen. Travelling expenses were higher, and in some cases as much as $6d$. a day was allowed for a mounted messenger. At this rate, it might be concluded that the cost of food and lodging had doubled. The normal pension given by Edward III to his messengers and like members of his household was $4\frac{1}{2}d$. a day; and if $5d$. or $6d$. represented the travelling expenses of man and horse, then $4\frac{1}{2}d$. was probably enough to support the man without any hardship. On the other hand, the only detailed travelling account[5] which has survived shows the messenger spending a good deal more than $6d$. a day on his food. When Jacke Faukes, a king's messenger, and Robert Arden, his companion, set out for Dover on 26 July 1343, they spent $10d$. on a meal before leaving London, $8d$. on a meal at Rochester, and $6d$. again on a meal at Canterbury. Thus the pair of them had spent a shilling apiece on food during the first day. On the return, a similar expenditure took place. Faukes, coming back alone, celebrated his landing at Dover by spending $2d$. on drink, then $1d$. on the same at Canterbury, $4\frac{1}{2}d$. on dinner at Rochester, and $9d$. on supper when he got to London. The single man had spent

[1] I.R. 31; *C.Ch.R.* 1226–1257 p. 134.
[2] *P.R.* 1203 p. 123; L.T.R.M.R. No. 1 (P.R.O. transcript pp. 188, 171).
[3] *C.R.* 1268–1272 p. 454; *C.P.R.* 1266–1272 pp. 614, 617; I.R. 33.
[4] I.R. 90 and 91; *L. Q.G.* p. 101.
[5] E.A. 312/4.

1s. 4½d. on meals for one day, exactly a shilling more than the average pensioner had for his entire support. Faukes and Arden might argue that they had been ordered to make great haste on that journey, and Faukes with justification might add that he had been travelling night and day for several days before that 9d. supper in some London tavern. Any messenger working for the government would be liable to spend more on meals than he would have done if journeying at his own cost, and certainly a good deal more than the same man would spend on meals in his own home. On the other hand, unreasonably extravagant expenses would have been disallowed by the exchequer auditors, and these items were all marked and passed, after the the examiner had detected and amended trifling slips in copying. Allowing for innkeeper's profits and messengers' extravagances, and allowing also for the economies possible at home, it looks as though the 4½d. pension was also becoming insufficient by the end of Edward III's reign.

The majority of messengers, if they had no private means, were dependent on the king's pension after they retired. This may explain why, towards the end of Edward's reign, a few old messengers got extra grants to supplement their money pensions. Nicholas Ufton, who had 4½d. daily from the alms, had also the office of porter at Newcastle upon Tyne,[1] and William Fox who succeeded him as porter, was given 4d. to increase his stipend.[2] Adam Merlin complained of the insufficiency of the wages he received as portejoie of the chancery (an office which he held while still working as messenger), and was allowed an extra 1½d. a day to supplement it, besides being recommended for a corrody at Kirkstall abbey.[3] Such grants prove that the 4d. or 4½d. pension was not thought to be an over-generous allowance.

Some messengers, on the other hand, had private means. Robert Blund's Shrewsbury house presumably brought him in a rent as long as the messenger remained at court. One man at least held land, which his family may have cultivated for him. John Barneby, king's messenger, brought a plea of trespass in 1277 against persons who had interfered with his land in Leicestershire.[4] Though members of the household were not allowed to keep wives at court, a number of the messengers were married, and the records mention incidentally the names of several wives who collected arrears for their husbands. These women must either have followed their husbands without official sanction, perhaps helping to make up the swarm of poor fed daily by the almoner; or else settled themselves in their native villages, living with their families and working their husbands' lands. Though no evidence

[1] *C.P.R.* 1345–1348 p. 56; 1334–1338 p. 263.
[2] *Ibid.* 1350–1354 pp. 295, 366.
[3] *Ibid.* 1354–1358 p. 148; *C.C.R.* 1354–1360 pp. 74, 389.
[4] *C.C.R.* 1272–1279 p. 416.

can be produced, it seems probable that some of the messengers at least kept up a home to which they could retire.

In addition to food, the retired messenger had also to provide himself with clothing, shoes, and shelter. The relative cost of these is difficult to assess. Edward I's messengers paid no more than ½*d.* a night for their beds: John Faukes on the other hand spent 5*d. en boire et pur son lit* at Chastelnoef.[1] Clothing is easier to price than sleeping accommodation. In the thirteenth century the cloth ordered for the messengers' clothing was allowed for at 16*d.* an ell;[2] and later each set of garments cost the wardrobe a mark, that is, approximately 2*s.* 2*d.* an ell if six ells were allowed for the dress, and 22*d.* an ell if seven ells were required. The mark for clothing became a fixed sum which the wardrobe paid out regardless of the current price of cloth, but during 1300–1, pieces of ray were given to messengers in place of wages, and these were said to be worth 2*s.* 4½*d.*, 2*s.* 8*d.*, or 3*s.* an ell.[3] Ray was a fairly expensive cloth: Thorold Rogers quotes prices from 2*s.* 2*d.* to 3*s.* 4*d.* during this period, whereas 1*s.* 5*d.* to 2*s.* was the average price of russet, and the homely bluett could be bought for 1*s.* to 1*s.* 4*d.* Yet even at 1*s.* an ell, it is difficult to see how a man living on a pension was able to afford to buy cloth at all. Shoes were more reasonable, since ordinary footwear could be had for 2½*d.* to 8*d.* a pair,[4] though Jacke Faukes and Robin Arden spent between them 6*s.* 8*d.* on the boots and spurs they purchased in London before starting off for Avignon. Certainly no retired messenger could spend anything like the 18*s.* a year allowed by the wardrobe for his shoes and clothes as long as he remained in the king's service. It is not hard to understand why Nicholas le Waleys and William Choll, 'formerly king's messengers' were given robes of the king's gift in 1266, and why John Russel's allowance of alms was enlarged in 1345 by 10*s.* yearly to pay for his clothing.[5] The average messenger who could expect no aid of this kind must on retirement have found his standard of living much reduced, for in court many things had been provided for him which he now had to find for himself.[6]

Food, clothing, and shelter, were the three main items which the king's clerks stipulated when demanding a corrody for one of his old servants. These 'necessaries of life' which the house must provide would give the messenger the same amenities as he had enjoyed in the king's household and without trouble on his part. According to his rank, the

[1]E.A. 312/4 f. 2. This is the only time that Faukes mentions the price of a bed in his account: possibly he would have paid less in England.

[2]*P.R.* 68.

[3]Add. MS. 7966 ff. 165, 165 v.

[4]Thorold Rogers *A History of Agriculture and Prices in England* II (1259–1400) pp. 436–538.

[5]*C.R.* 1264–8 p. 170: *C.P.R.* 1345–8 p. 16.

[6]cf. Tout 'The English Civil Service in the Fourteenth Century' *Bulletin of the John Rylands Library 1916* p. 21.

corrodian drew fixed rations from the buttery or shared in the common meal, the rules of each monastery differing in some respects. The phrase 'maintenance befitting his estate' was commonly used in grants of corrodies and gave little indication of what that maintenance ought to be, but a few letters were more explicit. Two letters close were addressed to the abbot and convent of St. Thomas, Dublin, and to the prior of the hospital of Kilmainham respectively, both in favour of the same messenger, Donald (or Douenald), of Athol. Here the king's clerks evidently considered it necessary to explain what was required. The messenger is to be provided with 'sufficient maintenance for life in food and drink, clothing, shoeleather, livery for a horse and groom, a suitable chamber within the enclosure of the abbey, candle, firewood, and all other necessaries'.[1] This was the only grant in which lighting and firing were specified, but presumably these were generally provided. Grooms were often mentioned. The groom attached to Gervase, messenger of Edward I, was to share in all the privileges granted to his master at Middleton, and William Alkham at Vaudey was to have 'what is necessary for the maintenance of a groom', as well as 'the requirements of his estate in food, clothing, shoeleather, and other necessaries.'[2] The king's messenger might not rank very high among the king's servants, but he still had a position to keep up, even in retirement. With a fitting chamber, the company and services of his groom, a share in the common life of the house, and everything found, the corrodian was a good deal better off than the alms-man whose allowance cannot have been enough to pay for a servant. This may be another reason why Edward I and his son tried to increase the number of corrodies available as pensions, and the later restriction on such grants may have been as unpopular with the messengers as with the exchequer.

4. Death

The king's responsibility for his household included the duty of giving decent burial to any man who died in his service. Such expenditure was made either through the almoner, when the wardrobe controlled finance, or through the exchequer; and there are a number of references to the practice. Among the messengers, there were three instances of men dying in the king's service and being buried at his expense. Robert Crowland and Robert Ryburgh were buried at York in November 1319, and the almoner recorded the expenditure of 5s. 'for the exequies done about the bodies of Robert Crouland and Robert Riburgh, wardrobe couriers, dead during the month of November in the present year.'[3] The ceremonies were no doubt arranged by the yeomen of the almonry. Later

---
[1]*C.C.R.* 1318–1323 p. 117; 1330–1333 p. 319.
[2]*C.Ch.W.* I, 28; *C.C.R.* 1307–1313 p. 248.
[3]Add. Ms. 17362 f. 3. Both had had grants of corrodies.

when payments of this sort were made by the exchequer instead of a household department, it was necessary to find someone to supervise the funeral, and another messenger was chosen for the duty. When Andrew Retford died in April 1375, 7s. 4d. was allowed and entered as 'money liberated for him (by the hand of Alan Barley) of the king's alms for the burial of his body on the advice of the treasurer and chamberlain.'[1] It seems from this that the household officers had certified the exchequer of the death and applied for the funeral expenses which were collected by a fellow messenger. Compared with other sums allowed for burying members of the household, the 5s. or 7s. 4d. spent on couriers and messengers in these instances do not appear unliberal; and were certainly not the medieval equivalent of a pauper's burial. Considering the number of messengers who are known to have fallen ill for longer or shorter periods, three deaths only recorded during some 178 years is a remarkably small proportion out of the total number of messengers in the king's service during that time.

It is not clear whether in such an event, the wives and dependents of the messengers received anything. Some of the messengers were married and in the man's absence, pensions overdue might be paid to the wife. Christiana, wife of John of Canterbury (de Cantuaria) collected his allowance of 1d. a day from the Sheriff of Essex while John, with another messenger, was sent to the Court of Rome.[2] Duca or Douce, wife of Thomas Oxford, a queen's messenger, received 100s. in quittance of her husband's pension in 1275; and Constance, wife of Simon Lowys, collected his grant from the exchequer in 1295. When Walter Cardinal's daily $4\frac{1}{2}d$. was in arrears in 1374, his wife Cecilia was given an imprest on the 66s. 8d. due.[3] In any pension paid to a messenger for life, his wife naturally shared. But what provision was made for her if she outlived him and what compensation, if any, should her husband be killed in the king's service, it is impossible to say. The only mention of anything like compensation occurs in 1384, when William Crayling (who does not appear to have been a regular messenger at all) was sent to the Netherlands with important documents and while on his way to deliver them was killed at Sluys 'on account of the message aforesaid'. His widow Natalicia received £13 4s. 10d. by way of compensation and assistance in paying William's debts.[4] Otherwise the only reference to a messenger's widow is in 1268, when Henry III gave a robe to Marsilia, widow of Henry le Messager;[5] and it appears almost certain that the king accepted no responsibility for dependents of his former servants.

[1] I.R. 456 m. 21.
[2] *C.L.R.* 1226–1240 pp. 32, 34.
[3] I.R. 28, 91, 451.
[4] *Issues of the Exchequer* ed. Devon p. 225.
[5] *C.R.* 1264–1268 p. 461.

CHAPTER V

THE SERVANT'S DUTIES

E VERY member of the household had his well-defined privileges as the king's servant; and correspondingly, he had definite functions which gave him full-time occupation. He need not feel, like the serf, uncertain of the next day's duty; nor, on the other hand, was he a ceremonial figure whose work was performed by a hired deputy.[1] The duties required of the king's inferior household servants were real enough; and in discussing them we pass from conditions of service general in the household to the special conditions attaching to a messengership. These were, however, typical of the trust placed in other men of similar standing.

The primary function of a king's messenger was the conveyance of letters, though he had a number of subsidiary ones. No distinction was made at this period between home service and foreign service messengers. An experienced man, if available, was naturally preferred for foreign journeys, and mounted messengers were more often sent abroad than couriers. Yet couriers were sent as far afield as the court of Rome[2] and were given equal responsibility with the privileged men. But messengers and couriers alike gained their experience chiefly at home. Journeys within the realm far exceeded those outside it, for continuous diplomatic negotiations were not maintained with any foreign power except the court of Rome. Out of 182 journeys made by regular messengers in 1252–3, only four commissions took the messenger outside England; and similarly, there were only nineteen foreign journeys out of 359 made in 1299–1300.[3] These figures are typical and might apply to any year in which no extra-ordinary negotiations were taking place.

1. Transport of Letters Abroad

A great many of the regular letters sent abroad were administrative orders to the king's Gascon officials. Each dispatch contained a number of letters, which the English messenger as a rule took no further than

[1]This, by the end of the fourteenth century, was the position of the highly-privileged papal messenger, whose work was done by outside letter-carriers (Yves Renouard *op. cit.* p. 7 *et seq.*).

[2]'Expenses of foot-messengers going to the court of Rome' form one sub-heading in the enrolled wardrobe account for 1236–8 (*P.R.* 81).

[3]E.A. 308/1; *L.Q.G.*

Bordeaux. There the Seneschal of Gascony or the Constable of Bordeaux received the dispatch, extracted his own orders and sent on the rest by his Gascon messengers, whose expenses might afterwards be refunded in part by the exchequer. When occasionally a messenger made the round of the Gascon towns with the king's letters, he must have carried something more immediate than a set of routine orders.

After Calais fell into English hands, similar correspondence was maintained with the officials there. In time of war it was particularly necessary to send news quickly of the various truces entered into by the king, their terms and duration; and the messenger Berengar Calder was sent to Calais in November 1353 with letters 'to proclaim the truce'. Meanwhile, precautions must always be taken and repeated orders for the better fortification of the town are mentioned among the letters sent out. Victuals in case of siege must be collected in from time to time and sold if unused, and a whole set of instructions on this important matter were conveyed by three messengers during 1375–6. Secret business of the king is given as the reason for sending John Eliot to the captain of the town of Calais and to the captains of Ardres and Guines in April 1377.[1] To all these letters, the home government expected a reply brought back by the messenger who took out the dispatch. It was presupposed that the seneschal, the constable, or the captain, would pay for the returning messenger, and so the wardrobe or exchequer rarely advanced more than outward-bound expenses.

Instructions were also sent to English envoys abroad, and here too, a reply by return was anticipated. Robert le Herberjur took the king's letters to his envoys in Rome in 1210; Robert Petit took letters to two of the king's agents in Germany in 1297; Simon Lowys carried instructions to envoys at the French court in 1304. William Fox, the messenger who had taken Edward III's letters to Bartholomew de Burghash, came back with news of the truce arranged between Edward and the king of France.[2] These are only a few instances. When an embassy set out, it was usual for a regular messenger to travel with the ambassador, or to catch him up on the way, so that last minute instructions could be conveyed from the king and an early report be received of his safe arrival. If he had not gone far, a courier might do this. Robert Snelling a courier was sent in July 1299 with William de Melton as far as London 'to bring back news of his expedition to the king'.[3] But outside England, a messenger was preferred. William of Dogmersfield went with Otto de Grandson as far as Paris in 1290;[4] Geoffrey le Galeys accompanied the Archdeacon of Richmond 'to foreign parts to bring back his letters' in April 1299, and next month was sent again, with a fellow messenger William of Alkham, in the

[1] I.R. 373 m. 12; 459 mm. 18, 23, 27; 462 m. 1.
[2] *Rot. de Lib.* pp. 128, 153; Add. MSS. 7965 f. 11 v; 8835 f. 109; E.A. 389/8.
[3] E.A. 355/18 m. 3.   [4] E.A. 308/12 m. 1.

train of two envoys going abroad.[1] Not only could the king's messenger take back the envoy's dispatches to the home government, he might
be useful as a liaison between the envoy and other royal agents. John de
Benstede's accounts illustrate this.[2] Guillot, one of the king's messengers had accompanied him as far as Paris in 1305, and was then sent
ahead by the envoy to find the king's agent, Otto de Grandson, at
Toulouse. Benstede could thus go straight to Bordeaux, where Grandson joined him; they consulted upon the king's affairs, and sent home
a joint dispatch by the same messenger. Ambassadors travelled more
slowly than a single messenger, mounted or unmounted; and a man
sent post haste after an envoy who had some start of him, usually
caught him up this side of the Channel. But when Edward II sent a
courier, Robert le Hunte, after certain formal messengers who were
'going from London to Dover or toward foreign parts', he was too
slow to contact them in England, and the exchequer clerk added a note
to explain why Hunte had spent 6s., 'because he went to Paris'.[3] When
the envoy returned to England again, a messenger was frequently sent
to meet his ship at Dover and bring back news. Adam of Bayworth
met the treasurer coming from abroad, and was sent again to Dover to
wait for returning envoys.[4] News came more quickly and frequently
than is usually supposed. In addition to any dispatches sent back by
regular king's messengers, envoys abroad were expected to keep the
home government fully informed of their doings, and to have messengers of their own for the purpose. The expense incurred was accounted
for in the envoy's particular of his own expenses, and were sometimes
considerable. An envoy to Aquitaine in 1327, sending in his claim for
over £19 spent on private messengers, showed that he had employed
twenty-one during the four months he had been abroad.[5]

A diplomatic significance, no doubt, attached also to the correspondence maintained by the royal family with relatives in other courts.
Queen's messengers took most of these letters, and communication was
fairly regular between Eleanor of Castile and the Spanish court, between Philippa and Hainault, and between Isabella of France and her
brother, especially between 1311 and 1315.[6] Beyond these personal
connexions, diplomatic correspondence was intermittent except with

---

[1] E.A. 356/mm. 10. 12d.
[2] E.A. 309/9 (C. L. Kingsford 'John de Benstede and his missions for Edward I'
in *Essays Presented to R. Lane Poole* pp. 337–8, 353).
[3] I.R. 205 m. 7d.
[4] E.A. 308/7 and 8 (1284–5).
[5] E.A. 309/36.
[6] Arnold Bon, Thomas Squiret, and Ralph Laundeles took letters to Spain during
1288–9; Gilbert the queen's messenger went twice to Hainault between March and
May 1332; William Bale the queen's messenger and his fellow John Noyon, took
Isabella's letters to France and Navarre on several occasions. (E.A. 308/10; John
Rylands Library Latin MS. 235 f. 32; Cotton MS. Nero C VIII; E.A. 375/9 f. 34
and 376/20).

K.M.–G

the Court of Rome. In any year, the vast majority of letters sent abroad went to Rome or Avignon. Usually the messenger would find there a representative of the king, who received his own instructions and presented personally the formal letters addressed to the pope. In the rare cases where no such intermediary was available, the messenger was instructed to hand the king's letters to a cardinal.[1]

The number of foreign letters accounted for by wardrobe and exchequer increased noticeably under Edward III, and especially at the beginning of his French campaigns. The extent of Edward's correspondence at that point with the emperor, the counts of Flanders and Hainault, the dukes of Brabant and Guelders, and with Jan van Artevelde and the Flemish towns between 1338 and 1340 is not always realized.[2] Both before and during the expedition, messengers passed constantly between England and Flanders, between Edward and his would-be allies. The unsatisfactory outcome of so much effort might be guessed from the disappearance of these commissions in later wardrobe books, when the number of foreign dispatches fell again to twenty or so a year.

2. *Transport of Letters at Home*

The king's messenger service was the indispensible link between the central government and its county agents, the sheriffs. Communication between them was constant, and some fourteenth-century sheriffs must have received instructions or writs almost every week in the year. The dispatching clerks kept a tally of the number of writs taken by each messenger, to whom they were addressed, and some indication of the contents. From these notes, the sheriff's duties and the government's anxieties can be seen. Messengers carried orders for collection of taxes, promulgation of statutes or royal commands, orders for opening and closing the ports, establishment of the staple, and control of base money. In 1299, every sheriff in England received the king's letters under the great seal with the form of Magna Carta and the charters of the Forest as re-issued by Edward I, together with the new statutes made that year at Westminster.[3]

Each messenger visited several countries. Thomas Hertford, going on foot, brought the 'new statute' of 1285 to the sheriffs at Gloucester, Hereford, Worcester, Shrewsbury, and Stafford.[4] The country was divided up into regular beats of four or five counties, each centre being estimated as so many days journey from London and the messenger paid accordingly. The sheriff usually had to make a return to the writs received, and paid part or the whole of the man's return expenses, which

[1]e.g. E.A. 361/16; I.R. 186 m. 4.
[2]Misc. Bks. Exch. T. of R. 203; E.A. 389/8.
[3]E.A. 356/8 m. 1.
[4]E.A. 308/8.

not only saved the exchequer but ensured that the messenger came back with as much as he took out and did not waste his labour.[1] As the fourteenth century progressed, each session of parliament was marked by a batch of statutes to be taken round by the messengers. Only the more important were named by the dispatching clerks, but one which in their eyes merited notice was the revocation of the Statute of Labourers, sent out on 9 November 1359 at a cost of 38s. 3d. The law on purveyance, passed by the Winchester parliament of 1371, was another burning topic.[2] When the staple was re-established at Calais in 1362, the change was proclaimed all over the country in obedience to letters sent out on 27 July, for which the exchequer paid £4 6s. 9d. to the messengers employed;[3] and every fluctuation in Edward III's staple policy meant a fresh set of regulations taken round by the messengers and published by the sheriff. Instructions to arrange for the election of knights of the shire went to the same hardworked officials, and they were responsible too, for distributing within their shire the individual summons addressed to magnates.

In time of war, this routine administrative business was diversified by writs to raise troops, either for the king's army abroad or local defence. The issue rolls for the years 1367[4] are full of messengers' expenses in taking out these urgent commissions calling for the enlistment in army or home guard of all men between the ages of 16 and 60. Foodstuffs had to be collected for the forces, tenants in chief notified of the military service required of them, earlier orders countermanded or postponed, temporary truces during the war proclaimed. All these orders went through the sheriff's hands and without a responsible and adequate messenger service, the organization of a war on these lines would have been impossible. The peace at last achieved was proclaimed to the ordinary citizen by the same means. In 1372 messengers were busy taking orders to proclaim peace between the king and the count of Flanders, a news item of interest to every merchant; and in 1375 letters went out to the sheriffs 'for the truce made between the lord king and his adversary of France to be proclaimed.'[5] The avoidance of the words 'king of France' is a reminder of Edward's dynastic claims. Another side of the king's war preparations was conveyed in the order to all bishops, abbots and priors and to the University of Oxford 'to pray for the king and his army being on the sea to resist the malice of his enemies, and for the state of the realm of England.'[6] All this has a very modern ring.

---

[1]Compare the scale of days laid down by the exchequer for the travelling expenses of its accountants. *Red Bk*. III, 835–9.

[2]I.R. 400 m. 8; 443 m. 16.

[3]I.R. 410 m. 37.

[4]I.R. 429, 431, 433, 434.

[5]I.R. 444 m. 30; 457 m. 21.

[6]I.R. 446.

The messengers' main commissions were to the sheriffs, but they were well known also to mayors of towns, bailiffs of royal manors, officials of every port that could produce ships for the king's service, heads of every religious house that could lend horses for the carriage of victuals. One entry for messengers' expenses is particularly interesting because it confirms the evidence of a chronicler and gives an insight into medieval publicity methods. Edward I, so John de Oxenedes told his readers, particularly wished that his doings in Scotland should be fully and favourably recorded; and to this end wrote to all religious houses, asking them to insert in their chronicles an account of his Scottish claims. Two messengers, Arnold Bon and Richard of Norwich, were sent round on this errand, and their expenses which came to 7s., were entered as spent on letters to all abbots, priors, and men of religion, that the deeds done in Scotland might be entered in the chronicles.[1] The king hoped to obtain perpetual recognition of his claims at a very reasonable rate.! Incidentally the king's messengers may often have supplied chroniclers with material and been welcomed for it, even when the arrival of a messenger at the abbey gate meant further royal demands upon the house.

3. Conveyance of Money and Valuables

Letter post and parcel post have always gone together; and the conveyance of money and valuables was a duty expected of messengers even in the days of the messenger serjeanties. Then it had been necessary to find a local man who would be responsible for transporting money to the exchequer, and the messenger sergeant was the obvious person. The holder of land at Cirencester had been required to conduct the king's treasure at his own expense within the shire and at the king's expense outside it; and though this was at first quite distinct from his letter-carrying duties, in time the two obligations were inseparable. Tenants of the Herefordshire village of Marden were expected to convey treasure from Hereford to London, in addition to taking out summons to certain lords.[2] When the household messenger took up the serjeant's duties, he too was made responsible for the safe conduct of valuables on the road.

This duty was no light one, and illustrates the trust placed in the messengers. A mandate of 1274 to the papal nuncio authorized him to 'deliver to the king's messengers all the money arising from the tenth of the bishopric of Lincoln deposited at Oxford, and of the bishopric of Norwich deposited at Dunwich, the king discharging the Church of Rome and the said Master Reymund of all risk of robbers or other

---

[1]*Chronica Johannis de Oxenedes* (Rolls Series) pp. 280–283; I.R. 70.
[2]Kimball *op. cit.* pp. 99, 101.

risk.'[1] The sums involved might be great. Nicholas Ramage transported £200 from Conway to Crukyn (?Criccieth) in 1283,[2] and as far as the accounts show, he had no assistance in doing so. More commonly, a messenger took a valet or another messenger for additional security. John Elyot went with a valet named Thomas to Sandwich in April 1375 'for the safe conduct of money'; and three messengers received 8*d*. for their expenses 'for porterage of gold and silver from the treasury to the exchequer of receipt' in 1377.[3]

When the court went abroad, to Gascony or Scotland, the difficulties of transporting money were greater and the need for it more pressing. In November 1295, Roger Windsor was sent from Winchelsea with £80 for the king's army in Gascony. This meant taking ship to Plymouth, in the cog *St. Edward,* and there transferring the money to another ship bound for Gascony, and the messenger must have been glad to get even £80 off his hands.[4] Arnold Bon undertook this duty twice when larger sums were involved. On the first occasion he was allowed 16*s*. for the expense of transporting £1,000 which was being sent to Gascony via Portsmouth. On the second, he was responsible, with one other man, for seeing that £2,333 arrived in Gascony safely.[5] Both the orders necessary for carrying on the campaign, and the ready money for its current expenditure, were conveyed by the messenger service, which formed an indispensable link between the administration at home and the army abroad.

Even though the exchequer moved to York during the Scottish war, there were still long and dangerous miles to be covered between York and the border. Robert Manfield in 1301 was put in charge of money urgently needed to pay Welsh foot-soldiers in the king's service in Scotland; and to secure the safe arrival of so much cash, the messenger hired seven archers and got an extra horse to carry the specie.[6] His precautions must have been approved of by the authorities, for in 1307 they entrusted him with £4,000 to be carried from London to Carlisle. The coin was loaded into four carts, each drawn by five horses, and the hire of carts, horses, and carters cost Manfield 2*s*. 6*d*. a day on the road, and an extra day waiting in London while the carts were being loaded. Besides this, he engaged twelve men-at-arms at 1*s*. a day each, and sixteen archers on foot at 3*d*. a day each, and with all this protection he must still have felt anxious as the cumbrous five-horsed

---

[1] *C.P.R.* 1272–1281 p. 53.
A tax on the clergy for crusading funds was decreed at Lyons in 1274, and the money was collected slowly between 1274 and 1287. Edward was allowed to borrow from the sums raised in England because he intended to lead the crusade (Powicke *King Henry III and the Lord Edward,* II 726–7).
[2] E.A. 351/9.
[3] I.R. 456 m. 20; 462 m. 9.
[4] Misc. Bks. Exch. T. of R. 202 f. 24 v.
[5] John Rylands Library Latin MS. 230.
[6] I.R. 108.

wagons trundled out of London with their twenty-eight guards on horse or on foot, the carters, the equipment, the provisions, and one king's messenger riding alongside, responsible for the whole cavalcade. They set out on 8 August, and were eleven days on the road before Carlisle came into sight; and even then the messenger's work was not done. He and his little troop waited a week while the money was checked and divided, part to remain in safe keeping at Carlisle, part to be repacked and taken to the king for immediate use. So new panniers and new cords had to be bought, since the Scottish roads were too bad for wagons, and £1,333 6s. 8d. of the money was loaded on to pack horses, Manfield superintending. He paid for the purchases, paid the wages of the archers and men-at-arms while they waited in Carlisle, and paid all the expenses of the four days' journey from Carlisle to the castle of Tibbers, where the king was staying. Finally, Manfield was responsible for dismissing the convoy with twelve days' wages for their return journey to London, since without the heavy carts, horsemen and footmen could cover the distance in much shorter time than they had taken to come north. The total expense to the wardrobe was £28 19s. 1d., according to Manfield's final account; and the whole responsibility of the transaction had rested on the messenger alone.[1]

In time of peace, the transport of large sums in cash was avoided, when possible, by the use of tallies; and instead of carts loaded with specie, exchequer writs and tallies for large amounts were dispatched by messenger, to the advantage both of administration and messenger. Richard Swart took such a writ and a tally for 100 marks made out in the name of the collector of customs at Yarmouth, who was to pay a certain William Lussher at Yarmouth for fish which he had supplied to the court.[2] But messengers still had to take jewelry and valuables from place to place, and these, though less bulky, must have been equally anxious commissions. William Burre and Robert of Newington were sent to the king in 1308 with a gold crown and jewels valued at £75, a gold cypher worth £40, heavy enough to require an extra horse to carry it, and other valuable objects.[3] The messenger Piacle was sent in great haste to bring four pieces of cloth of gold to the court at Gillingham in March 1297,[4] and these were probably intended to make up the gift of twenty pieces of cloth of gold which the king was sending to Rome in April—hence the need to hurry. The present was dispatched as far as Plymouth in the charge of another messenger Robert Little, who was given 8s. for his expenses and the cost of hiring hackneys to carry the bundles.[5] When the king made an offering at the

[1] E.A. 373/15 f. 11.
[2] Cotton MS. Nero C VIII f. 293.
[3] E.A. 373/15 f. 26 v.
[4] Add. MS. 7965 f. 109 v.
[5] Add. MS. 7965 f. 109 v.; f. 17.

shrine of some saint, or a gift to a much frequented place of pilgrimage, he did not necessarily present them with his own hands. Far more often it was a king's messenger who took these valuable articles. William Clerk, a courier of Edward I, took a piece of cloth of gold as a gift from the king to be laid on the shrine of St. Kenelm at Winchcombe in the king's name.[1] John Faukes was sent to London to fetch a golden ship, intended as an offering on the king's behalf at Walsingham, and presumably meant as thank-offering after a successful voyage, most probably on the king's safe return from France.[2] The knowledge that he carried objects of such value must have increased the messenger's fears of those wayside robberies, against which his mere presence was held sufficient insurance in 1274.[3]

4. *Escort and Espionage*

Messengers were often sent as escorts to foreign envoys in England, acting as their protection and guide on the road, reinforcing the king's safe conduct and offering respect to the foreign power. But besides these objects, the messenger was sent so that the king should have some check on the envoy's movements and contacts while in England. Every envoy and every messenger from abroad was a potential spy; and the medieval administrator believed firmly in the principles laid down, for the guidance of a later generation, by Philip de Commines. According to him, every ambassador, friendly or hostile should be dismissed as quickly as possible. 'If they come from true friends of whom there can be no suspicion, treat them with good cheer and grant them frequent audience but dismiss them soon, for friendship among princes does not endure for ever. If from hostile courts, send honourably to meet them, lodge them well, set safe and wise men about them to watch who visits them and keep malcontents away, give them audience at once and be rid of them. Even in time of war one must receive envoys, but see that a keen eye is kept on them, and for every one sent to you, do you in return send two, and take every opportunity of sending, for you can have no better spies, and it will be hard to keep a strict watch over two or three.'[4] The advice was not new. Edward I was particularly cautious about foreigners, and during his reign both messengers with letters and envoys on diplomatic missions were escorted by his own messengers and couriers. Arnold Bon was sent with the Duke of Brabant's messenger as far as Whitsand in1285 (for which he claimed 4*s* for the expenses of both) and was guide to a Gascon messenger in 1295.[5] William Ledbury in 1289 was put in

[1] Add. MS. 37655, E.A. 368/27 f. 83 v.
[2] Misc. Bks. Exch. T. of R. 204 (1341–5).
[3] *C.P.R.* 1272–1281 p. 53.
[4] Quoted by Neale 'The Diplomatic Envoy' *History* XIII 204–218.
[5] E.A. 308/8; I.R. 90.

charge of a foreigner who received through the messenger his present from the king as the bearer of news.[1] Robert Romeyn, a courier, was ordered to go with another messenger from the Duke of Brabant,[2] to escort him out of England, and take at the same time the king's reply to the communication. John of Canford, Edward II's messenger, went with a courier of the king of France in March 1324 *pro securiori expedicione.*[3]

Care was thus taken to prevent spying by letter-carriers; but diplomatic envoys were even more suspect, for their position gave them many opportunities of collecting information. Partly as mark of respect, partly as watch-dog, William of Dogmersfield travelled in the train of the Duke of Brabant after his visit to the English court in 1294. The same messenger later escorted three friars who came as envoys to the king's son, and while he hired their horses, paid their expenses, and arranged their passage, William was no doubt able to keep effective watch over their movements.[4] Godfrey the queen's messenger was doing much the same when his mistress sent him to Northampton in the company of messengers from Germany.[5] Robert Rideware, messenger of Edward of Caernarvon, had a more trying time with the two Frenchmen whom he conducted from Nottingham to Dover in April 1303. The strangers fell ill on the road, and Robert was obliged to wait until they could go on again, which kept him from April to June on the same business. He then had to rejoin the court in Scotland, a twenty-one days' journey from Dover, so that his watch over the foreigners had taken up seventy days of the messenger's time, with correspondingly heavy expenses.[6]

Later accounts show the same care for the comfort and good behaviour of guests from abroad. Philip Melton was sent from Nottingham by Edward II to meet and conduct the king of Portugal's envoys from London to Carlisle where the king expected to be,[7] and Adam Baggard a courier, was sent 'in the company of Robert of Aungiers, a messenger of the king of France (by special command of the queen) to show the said Robert the right road between Clipstone in Sherwood and Northampton.'[8] A special guide was hired in 1316 for the benefit of the cardinal's messengers who were carrying Papal Bulls from London to Scotland, but this was a rare occurrence, and presumably no messenger or courier happened to be available at the time.[9] When the ports were closed against all foreigners, as they were for considerable

[1]Chanc. Misc. 3/46 No. 29.
[2]Misc. Bks. Exch. T. of R. 202.
[3]E.A. 379/19 f. 8.
[4]Misc. Bks. Exch. T. of R. 202; Add. MS. 7965 f. 34.
[5]E.A. 359/10.
[6]Add. MS. 35292 f. 45 v.
[7]E.A. 373/15 f. 24 v.
[8]E.A. 376/20 m. 4d.
[9]Society of Antiquaries' MS. No. 120 p. 149.

periods, it was necessary to meet all envoys and letter-carriers from abroad with permits for their entry into England and letters of safe conduct. Such passports were made out for the envoys of Robert, brother of the Duke of Burgundy, in 1323–4, and sent by messenger to the keeper of the passage at Dover, in readiness for their arrival.[1]

Messengers and envoys from hostile courts were not the only ones to be treated with suspicion when they came to England. In 1295, Simon Lowys, then in the king's service, was put in charge of a party of important persons from Guernsey, who were waiting in London for the king's return. The messenger made himself very useful to the visitors, paying weekly for their lodgings and food, according to the treasurer's instructions.[2] No doubt he kept watch over their movements at the same time, and may have beguiled their enforced leisure and his own by acting as guide to the sights of London.

English messengers abroad were treated in the same way. When Jacke Faukes went to Avignon in 1343, he had to get a safe conduct to pass through France on his return journey; and was obliged to travel much out of his direct route to collect it. Meanwhile a serjeant was sent with him, for whose expenses Faukes was apparently responsible. It was this item which made him overspend his travelling allowance, and caused his account to be preserved for the exchequer auditors.[3] The French court had reason to be suspicious for the constable of France was explicitly charged, according to a fourteenth century description of the office, with the duty of sending out messengers and spies, on horse or foot, wherever he thought necessary.[4] English kings were equally likely to use spies, though more reticent about it. In war time, occasional references in the accounts show that information was being collected from many sources. Nicholas Ramage in 1299 was engaged on some business in Scotland which involved a five days journey in the company of a spy employed by the constable of Roxburgh Castle.[5] Edward III gave his messenger William Fox a commission under letters patent to go to Flanders' to inquire into certain contentions, robberies and other misdeeds perpetrated by English and Flemings', and allowed him to take three men with him for the investigation.[6] Two messengers were sent to Normandy in 1339 to find out about the French galleys lying in port there,[7] and later in the same reign, a gentleman in the retinue of the Duke of Lancaster was reimbursed for over £70 paid 'to divers messengers and valets sent to divers parts to watch the desires and actions of the

[1]E.A. 379/19 f. 9 v.
[2]I.R. 95.
[3]E.A. 312/4.
[4]Anselme *Histoire de la Maison royale de France* (1730) VI, 234.
[5]L.Q.G. p. 281
[6]E.A. 311/14.
[7]Misc. bks E.T.R. 203 f. 112 v.

French enemies during the time the said duke remained in the service of the king there'.[1] The sum is large, in comparison with the £183 spent on ordinary messenger expenses for that year, and proves that Edward was in the habit of employing a large number of secret agents, some of them messengers in his household, at times of danger. Indeed, this may explain a number of special or 'secret' commissions undertaken by messengers for the king and not described more fully by wardrobe or exchequer clerks. Though the word 'secret' does not necessarily mean more than 'private', and may often have covered nothing more sinister than personal commissions for the king, yet the 'secret business of the king in the direction of Scotland', and 'the business secretly enjoined upon them by the king', which certain messengers undertook, suggests something more important than these.[2]

Even within the realm, the king might find it convenient to check the returns of local authorities and supplement their information with an independent report. When Edward III wanted to have an accurate return of ships available in the port of Winchelsea in 1370, he did not trust the word of the mayor and bailiffs, to whom he had sent writs of inquiry. William Fox, whose employment abroad has been mentioned, was sent with the letters and instructed to make his own observations at the same time; and the administration seems to have been confident that the second report would be accurate, if not the first.[3] In Ireland, again, there might be good reason to get a second opinion. It was for this that John Eliot, the king's messenger was sent to Ireland in 1376, with the ostensible duty of summoning the barons of the Irish exchequer to the council, and the real object of bringing back to the king a report on the state of the country.[4] Incidentally, these secret commisions are a further proof of the confidence placed by the administration in the messenger service.

5. *Arrest and Custody of Prisoners*

These duties, like messenger-service, began as a serjeanty attached to land-holding, and in this way became early connected with letter carrying. A serjeant holding land in the forest of Galtres near York had the duty of keeping prisoners of the forest; in Herefordshire, certain men were bound to arrest and distrain for debt, and to carry the king's writs into the bargain.[5] Under John, the custody of the Fleet prison was a serjeanty obligation, while the keepers of the gaols at Winchester and Exeter were still the king's serjeanty tenants at the end of the thirteenth century. When the household messenger took

[1] *Issue Roll of Thomas de Brantingham* p. 493.
[2] e.g. E.A. 379/19 f. 15 v.
[3] *Issue Roll of Thomas de Brantingham* p. 180.
[4] I.R. 459 m. 28.
[5] Kimball *op. cit.* pp. 49, 89, 98, 99.

over the duties of the messenger-serjeant, it was natural that he too should sometimes have been asked to arrest or take charge of prisoners for the king, and that in his old age, keepership of a gaol might be thought suitable preferment for him.

Scattered references to arrests are found in the accounts. Alberic the king's messenger was allowed money for handcuffs which he had bought for the use of prisoners in 1221,[1] and the keeper of Newgate gaol was ordered to receive and keep safe certain prisoners who would be delivered to him by the messenger Robert Blund.[2] Arnold Bon was specially sent to Thurrock on two occasions, first to collect and convey ten alien fishermen captured at sea by English sailors, and then to receive custody of another foreigner taken at sea.[3] An order addressed to the justices of North Wales in 1347 commanded them to 'receive from Thomas Bolefot and John le Taverner, king's messengers, the body of Arnold de la Meynade and to keep him safely in the castle of Caernarvon, as they will answer for him body for body.'[4] It may be presumed that the messengers who delivered up the prisoner had also been expected to answer for him 'body for body', and that an escape might have landed them in much trouble. In other cases, the duty was less onerous. The Black Prince's messenger received a mark for his expenses in bringing Sir John Berner's son before the council, and keeping him safely;[5] and messengers may often have provided escorts for wards and other quasi-captives.

These duties, conscientiously performed, might lead in the end to the establishment of the retired messenger as keeper of a town or castle gaol. Such a man was 'Master' Robert Hoton, messenger, to whom the king gave the keeping of Stafford gaol for life, according to his own story. Robert complained that in spite of a writ to the sheriff to deliver the bailiwick of the prison to him, 'the sheriff would not deliver it nor perform the king's command at which many of the people of the county marvelled, whereby he is at great mischief, and on the point of begging his bread.' The sheriff, it appears, had taken the precaution of demanding a guarantee for the safekeeping of the prisoners, and wanted 2,000 marks surety, refusing to accept the assurances of substitutes, even though they were 'the best serjeants of the county'.[6] It may be that the king had overstepped his rights in making the grant, and that Stafford gaol was one of those attached by custom to the sheriff's farm; if not, there seems no justification for the refusal to admit Robert. There was nothing unusual in giving the post to a member of the household, or to a man drawn from that level

[1] *R.L.C.* 1204–1227 I, 453.
[2] *C.R.* 1242–1247 p. 463.
[3] Misc. Bks. Exch. T. of R. 202 f. 23.
[4] *Black Prince's Register* I, 82.
[5] *Black Prince's Register* IV, 475.
[6] *C.Ch.W.* I, 561. The original grant is also enrolled. *C.P.R.* 1313–1317 p. 366.

among the king's servants. One of Edward III's messengers, William Fox, was for some years porter and gaol-keeper in Newcastle castle, with full responsibility for the prisoners there; and no unreasonable guarantee appears to have been demanded from him.[1]

A messenger travelling with prisoners did not receive any extra allowance for his vigilance, but he was repaid for necessary expenses. On the other hand, men sent out to search for malefactors were paid at the usual daily rate for indefinite periods and allowed to hire assistants. Two men whose rank in the household is uncertain, though they may have been couriers, were sent off in 1236 with five footmen to look for malefactors wandering in the county of Norfolk and to arrest them; and were allowed 2d. a day for each man employed for fifty-two days.[2] The entry neglects to state how many vagabonds they succeeded in capturing during this period.[3]

6. Miscellaneous Duties

Messengers and other members of the king's household might now and then find themselves asked to attend to something that was not, strictly, within their duties. The most usual was the task of supervising other people's work, seeing that it was competently done, and notifying the wardrobe or exchequer of the cost. Messengers' names were entered on several occasions against accounts which had been paid on their authority. Henry the king's messenger was one of the two men put in charge of workmen bringing timber from Stafford to Westminster in 1221–2, and the bill was paid by the sheriff of Kent 'by the king's writ and by sight of Henry the messenger.'[4] A winepress at Kenilworth was repaired in 1236 at a cost of 47s. 8d. 'according to the sight and testimony of John Bayes and Gregory, couriers'.[5] Roger Windsor, Edward I's messenger, was made viewer of the works at Windsor castle, with 2d. a day for his maintenance.[6] In each case, the messenger's word was accepted by the authorities as reliable, without further investigation.

This confidence is illustrated again in the mission of Robert of Chester, a wardrobe courier sent to Gascony in 1315 with a coffer full of letters. Robert set off in the train of a special envoy and a packhorse from the king's stable was lent to him to carry the heavy box. The cortege left London on 4 August, and from then till 4 October, through sixty-one days, Robert bought hay and oats for his horse and

[1] *Ibid.* 1350–1354 p. 295.
[2] P.R. 81.
[3] The use of messengers to make arrests continued until 1772. Examples of messengers' warrants to arrest are cited (e.g. Thompson *The Secretaries of State 1681–1782* pp. 175–6) and the regulations governing their expenses with prisoners (Wheeler Holohan *op. cit.* pp. 12–13). See also *N.E.D.* s.v. messenger.
[4] P.R. 66.   [5] P.R. 80.
[6] *C.P.R.* 1292–1301 p. 407.

paid for shoeing and farriery. By that time, the letters had been distributed, and the horse was sold in Bordeaux for 20s. 'according to the sight of Robinet', who testified to the sale before the wardrobe officials, and whose word was accepted by them in making up their accounts with the envoy.[1] A task more in character was given to Robert of Manfield who hired and paid additional messengers for Edward II without any other authority than the king's personal command.[2] Nor was it unusual for a messenger to be sent to buy articles for the king's use. Arnold Bon was sent for fruit for the king in 1286, and Peter of Auckland, a wardrobe courier, was sent back to York while the court was in Scotland to procure two bridles for the king's own use.[3] A memorandum from Thomas Wynebaud, the treasurer's messenger, shows that he had been sent to Stamford fair to buy palfreys for the king, for which journey and several others, he complained, his expenses remained unpaid.[4] In the Black Prince's household, the trusted messenger Dagonet was put in sole charge of 200 quarters of wheat, attached by the prince's officers from no less a personage than the archbishop of Canterbury. Dagonet was to hire threshers, buy barrels for the grain, and deal with the business till Christmas, three whole months away. Clearly he was expected to be able to handle men as well as correspondence.[5]

Wardrobe couriers were often asked to take charge of carts or goods belonging to the department, sometimes as an escort for them on the road, sometimes as a guard while they remained stationary, left behind when the court moved on. Adam Attenasshe acted in both capacities during 1286. In January he was told to hire a cart and fetch the wardrobe's stores of grain from Oxford to Colecoumbe, a two-days journey, for which he was allowed 22d. a day for cart-hire in addition to his own expenses of 2d. a day. From Colecoumbe, he was sent on with one hired pack-horse to carry part of the grain to Childebergh—a much cheaper method of conveyance, for the wardrobe had only to pay 2d. a day for the hire of the horse. Next Adam was helping to remove the wardrobe from Colecoumbe to Wimborne, escorting a cart loaded with corn. The hire of this waggon cost the same as the first, but the removal took six days. No long halt was made at Wimborne, and Adam was sent straight on to Dunton[6], the next stop, a two-days' journey ahead, with another cart full of wardrobe harness so heavy that additional horses had to be hired and 5d. added to Adam's expense sheet 'for the two

---

[1]E.A. 309/22.
[2]Cotton MS. Nero C VIII f. 104 v.
[3]Chanc. Misc. 4/3 f. 8; E.A. 356/8 m. 3 (1298–9).
[4]E.A. 371/8 No. 35A (temp. Edward I).
[5]*Black Prince's Register* I, 18. During the spring of 1307, messengers in the king's service were kept busy fetching necessaries for the prince's tournament, and lampreys against the arrival of the cardinal, though the cost was met by the prince's steward, not by the king's officials. Add. MS. 22923 ff. 2 v, 7 v, 8, 8 v, 15.
[6]Probably Downton in Wilts. Colecoumbe and Childebergh defy identification.

horses helping on the road'. Perhaps the clumsy waggon got itself bogged in the winter mud. Finally his two carts, one with grain and one with harness, took the road from Hungerford to Langley, with Adam still escorting them for five days more before they reached the royal manor where the court intended to remain for a while. Another messenger, Stephen of Westbury, had been escorting two other carts carrying harness and wine, which arrived at Langley several days before the king, Stephen being paid an extra 2*s*. 6*d*. for guarding their contents until the wardrobe officers could take charge of them. Adam was to spend another eight days later in the same year keeping an eye on some wardrobe carts which the department found it convenient to leave behind during a removal.[1]

When the court travelled abroad, it was more than ever important to place a guard over its coffers and waggons. Thomas Skiret, a king's messenger, was put in charge of wardrobe coffers while Edward I was in Gascony, and was responsible for their safe carriage to Bordeaux.[2] If he had difficulty in collecting his expenses for this journey, it was not for any dishonest practices of his; during the winter of 1294–5 while the court was in Wales, Thomas was entrusted with the wardrobe's chests and valuables inside Conway Castle, where Edward was blockaded. Conway was not relieved until the main English army came up in January, and meanwhile the messenger earned 15*s*. in wages and expenses for keeping guard over the coffers, the amount being paid to him in two imprests, 10*s*. by the wardrobe officers, 5*s*. by Melton himself.[3] All was not easy inside the castle during that winter blockade. No doubt the atmosphere grew strained as the days went by, the discomforts of the siege were felt, and rumours spread among the troops; special vigilance was needed. Yet the duty was one which might be required of any messenger in peace or war.

Plenty of examples could be cited of messengers being sent for important documents, either in connexion with the wardrobe's account at the exchequer, or with the working of the household and the administration. Two examples must suffice, the 'roll under the privy seal containing the names of those going with the lady queen to parts beyond the seas', which Edward II sent for in 1325, and the memoranda relating to the complete account of the wardrobe which Fulk of Hertwell took to the cofferer at York in 1354.[4] The exchequer had been out of court so long, that when a removal had to be made, as it was to York in 1333, it caused a much greater upheaval than any number of wardrobe journeys. Messengers were sent out to give notice of the change and to requisition carts from the sheriffs; and the same

[1]Chanc. Misc. 4/3 ff. 4, 4 v, 19.
[2]*Ibid*. f. 22 v.
[3]Misc. Bks. Exch. T. of R. 202 f. 20 v.
[4]E.A. 381/4 m. 16; 387/9.

procedure was repeated when the department came back to London in
1338.¹ But though the exchequer itself moved seldom, its records were
carried from Westminster to the court, wherever that might be, for the
convenience of the king and his officials, and sent back again by
messenger or courier. Thus Roger Mynot, a courier, took exchequer
rolls back to the exchequer of receipt in 1364, and paid 5*d*. to the
labourer who was hired to carry the rolls.²

Taking charge of animals, particularly dogs, was a duty somewhat
outside a messenger's usual sphere, yet one which he might be asked
to undertake. John of Bristol when a courier was sent into Hampshire
to inquire from the bailiffs of the bishop of Winchester about two deer-
hounds lost in the forest there.³ Another messenger was sent for some
dogs which had belonged to Robert Fitz Payne and were now in the
charge of his executor. Edward II, whose interest in country life has
often been noticed, wanted to see them; and having satisfied his
curiosity, returned them by the same means.⁴ Robert of Chester was
sent out hastily by night in 1337 to the sheriff of Southampton to look
for a lost greyhound belonging to the king's chamber; William Fox
was paid for fetching the king's dog, and William Walshman sent
twice with the king's hounds to Bamburgh in August 1335.⁵ Horses,
too, might have to be fetched. Geoffrey le Waleys, a messenger of
Edward I, was sent to Dover to wait for the arrival of the king's
horses, and Gilbert the queen's messenger was dispatched by Philippa
with a grey warhorse, her gift to the king.⁶ A messenger was not
exactly a jack-of-all-trades, for all these miscellaneous commissions
took up little of his working life in comparison with the routine carrying of letters; but at the same time he had to be prepared for a variety
of other tasks.

One thing, however, which might have come within his province,
he did not do; the messenger never acted as harbinger for the wardrobe even when he escorted its carts. The harbinger was a specially
appointed officer, whose unenviable duty it was to find billets according to fixed rules of precedence for all members of the household entitled to lodging. Though John had a messenger called Robert le
Herberjur, the man did not act as harbinger during the period covered
by surviving accounts, and the title may have been a nickname, given
either because he always arrived first or because he never did. Once at
a time of crisis, a messenger did go ahead to find accommodation, not
for the household but for special envoys. Sampson the king's messenger
was sent in December 1347 to Guildford to find lodgings for the envoys of the king of Spain.⁷ On the other hand, when William Ashby,

¹I.R. 301 mm. 9 and 21.   ³E.A. 308/8.
²I.R. 421 m. 20.   ⁴E.A. 376/7 f. 83 v.
⁵E.A. 385/16 m. 2; 387/9 m. 6; Cotton MS. Nero C VIII f. 292 v.
⁶E.A. 308/8; Cotton MS. Nero C. VIII f. 273 v.
⁷I.R. 340 m. 23.

messenger of Thomas of Brotherton, was sent to the king's steward in London to see about providing accommodation at the New Temple for the king's sons Thomas and Edmund, it is clear that the messenger was only the bearer of instructions, not billeting officer.[1]

7. *The Messenger on the Road*

On the morning of the fourth of October 1307, several messengers were standing by at Westminster to take out dispatches as soon as the exchequer clerks had done them, and there was unusual bustle in that slow-moving department. At the sixth hour, about midday, John Cook was called up by the usher—one writ to go immediately to the sheriff of Northumberland commanding him to take the oaths of the assessors and collectors of the twenty-fifth in that county. There were a batch of less urgent letters and writs, too, waiting dispatch to the north, so these were slipped into his bag as well. Some had been in the marshal's hands for nearly a month, held back till a messenger should be sent in that direction. Sheriffs[2] sometimes complained that their letters arrived too late to be obeyed, or else never arrived at all, having been mislaid at the exchequer by the marshal or the usher. Thus in 1315 Robert Rideware's case could not be proceeded with because the writ for his appearance did not reach the sheriff in time.[3] Dated 22 January at Westminster, it was not delivered in Kent till 5 February. The ordinance of 1323 devoted a paragraph to the matter of delayed letters and the necessity of getting a receipt from the sheriff for all that reached him safely.[4] But if the marshal had done his duty properly in October 1307, he would have made a list of all sealed writs received for dispatch, with their dates, addresses, and the number for each county; and the usher too would have noted how many he gave John Cook and the other messengers. If there were anything unusual about the commission, an entry might be made in the memoranda roll itself 'Memorandum that this day 3 letters patent were delivered to Robert le Hunte to carry under peril etc.' the threat was so familiar to the clerk that he went no further.[5] There ought to have been a further check on the dispatch when the writ was returned by the sheriff with

[1] E.A. 368/12 f. 4.

[2] Willard *Parliamentary Taxes on Personal Property 1290–1324* p. 49 and 'The dating and delivery of letters patents and writs in the fourteenth century' in *Bulletin of the Institute of Historical Research* X, 5, 9.

[3] K.R. writs bundle 9.

[4] *Red Books of the Exchequer* ed. Hall, III 888–9 'Face le Mareshal del Exchequer desore distinctement remembrer devers lui tutz les briefs qi lui serront liveres a entrer pur le Roi et a liverer as husshers de envoier avant, et face remembrer quantz des briefs il les livere et queu jour il les livere et combien a chescun viscounte ou autre et face remembrer qe les husshers lui facent avoir bille de chescun viscounte qi testmoigne le receyte des briefs qil avera receu pur le Roi, et quant, et ou, et par qui'.

[5] L.T.R.M.R. 108 m. 19; and see also mm. 10d, 11d, 12d, 17, 17d, 18, 18d, 19, 19d.

the messenger's name endorsed on it, but sheriffs were not always careful to do this.[1] Meanwhile, John Cook was receiving his expenses from the usher. There was no difficulty about the amount, because the exchequer still clung to the old system of *dieta* or day's journey from Westminster; and according to this scale, Northumberland was eight days from London.[2] John Cook knew all about it, for he had always been attached to the exchequer and worked for the officers of that department. The rate, as set down in the *Red Book*, was 3*d.* a day,[3] and nothing allowed for the return journey because the sheriff paid the messenger for that. So, with his bag of letters, his money, and his instructions, John Cook went off on his errand.

Chancery too had a few messengers permanently on its staff, who could take messages for the officials and deal with urgent business. Occasionally, when some important commission was anticipated and the court was away from the capital, a messenger from the wardrobe would be sent to the chancery to wait for the letter to be completed and sealed. Then an entry appeared on the patent roll to this effect, 'Be it known that these two pairs of letters were made according to the form which Master Gilbert de Millers sent to court and were sent to Gascony by Henry de Chelmerford the king's messenger on Sunday next after St. Bartholemew, the king being then at Newcastle upon Tyne.'[4] Even Sunday was no day of rest for the messenger when urgent business was to be done, and in those cases, the hour of dispatch was often noted 'at the hour of prime', 'at terce', 'at matins', 'at noon', 'in the evening', 'late'.[5] An even more explicit note appeared in the *Black Prince's Register*. 'Be it remembered that these letters were delivered to Sir Peter de Lacy on the eve of Whitsun, after eating, in the chamber of Sir Peter de Gildesburgh, to have them quickly dispatched.'[6]

As a rule, however, chancery had nothing to do with dispatch, which was the business of the wardrobe; and so many letters went out from these two departments under the great and privy seals that much less delay occurred here than in the exchequer between the sealing of a letter and its delivery to a messenger. As in the exchequer, an entry was made by one of the wardrobe clerks on a roll of messengers' expenses which he kept for the purpose,[7] so that every penny spent on letters might be accounted for at the exchequer audit and the king's ministers know what dispatches had gone out, and when and to whom, and by what messenger. The wardrobe clerk who did this also gave the

[1]Fowler *Rolls for the Office of the Sheriff of Beds. and Bucks. 1332–4.* p. 12.
[2]*Red Book* III 835–9.
[3]*Ibid.* p. 837.
[4]*Pat.R.* 1247–1258 p. 424.
[5]e.g. I.R. 170 mm. 8, 172, 178; 446 m. 7; Add. MS. 7965 f. 109 v.
[6]*Black Prince's Register* I, 80.
[7]e.g. E.A. 308/1 and 2 (1253–4, 1264–5); 309/11 (1360–1).

messenger his instructions and journey money, for the wardrobe (at least from 1234 to 1342), controlled, paid, and sent out the king's messengers.

Up to 1307 or thereabouts, the wardrobe calculated the cost of journeys on the same scale of days as the exchequer. To mounted messengers, it paid 3d. a day, though its couriers received less.[1] The messenger John of Wallingford, sent to the Sheriff of Northumberland just after Easter 1265, was allowed 2s. or 3d. a day for eight days; and his companion Colin of Woodstock, starting at the same time for Westmorland and Cumberland, received 2s. 6d. for his ten days' journey.[2] The same word, *dietae*, was used. But as the number of letters increased, a county basis became less convenient for calculating expenses. Under Henry III, messengers often went out with one commission, a single day's journey away from court. Under Edward I and still more under his successors, these petty tasks disappeared. The average messenger starting from court in 1307, took a bag full of correspondence and seldom less than 5s. for his expenses. The household ordinance of 1318 laid so much stress on the payment of messengers at 3d. a day for a limited period,[3] that it looks as though the 3d. rate was being extended and the exchequer *dietae* neglected. By 1337–8, messengers generally received a lump sum for their journeys, 1s. 8d., 3s. 4d., 6s. 8d., or 13s. 4d.; and presumably accounted with the department for anything they spent beyond this, just as envoys going abroad did.[4] Further, the items in the 1337–8 account which were not fractions of a mark, were made up of amounts from 2s. to 12s. progressing without exception by 6d. and not, as earlier, by 3d. Either the the 3d. rate had been abandoned, or messengers were being paid for inward as well as outward journeys. The former seems more probable, especially since wages in court also rose to 6d. under Edward III and even messengers' pensions were increased to 4½d. For the Black Prince's household, the daily travelling allowance was definitely 6d., and at this rate Roger Pope accounted with the prince's treasurer in 1340 and 1362.[5] John Stygan, the chamber messenger, also received 6d. a day for his expenses out of court.[6]

The same change can be seen in the calculation of messengers' expenses abroad, though for these journeys the alteration came more

[1]Under Henry III, the same rate seems to have been paid to both but Edward I seldom paid more than 2d. to couriers after 1280 and never after 1291. The 2d rate was in force for unmounted messengers until the last years of Edward III.

[2]E.A. 308/2.

[3]Tout *Place of Edward II* p. 272 'Quant ils serrount enuoiez en messagez, serrount lour iournez limitez en certain'.

[4]E.A. 388/5.
The exchequer ordinance does allow for this in some cases (*Red Book* III, 926–7).

[5]E.A. 389/6 mm. 1, 3; *Black Prince's Register* IV 470.

[6]E.A. 396/2.

rapidly. At first the increase might take the form of a bonus. When William of Ledbury and Geoffrey le Waleys were sent abroad by Edward I, they spent forty days 'in the passage of the sea, going and returning, receiving by the day 3*d.*' and after their return they received a further 4*s.* 'for the great haste which they made.'[1] Many overseas journeys recorded were the regular ones to Bordeaux and Calais or to Ireland; and for these it soon became customary to hand the messenger a fixed sum, and omit any calculation of days to be spent. Thus 10*s.* became the recognized amount for a messenger taking letters to Dublin, unless sent beyond the city.[2] In other cases, the messenger was treated like an envoy, and given a lump sum for which he accounted in detail on his return. The actual expenses of the journey usually came to rather more than the allowance, though only two of the detailed accounts submitted by messengers survive. The first is that of William Fox who in 1335 was sent to Flanders in charge of three men, with letters patent authorizing him to make inquiries into 'robberies and malefactions'. Fox drew £20 from the exchequer of receipt for the journey and accounted on his return after forty-seven days for £26 8*s.* 9*d.* actually spent.[3] The second account is that of Jack Faukes, whose costs were unexpectedly increased by having to pay for a French serjeant escort.[4] In his case, the £10 given to him when he set out covered about two-thirds of his actual expenses which were £13 14*s.* 10*d.* This was the usual proportion of an envoy's travelling expenses which he received in advance, and the remainder had to be reclaimed afterwards. Faukes, too, sent in his claim for the 74*s.* 10*d.* due to him, and received it in instalments during the next twelve months.[5]

Up to 1342, the messenger drew his travelling expenses for all home and many foreign journeys from the wardrobe; and in urgent cases might even be paid by one of the higher officials, who claimed the amount spent as due to himself.[6] After 1342, the exchequer took over the task of finding ready money for messengers and so Jack Faukes, setting off for Avignon in 1343, went to the exchequer of receipt for his £10. His detailed account shows him collecting the money (having already received his instructions and letters), travelling by boat from Westminster to the city and there buying two pairs of spurs and two pairs of boots for himself and his companion. He then completed his preparations for an arduous journey with a meal in London before he hired the horses to carry them both to Rochester on the first stage out.

[1] E.A. 308/12.
[2] e.g. I.R. 232 m. 10; 307 m 2.
[3] E.A. 311/14.
[4] E.A. 312/4. See Larson 'The Payment of Fourteenth century English Envoys' *E.H.R.* LIV 403–414 (1939).
[5] I.R. 331 mm. 9, 22; 335 m. 34; 336 m. 4.
[6] e.g. Add. MS. 8835 ff. 108 v–109.

Although his account shows Faukes overspending his allowance by
74s. 10d., he was able to pay his own expenses on the return journey.
Some messengers managed to avoid payment.[1] But if a messenger
abroad were in urgent need of money, it might be possible for him to
get a loan through the Frescobaldi, the king's bankers. William Lue,
taking letters to the bishop of Hereford in Paris during 1318–19 and
John Russel and Robert of Chester on their way to Avignon in 1319,
were assisted by the bankers' agents, and many similar payments were
made to messengers abroad between 1334 and 1336,[2] so that there was
always a possibility of receiving further supplies of money abroad
should need arise.

Once away from court, the messenger who was sent out on a routine
journey did not hurry himself. He had to think of his horse, which was
his own and not the king's, and must carry him the whole way and
back again without a rest. Thus the average rate of progress was the
same for a messenger as for a courier, about three miles an hour and
not more than twenty to twenty-five miles a day. Robert Rideware,
returning from Dover to the king in Scotland in 1303 took twenty-one
days over the journey, or precisely the same time that a modern walker
takes to cover the distance between London and Edinburgh.[3] London
to York was a six days' journey for Alan Poydras in 1265,[4] and a
messenger sent in haste from York to Hull still took two days to cover
the distance.[5]

If the message were really urgent, the messenger could not rely on
his single beast but hired extra horses where he could or rode post.
Both methods were possible on some roads. Edward I is believed to
have set up posting stations on the road between London and Scotland,
and also between London and the Welsh Marches; and messengers
had a prior claim to post horses if they needed them. On the Dover
and York roads there were certainly posting establishments, and when
Faukes in 1343 required mounts for the London–Dover part of his
journey, he found no difficulty in getting them, either going or returning. Difficulties must have arisen at times, for in 1372 strict injunctions
were sent to the bailiffs of Canterbury and Rochester to provide hackneys for their respective parts of the route between London and the
coast, and to hire these for reasonable payment to 'any of the king's

[1]Messengers in the sixteenth century were notorious for getting post horses
and provisions without payment. The corporation of Bridgnorth in 1597 passed a
loyal resolution to accept responsibility for such debts themselves. The rate was to
be 2d a mile. (Bridgnorth Corporation MSS., Leet book III f. 30).

[2]I.R. 187; E.A. 387/9 mm. 3, 11.

[3]Add MS. 35292 f. 45 v. See also Fowler *Rolls from the Office of the Sheriff of
Beds. and Bucks.*, p. 14 for a discussion of the average messenger's rate of progress, and Landon, L. in app. to *Itinerary of Richard I* (P.R.S. New Series 13,
p. 186) for express rates abroad.

[4]E.A. 308/2.

[5]I.R. 231 m. 3.

messengers of whose coming to the king with letters or otherwise with reports from over sea they shall have knowledge hereafter . . . so that the king's business be not hindered by their default.'[1] Much later than this, a master of posts complained to Thomas Cromwell that the only certain post horses in England were those on the Dover–Gravesend road. Elsewhere, he complained, the king's premptory command only produced tired beasts, taken from the plough or the cart by the parish constable.[2]

On roads where no regular post horses were available, the king might give special instructions for horses to be ready to meet an expected messenger. Edward I wrote to the justice of Chester on behalf of William Clerk, a wardrobe courier 'whom the king is sending to Ireland for certain affairs that he has much at heart', and demanded 'speedy and safe passage to those parts' to be provided for him 'at the courier's own cost.'[3] Such instructions often cost the messenger a good deal, and the expenses of hiring horses no doubt prevented the development of an efficient posting system for the king's service. A comparatively short journey from London to Ipswich cost John Lewer 4s. 'for his expenses and for the hire of one horse on that same journey.'[4] Joseph of Faversham spent as much as 45s. on a journey when he had to hire horses; and the 6s. 8d. spent by Robert of London on mounts, in addition to his own expenses of 3s. 4d., had to be specially warranted by the chamberlain before his account could be passed in 1362.[5]

For the same reason, the medieval messenger did not, like his eighteenth century successor, pride himself on riding night and day. With one horse, night travel was out of the question, and the courier was unlikely to go by night, except when sent with an urgent message to the king's huntsmen, for instance.[6] If the accounts speak of a messenger going out at night, it is almost certain that he is riding post or hiring extra horses as he goes. Thus John Piacle was sent out 'on the 10th day of April late' in 1297 with letters to the keeper of the Tower of London 'with the greatest possible haste' and was allowed to claim 'for his expenses and for the hire of hackneys both by nights and days' the sum of 10s. 7d.[7] Two night journeys were made for Edward II in the year 1323–4,[8] and under his son such payments became more frequent, though never common. Walter of Colchester took some urgent letters by night in October 1337,[9] and a messenger going to the king

[1]*C.C.R.* 1369–1374 p. 389.
[2]Letter to Brian Tuke, 1533, cited by Walker *Haste, Post Haste!* p. 44.
[3]*C.C.R.* 1302–1307 p. 62.
[4]I.R. 355 m. 40.
[5]Misc. Bks. Exch. T. of R. 203 f. 116 v; I.R. 410 m. 38.
[6]E.A. 308/8.
[7]Add. MS. 7965 f. 109 v.
[8]E.A. 379/18 f. 3 v.
[9]E.A. 388/5.

with news from Scotland in 1337 was paid extra for his haste.[1] Even a courier might be mounted for a very urgent commission.[2]

The expense of the Channel crossing varied greatly, for the messenger might wait for the regular service or hire a boat specially. A passage in one of the ships plying regularly from Dover to Whitsand cost 2s. for a horseman and 6d. for a man on foot according to an Act of 1330, though legislation was found necessary because the keepers of the passage and the boatmen had been demanding more.[3] Shipmasters' bills are found among the wardrobe and exchequer accounts, and from these, and the messengers' own returns, it appears that to hire a special boat cost from 9s. to £1. Edward I's messenger Thomas Wynebaud, returning from Gascony, expected repayment of this part of his expenses 'E lavaunt dit Thomas demaunde ix s. pur un batel alowe de Whitsaund a Doure pur ceo q'il ne troua point de passage.'[4] If the returning messenger were unable to pay for his crossing, the shipmaster might be willing to wait till his bill could be honoured by the exchequer or wardrobe. From this we hear of Brecun of Dover, who gave a passage to several messengers in 1274–5; William Kentan, who was hired on different occasions by Robert Little and William of Ledbury; and William Goldewombe, who conveyed the courier James of Newbury to France during 1298–9.[5] The cost of crossing was naturally increased if the messenger took his horse over with him. William Fox in 1335 had to pay 4s. 4d. each for the four horses taken by his party, and had the additional expense of 7d. pontage for them at each end of the crossing, with 6d. for getting his baggage into the ship and out again, and 2d. each for himself and his three companions to be rowed to the ship at Dover and from the ship at Whitsand.[6]

Customs and port dues were another charge for which the messenger had to be prepared. At Dover 1d. a head port dues and 2d. custom were demanded.[7] Any member of the household who was also a freeman of London, Canterbury, Norwich or Rochester, could avoid the second payment by virtue of an ancient privilege of these towns. Jack Faukes, who was a Londoner, was able to escape at Dover with payment of 1d. only, though his companion was less fortunate.[8] Abroad, similar charges were made for landing, and no privilege mitigated these.

On his return, the messenger sent in his account for the expenses of the journey to the department which had issued his travelling expenses. The first draft of this, made presumably to his dictation (for there does not seem anything to imply that messengers were able to write down their own claims) was in French. From this the clerks drew up a neat

[1] E.A. 388/6.
[2] E.A. 308/8; I.R. 76.
[3] *Statutes of the Realm* I, 263 (4 Edw. III c. 8).
[4] E.A. 371/8 No. 35A and B.
[5] I.R. 28; E.A. 356/1 m 2d.
[6] E.A. 311/14.
[7] *Ibid.* and 312/4.
[8] E.A. 312/4.

statement in Latin fit to produce in the exchequer at the next audit. The two seem to have been identical in substance, to judge from the one instance in which both French and Latin versions survive,[1] but the former is more immediate, the latter more stereotyped in expression. Two other first versions for messengers' expenses have been pre-served[2] among hundreds of claims for the much heavier travelling costs of envoys.

On the state of the roads, little fresh can be said. When even the justiciar of Ireland could be plundered by malefactors on the seas, and a sheriff's receiver be presented by a jury for maintaining a gang of highwaymen at Bridgnorth, when a bishop was afraid to travel on account of disturbances, the king's messenger might well be prepared for attack.[3] Yet when the records mentioned an assault made on a messenger, it was always in time of war, foreign or civil. A courier was mutilated by the rebel Kenilworth garrison in 1266, as an act of defiance to the king in the person of his representative, and Rishanger was amazed that the insult was not avenged more drastic-ally.[4] Alan the king's courier was wounded by the Scots in February 1304.[5] Abroad, several messengers were stopped and imprisoned on account of their dispatches; and though imprisonment was more often the lot of the envoy than the humble messenger, Edward II in 1311 was forced to complain that the king of Norway had 'committed to hard prison the bearer of his former letter, one Geoffrey le Taverner of Grimsby.'[6] Later John Taverner, a messenger 'whom the lord king sent to parts of France for certain business touching the lord king him-self, was captured at Whitsand and there imprisoned' in July 1337, and received 60s. compensation for his ill-treatment. This first experience did not daunt him, but the same man was later maimed in the king's service and forced to retire from his post on account of injuries.[7]

When such incidents occurred, English kings were quick to retali-ate, and orders were reiterated for watch to be kept on the ports, all foreign envoys and messengers stopped and searched, and no entry or exit permitted without licence. The fourteenth century saw the strictest security measures taken at the ports, though as early as 1213 King John had rewarded one of his knights 'who caused the messengers of

[1]E.A. 371/8 No. 35A and B.
[2]E.A. 311/14 and 312/4.
[3]*C.P.R.* 1258–1266 p. 319; *Rot. Hund.* II 88; Eyton *Antiquities of Shropshire* I, 287; *C.C.R.* 1302–1307 p. 81.
[4]Rishanger p. 43 'Et mirum quod Rex taliter indulsit eis, cum ipsi patriam depraedati fuissent . . . et parum ante cursorem Regis apprehendissent et sibi manum amputassent, ac Domino Regi ex parte exhaerditorum ridiculose mississent' (*Chronica et Annales* ed. Riley, Rolls Series 1865).
[5]Add. MS. 8835 f. 104 v.
[6]*C.C.R.* 1307–1313 p. 349.
[7]I.R. 295 m. 30; *C.P.R.* 1348–1350 p. 146.

the king of France to be captured with letters.'[1] At such times, all messengers sought for safe conducts. The bishop of Winchester's messengers had safe conducts during his embassy in France, about the same time that Faukes was having to go so much out of his way to get a passport from the chancellor of France and have it ratified by the king of France personally.[2] Scottish messengers in England were sometimes granted similar protections.[3] But security regulations were not permanent. More often than not, a messenger could enter England or France without hindrance. Though individuals might be assaulted now and then, only one man is known to have lost his life while carrying letters. This was William Crayling 'who was lately sent as a messenger from the king and was taken in the said message by persons of Lesclus in Flanders and killed on account of the message aforesaid.'[4] During nearly two centuries of travel, this makes a very small percentage indeed of all the journeys, at home and abroad, undertaken by the king's messengers and couriers. Perhaps the medieval messenger had less cause to fear for his life and limbs on the highway than the modern traveller.

A different sort of protection was sometimes granted to members of the household who went abroad with the king or on his business. These 'letters of protection' safeguarded thier private interests, and no suit could then be won against them by default. A list of members of the household protected during the king's stay abroad in 1322 included William the Messenger, but not all the household and no other messenger received such guarantees of immunity.[5] Individuals too might have simple protection when abroad on the king's business. Robert of Newington did twice, and Donald of Athol was protected while in Ireland in 1324 and 1328.[6] This implied a long absence or such special business as that entrusted in January 1359 to Roger Mynot, who was granted protection valid for the whole of the year. John of Arches was given protection with clause *volumus* in 1357, and had power to nominate attornies to act on his behalf.[7] No special privileges were allowed either to the messenger working at home or to the ordinary members of the household in virtue of their position there.

The modern traveller, armed with maps and guidebooks, finds it hard to imagine journeys without them, on roads unmarked by signposts or milestones. Constant travelling, with the court or alone, no doubt familiarized the messenger with the lie of the land and the routes

[1] Cole's *Records* p. 261.
[2] E.A. 309/27; 312/4.
[3] e.g. *Rotuli Scotiae* I, 58; II, 174.
[4] *Issues of the Exchequer* ed. Devon p. 225.
[5] *C.P.R.* 1321–1324 p. 42; the household of Edmund, the king's brother, was similarly protected in 1286. *Ibid.* 1281–1292 p. 239.
[6] *Ibid.* 1313–1317, pp. 374, 426; 1321–1324 p. 410; 1327–1330 p. 309.
[7] *C.P.R.* 1354–1358 pp. 622, 604; 1358–1361 p. 131.

between the principal towns, castles and manors. In Scotland and overseas, guides were necessary. While Edward I was in Scotland in 1300–1, his two messengers Edmund Moses and John Somer, coming from Selkirk to Peebles, were obliged to hire a guide named John Heddon, to whom they paid 2s. on their safe arrival. Later in the same year a courier going out with letters took a Scots guide again.[1] John Piacle had a guide when he took the king's letters to the count of Savoy and the duke of Brabant[2] and in 1324 the messenger John of Canford made use of a returning French courier who directed him 'for his more certain expedition' and perhaps watched his movements too.[3] Some information on the state of the roads and the best route between the principal cities was available to the medieval traveller in the form of *livres des postes*,[4] but the unlettered messenger was not likely to be able to avail himself of these. A pair of messengers travelling together, or a messenger and groom, gave each other a certain amount of protection from danger and at the same time pooled their information about the roads. This must have been excellent training for a young man, besides providing against the possibility that 'the messenger should lack courage.'[5] Very occasionally, important dispatches were sent out in duplicate. Thus the messenger Donald of Athol took out urgent letters in February 1318, and the courier Robert of Chester was sent with identical letters by another route in case of accidents.[6]

The greatest difficulty experienced by the messenger on the road might be to hand over his missive. People who anticipated something unpleasant would take pains not to receive the letter, or would abuse and ill-treat the bearer. Henry III sent a writ demanding the services of John Balliol in the campaign against Llewellyn, and since Balliol preferred not to obey this command, he arranged for the messengers to be attacked in Sherwood Forest and the writ stolen from them. The king was naturally furious at this insult.[7] Palatinate lords like the bishop of Durham might consider that the king's writ did not run within their franchises and that the king's messenger might be assaulted there with impunity—only to be shown by the seizure of the liberty that Edward I's power to protect his minister 'extended within liberties as well as without.'[8] Edward II also had cause for complaint. When

---

[1]E.A. 359/6 f. 21; Add. MS. 7966.
[2]Add. MS. 7965 ff. 113, 113 v.
[3]E.A. 379/19 f. 8 v.
[4]e.g. 'Matthew Paris' Itinerary' (printed in *Palgrave* II, 21). The distances between important towns were indicated on 'Gough's' map (now in the Bodleian) which was made c. 1350; but it was unusual for surveyors to show roads on their maps, even in the seventeenth century. (See Stenton F. M. 'The Road System of Medieval England' *Economic Hist. Rev.* VII, 1–21 (1936–7), and Tooley *Maps and Map-makers* (1950) pp. 9–18.
[5]E.A. 308/10.
[6]Society of Antiquaries' MS. 121 p. 102; see also Misc. Bks. E.T.R. 203 f. 111 v.
[7]*C.R.* 1261–1264 p. 381.
[8]Cam. H. *Liberties and Communities in Medieval England* p. 207.

letters of privy seal were sent to Thomas Wake, summoning him to consult with the king, 'Thomas, as the king learns, has received certain of the letters and has taken care not to receive others, hiding himself so that the bearers thereof cannot come to him to deliver them.'[1] Contempt went further in 1318, when the recipients of writs assaulted the messenger Robert of Newington, threw down his letters and trampled on them.[2] Contrary to the precedent set by Edward I, no redress was offered except through a civil action brought against the offenders by Robert personally. He secured a commission of oyer and terminer on his complaint, but the issue is not known. Perhaps Edward II's reluctance to provide a remedy in such cases explains the number of instances quoted by Salzman.[3] They stand out from the routine entries in the rolls, but in comparison with the total number of letters dispatched, such difficult commissions were really few and far between. All the examples given happened during times of political unrest.

The medieval messenger did not always bear a good name on the road for his behaviour. Langland complained that messengers were allowed to ride through standing crops if they wanted to take a short cut.[4] and farmers will sympathize with his indignation. A French mystery play of the same period introduced the character of the bragging courier, Auberon, who boasted that he carried the king's seal and letter, and hoped to impress the innkeeper and his guests and escape payment. 'Shame on all couriers, for they always run away' grumbles the innkeeper's boy when the messenger, who has drunk well, cannot pay his score and promises to settle the reckoning on the return journey.[5] Neither French nor English messengers had the right to demand free lodging, as could the papal couriers,[6] and no doubt there were many occasions when a messenger could not make his allowance cover his expenses. The accounts show only the messenger as he appeared to his superiors; they cannot give much information about the messenger with whom innkeepers and other travellers had to deal on the road. Yet for the credit of the king's household it may be pointed out that neither Langland nor any other writer found anything more serious to complain of than a liking for short cuts and a traveller's thirst.

[1]*C.C.R.* 1323–1327 p. 549.
[2]*C.P.R.* 1317–1321 p. 176.
[3]Salzman *Medieval Byways* (1913) pp. 155–7.
[4]Cited by Jusserand *English Wayfaring Life* p. 234.
[5]Cited by Michel and Fournier *La Grande Bohème* Vol. 1. Hostelleries et Cabarets (1851) p. 233.
[6]Renouard *op. cit., Revue Hist.* CLXXX, 5.

CHAPTER VI

RECRUITMENT AND PERSONNEL OF THE HOUSEHOLD

1. The Making of a Servant

THE life of a servant in the king's household is pictured, as far as it concerned his work, in the accounts of wardrobe and exchequer; and once admitted into the king's service, his falconers, huntsmen, minstrels, and messengers were in no doubt of their duties or privileges. The personal background of such men is more difficult to discover. How they were admitted to the household, the levels of society from which they were drawn, the principles upon which they were selected or recommended to the king's officers, are matters on which the accounts give only a few hints. This chapter is an attempt to collect and assess this scanty evidence for one household group, though the difficulties in the way of accurate social classification in the fourteenth century are no less great than those of the twelfth and thirteenth.[1]

Some recapitulation of material already used in other chapters is inevitable.

The information offered consists, first of some explicit references to the admission of messengers to household privileges, and rather more entries showing the future messenger in training. Secondly there are a few scraps of information about messengers' private affairs, either during or after their period of service; and thirdly, there is the evidence of social status offered by their surnames. This is dangerous ground, but it cannot be disregarded. Even in the thirteenth century, it was customary for the king's servants to be identified by a second descriptive name, and there are few entries which mention a christian name alone, though in the *liberate* rolls one of Henry III's messengers was qualified only as Reynold Sanzsurnum. By the fourteenth century, many surnames were already conventional; and in discussing this type of evidence, one must not assume that every man called London was born and bred in the shadow of St. Pauls, or that Hunt, Page, and Lewer were domestic servants (in the modern sense) before they were messengers, though this may sometimes have been the case. The names indicate nothing more than a connexion with a place or with an occupation; and this connexion may be one generation old at least. The surnames of John Somer of Cheriton, Robert Rideware of Newington,

---

[1]A. L. Poole *Obligations of Society in the Twelfth and Thirteenth Centuries* pp. 1–11.

and John Lyrish of Windsor were obviously formalized and required further qualification. But though the surname may tell little about the man, it tells much about his family; and evidence from the names helps to fill in the picture.[1]

2 Method of Appointment

No formal record of appointment to any office was kept by the king's clerks, and not till the late fourteenth century was any written warrant issued to a messenger on his entering the service.[2] However, there is no doubt that men were admitted to the privileges of the post with some ceremony. Four references to the creation of new messengers happen to have been made in wardrobe accounts, one in an issue roll, and one in a chamber account; and there are many references to the swearing-in of newly appointed servants in other household and administrative departments.

In the new year of 1297, Robert Little and William of Alkham entered the king's service as messengers, and their appointment had to be mentioned in the wardrobe account for that year because they were too late to receive the current issue of clothing and were allowed only the summer's issue of shoes, 'because they were admitted after Christmas', as the clerk explained it. And when the wardrobe officers wanted a pair of letter pouches for them, only one could be found which they bestowed on Alkham, and made a further note in the same account to explain to the exchequer auditors an expenditure of 2*s*. to buy a pouch for Robin Little the king's messenger 'at the time that he was first made a messenger, because there was not a single pouch found in the wardrobe at that time.'[3] These entries sufficiently prove that the appointment was from a definite period and to a well-established office. They are corroborated by the payment of a gratuity in 1325 to one 'de nouvell fait messager le Roi', and by the description given to Fulk Hertwell in 1336, 'lately made a messenger at Nottingham.'[4]

Another illuminating entry was set down for a different reason. In 1300, a messenger was being transferred from the service of the

---

[1]The use of surnames developed more rapidly in England than abroad. It has been suggested that local names and nicknames became hereditary some time before occupational names, and that the process was rather more rapid in the south than in the north. Clear evidence of inherited surnames among ordinary folk can be cited for c. 1276, and the permanency of surnames by the fourteenth century is proved by cases in the Assize Rolls, where the action was withdrawn because the plaintiff mistook the defendant's name (Fransson, G. *Middle English Surnames of Occupation* [1935] pp. 20, 23, 33, 39).
[2]Wheeler-Holohan was mistaken in thinking that the earliest reference to such a warrant was 1485 (*History of the King's Messengers* p. 5.)
[3]Add. MS. 7965 ff. 42, 108 v.
[4]Society of Antiquaries' MS. 122 p. 64 (a chamber account incorrectly described on the modern cover as a wardrobe book); and Nero C VIII f. 299 v.

constable of Edinburgh to the service of the king, and he was admitted by the king personally. 'Memorandum, that on the 15th day of March in the present 28th year, Geoffrey of Bardeney (who was in the Edinburgh garrison) was admitted by the king to remain in his household as a messenger and to receive as one of his other messengers; and on the same day a pouch with the same king's arms was issued to him.'[1] No doubt it was exceptional for the king in person to concern himself with a humble member of his household, though it is not the only indication of a personal connexion between master and servant. But the phraseology used seems to suggest that *per regem* is not mere formula here. In the same winter that Geoffrey became a messenger, a number of knights and serjeants were also admitted to the household, 'ad feodum et robas regis ad percipiendum sicut miles simplex de hospicio ipsius regis' or 'tamquam serviens ad arma', as the case might be.[2] In talking of these appointments, the clerks did not use the words 'per regem'. Without wanting to build too much on the omission, it is possible that Edward did himself authorize Geoffrey's transfer to his service. In a sense, all household appointments made by the king's officers were made by him. His independence of choice, whether exercised personally or through his officials, was insisted on all through the thirteenth and fourteenth centuries. The issue between Henry III and the reformers, and again between Edward II and the ordainers, was narrowed down to precisely this, the king's right to 'be master in his own household.' It was 'the acid test of royal status'. Public attention naturally concentrated on the higher appointments, but no interference could be tolerated anywhere by a king, like Edward I, whose household was intended to be the instrument of his will.[3] The king's command was translated by his clerks into writs and communicated to his provincial agents through his messengers, whose efficiency and loyalty were essential to the whole scheme of government. Messengers' credentials must have been scrutinized with some care before they were appointed. It is natural to suppose that this duty fell in 1300 to the keeper of the wardrobe or his subordinate; at a later date, it seems to have been part of the chamberlain's responsibility.[4]

Successful candidates for household posts were admitted by the officers of the appropriate branch. Messengers were 'made' by the keeper or treasurer of the wardrobe, as long as that department employed and controlled them. Later, when the wardrobe's authority had been undermined, the king may have used an entirely different type of representative for this purpose. Several attempts were made during the fifteenth century to systematize the household. On the one hand, successive ordinances regulated duties and privileges. On the other,

[1]*L.Q.G.* p. 283. [2]*Ibid.* pp. 188, 213
[3]Powicke *King Henry III and the Lord Edward* (1948) p. 694.
[4]*Collection of Ordinances* p. 31.

writers on chivalry tried to bring heralds, pursuivants, messengers and even couriers into a single system. One of these theorizers was Nicholas Upton, whose work, *De Studio Militari*, was written in the early fifteenth century.[1] It is difficult to know how much of this book is based on first-hand experience of court and administration. Upton was first canon and later precentor of Salisbury and from 1442–57 Master of St. Nicholas Hospital. He was one of the chapter's proctors at Rome to handle the business of St. Osmund's canonization; and in his ecclesiastical position, especially when his work took him abroad, he must have seen a good many king's messengers.[2] On the other hand, he was a jurist, and therefore trained to seek for system among apparent incoherence. His description must therefore be used with caution.

Upton pictured a hierarchy of chivalry, in which heralds, the king's most important messengers, were followed by pursuivants, and they in turn by riding messengers and couriers, each rank being selected from the grade below and promoted to the new office with appropriate ceremonial. He said nothing about the selection of couriers, but stated that riding messengers 'who may be knights, on account of the perils of their office' were created from couriers and admitted to their new office by one of the heralds' whose duty it is to make the lesser messengers'. A messenger who had completed three years' service might be eligible for promotion to the rank of pursuivant. There is no other evidence for this *cursus honorum*, either in the fifteenth century or earlier. Upton's description was not meant to apply to the previous period, but part of it was valid two centuries afterwards, for the seventeenth century Lancaster Herald, Francis Thynne, in his *Discourse of the Duty and Office of an Herald at Arms*[3] spoke of the 'solemnities' to be done at the making of messengers and pursuivants, who were to be introduced by the herald of the province or by the eldest herald respectively at the prince's command. The fourteenth century loved ceremonial and understood its value; and Upton's account, though perhaps exaggerated, need not be rejected altogether for the generation before his own. Much humbler servants than messengers were formally admitted to the king's service.[4]

Unfortunately neither Upton in the fifteenth nor Thynne in the seventeenth century were really interested in the details of the appointment ceremonies for messengers or couriers. Two features only stood out. The first was handing over the letter pouch and the king's arms, to be worn on the belt or thigh by the courier and on the left shoulder by the messenger. The second was the swearing-in. An

[1] *Nicholai Upton De Studio Militari* Lib. I cap IX–XII pp. 18–20.
[2] *Fifteenth century Cartulary of St. Nicholas' Hospital, Salisbury*, ed. Wordsworth (1902) p. 212.
[3] Gwillim *Display of Heraldry* (1724 ed.) p. 34.
[4] e.g. a balista maker in 1294 (I.R. 85).

oath constituted the strongest guarantee of fidelity and was commonly exacted from all who undertook responsible work for the king, whatever their grade or rank. Instances of this could be multiplied, but typical of many was the entry in the close roll for 1346 ordering robes for John Berengar, clerk, 'as he is sworn to the king's service -- and on the said day the king retained him of his familiar household.'[1] A clerk appointed to supervise works at Westminster and the Tower was sworn 'to bear himself well and faithfully in the said office' before the treasurer and chamberlain of the exchequer in 1310;[2] and in 1325 Master Henry de Clyf, on his appointment to the custody of the rolls of chancery, took his oath 'in the Great Hall of Westminster at the marble stone.'[3] Even the sailors taken into the king's service for the 1372-3 campaign were sworn in.[4] Similar oaths were taken by messengers and servants entering the papal household.[5] So much was this safeguard taken for granted that nowhere among the household records is any set form of oath preserved. That used for a messenger, however, probably varied little from the formula cited by Upton as suitable for a pursuivant, who promised fidelity to the king till death in any business entrusted to him, and obedience to his superior officers.[6]

Such an oath was not lightly broken. In the Lanercost chronicler's story of the traitorous Welsh courier, one of the points emphasized is that in handing over his letters to the enemy he had broken his oath; and the constable of the castle was said to have had scruples about profiting from this treachery.[7] According to this story, Edward I employed a Welsh courier named Lewyn and 'believed him to be his fastest and most faithful *cursor*.' But Lewyn, being sent from Edinburgh to London with letters, was tempted to begin his journey with a visit to a tavern, spent the night there, and found himself in the morning with no money left for his travels. In drunken valour, he declared he would attack the castle himself, and got up to the walls, where he shouted to the besieged that if they would take him in, he would deliver up all the king's secrets to them. The Scots who heard him were only too willing to profit by his offer, so Lewyn was brought to the constable, to whom 'he held out in his hand the pouch with the king's letters'. For the chronicler and for his readers, this was the supreme act of treachery in a messenger; and so strongly did the constable feel

---

[1]*C.C.R.* 1346–1349 p. 11.   [3]*C.C.R.* 1325–1327 p. 386.
[2]I.R. 157.   [4]I.R. 446 m. 1.
[5]Baumgarten *Auz Kanzlei und Kammer eröterungen zur Kurialen Hof-und-Verwaltungsgeschichte in xiii, xiv, und xv Jahrhunder* (1907), pp. 231, 234.
[6]The form of oath taken by messengers in ordinary in the seventeenth century was the same as that taken by all other members of the household, while the special form of oath for exchequer messengers is given in the first report of the Committee on Public Records (p. 254).
[7]*Chronicon de Lanercost* (ed. Stevenson for the Bannatyne Club 1839)p. 177–9. The account is interesting because the chronicle claims to have had first-hand knowledge of the affair from the constable himself.

this, that he refused to take advantage of the situation. Instead, the messenger was sent down the rope again with his letters unopened, and suffered for his treason on a special gallows as an example and warning to others. A second story of treachery from the same period concerns a man sent with letters by Edward during the siege of Stirling in 1303; and here his failure to obey led to the surrender of the town. When Stirling was retaken in 1304, he suffered Lewyn's fate.[1] One point emerges from these stories: neither were regular messengers. The incidents may have shown Edward the importance of employing only his properly appointed messengers or well-tried couriers; and in this way may have helped to define the position of the unmounted as well as the mounted men. No messenger whose record can be traced in the accounts ever failed in his duty or handed over his pouch to the enemy.[2]

Ordinary appointments were subject to good behaviour and not for life. Towards the end of Edward III's reign, the appointment of a special messenger was sometimes confirmed by letters patent which mention this important reservation. An instance occurred in 1370, when John Stygan messenger of the king's chamber, received his first instalment of 100s. a year which the king had granted him by letters patent 'as long as he should well and faithfully conduct himself in the aforesaid office.'[3] In the exchequer, on the other hand, messengerships were rapidly becoming sinecures, and this is reflected in the terms of appointment. When John Sewale was chosen by Richard II to fill one of the four messengerships in that department, his patent merely stated that John should have a daily wage 'to be received in the same manner as Thomas Monk, deceased, lately one of the aforesaid messengers', without any stipulation about the service to be rendered for it.[4] By the next century, these exchequer posts were openly stated to be held for life.[5] Later, patents for them were issued under the exchequer seal, and had the additional merit of exempting their holder from all civil duties, even when the office was a financial asset without any practical importance.[6]

[1] *Flores Hist.* III, 310 and 320 (ed. Luard. Rolls Series 1890).

[2] Henry of Bitering, messenger, whose lands were restored to him in 1322 after he had been in disgrace as a rebel, is more likely to have been a messenger in private service than a king's messenger. His name is not mentioned elsewhere. *C.C.R.* 1318–1325 p. 574.

[3] *Issue Roll of Thomas de Brantingham* p. 8, *C.P.R.* 1364–1367, p. 351.

[4] I.R. 606 m. 7.

[5] Warrant of privy seal, 1454 (E. 404/70).

[6] *Abstract of Orders of Quarter Sessions for Salop* I, 45 (1657).

'Forasmuch as John Bright of Totterton in the Parish of Lidbury, gent. came in Court and produced his patent under the seale of the Exchequer, whereby. it appeared that the said John Bright is one of the messengers appoynted to attend the Barons of the Exchequer, and is lately chosen to be one of the Churchwardens of the parish of Lidbury aforesaid; this Court doth order that the said John Bright be dismissed from the said office, and for the future be not elected into any office within this County that may Render him uncapable to attend the duty of his place.'

3. *Previous Training and Recommendation*

Training for the post of messenger, and equally for other responsible household posts, could be had either in the humbler branches of the king's service, or in some other great household. It will be remembered that the thirteenth century courier developed from a jack-of-all-works in the kitchen. There is evidence that, then and later, a boy might enter the household as a groom, become in time a running messenger, and finally a mounted messenger with full privileges. Thomas of Wynebaud started as a groom in 1288, and went on to be first courier and then treasurer's messenger, often borrowed by the king though not actually a member of his household.[1] In most cases, the cost of a riding messenger's equipment barred promotion from below, and these Dick Whittington advancements were never common. But prospective messengers often started as couriers, gaining experience of the road while they waited for a vacancy on the establishment. Simon of Marden (Mawurthin) served as *cokinus* before becoming messenger in 1264; and John Lirreys was known as a courier for two years before he was described as king's messenger for the first time in 1325.[2] William of Alkham had to wait even longer for a place.[3] Other candidates filled in the waiting period with service in a different capacity. Thus Roger Jolif the messenger of 1302 was probably identical with the Roger Jolif who had worked as wardrobe carter earlier that year; and Stephen of Hamslope and John of Waltham of 1323 with their namesakes the archers in 1319–20.[4] One messenger, Joseph of Faversham, may even have started as a professional courier in London.[5]

But the best and by far the most usual training for a messenger was work in one of the subordinate royal households or in the household of a bishop or magnate. In addition to men who served the heir to the throne and were automatically advanced at his accession, Brehull, Attleigh, and Lowys had all been queen's messengers. John le Blake had served Edmund of Cornwall; and Gomage had worked in turn for the queen and the treasurer before becoming king's messenger. Geoffrey of Bardeney came from the service of the constable of Edinburgh in 1298, John Arches from the earl of Pembroke's in 1319. John Ellyot was messenger of the bishop of Bath and Wells in 1373. John Faukes gathered experience successively under John bishop of Winchester in 1331 and under Richard de Bury, then keeper of the privy seal, before in 1333 he commenced his long career in the household of Edward III; and the appointment may be attributed to Richard's

[1] E.A. 308/10.
[2] E.A. 308/2; 379/19.
[3] Chanc. Misc. 3/51 and Add. MS. 7965 f. 42.
[4] Add. MS. 35292 and E.A. 365/8; Add. MS. 17362 f. 20.
[5] I.R. 191. See Appendix 3.

K.M.–I

personal influence with the king. In the service of magnate, diplomat, civilian, or ecclesiastic, the prospective king's messenger had a chance to acquire that stock of practical experience which stood him in lieu of maps and guide books; and no doubt he learnt much from meeting other messengers and travellers.[1] In due time, his master might recommend him to the king's officers or put him in the way of introducing himself to their notice.

Patronage was a most important factor then and equally difficult to trace now. But the value of a little personal influence behind a messenger is well illustrated in two particular cases. The first was a simple matter of the ordinary household clothing allowance which was not given as a rule to a man newly entered on his duties. The countess of Leicester, the king's sister, pleaded for special treatment for Richard of Malmesbury,[2] and it is natural to conclude that Richard had been trained in her establishment and was being transferred from her household to the king's, for she would hardly have made such a request on behalf of a green boy from the country of whom she had no personal knowledge. A more noteworthy case was that of Robert of Newington, whose indiscretions put him in greater need of protection than any newly-joined messenger. A gossip about politics between Robert and the sub-bailiff of his native village in Kent was reported to the king's council by one Robert le Viroler of Newington and confirmed by a jury of neighbours in 1315.[3] The informer declared that, on being asked about the Bannockburn disaster, the messenger had blamed the king's disinclination to attend mass, his general laziness, and his fondness for degrading manual labour. Robert of Newington had been in Edward's service since 1296 at least, and no doubt had plenty of experience of his master's habits but in this conversation we seem to overhear, not so much his personal opinion of the king as the current talk of the servants' hall. Such criticism, publicly uttered, could not pass unrebuked, and the messenger soon found himself cooling his heels in prison, even though he protested that he had intended nothing derogatory to the king's honour. From this predicament he was released through the personal intervention of the queen and on mainprize of the archbishop of Canterbury. Isabella may have agreed privately with Robert's criticism; and perhaps she was glad to foster discontent within the household for political ends. But she may simply have taken a personal

[1]One messenger at least travelled on his own account. In 1353 the king gave 26s 8d. from his alms to "William Clerk a courier of the king's wardrobe going on a pilgrimage to Jerusalem and Mount Sinai . . . in aid of his expenses" ' (I.R. 368 m. 18). About three years later, William Clerk, king's messenger, reappears in the accounts; he continued to serve the king till 1371 and in 1362 had a pension of 4½d. a day out of the issues of Surrey and Sussex. (*C.C.R.* 1360–1364 p. 318; *C.P.R.* 1361–1364 p. 195)

[2]*C.R.* 1256–1259 p. 61. She is said to have employed a messenger named Diquon.

[3]L.T.R.M.R. 86 m. 32d; see an article on this case by Hilda Johnstone *E.H.R.* XLVIII 264–267 (1933).

interest in the messenger who had served loyally in the past. Robert came from a manor in her own hundred of Milton, and a sense of feudal obligation might prompt her to interfere.

Both these stories show a very decided contact between the servant and his master or mistress, not confined to the giving and receiving of instructions. Such contacts grew most easily in a small household, and this probably explains why so many of the recorded instances relate to messengers of the queen or princes. Edward I's special treatment of his mother's and his wife's messengers in the matter of pensions may be attributed to this friendly connexion between the servant and the mistress; and is in contrast to his treatment of his own servants in their old age. The name *cursor* for a running messenger, instead of the slightly opprobrious *cokinus*, came into use in the princes' households long before it was used at court, which again may indicate greater consideration. Thirteenth century queen's messengers sometimes received tunics trimmed with lambskin, when the king's messengers did not; and nothing given to a king's messenger ever equalled the handsome belt given by the Black Prince to Dagonet. Yet even in the larger household, contact was possible. It may be that references to 'the king's own command' given to a messenger were not stock phrases. Nicholas Ramage justified some expenses by 'the king's own command' in 1289 and Robert of Rideware demanded the robe which the king had promised him when he went to France.[1] John Faukes said that the king bade him spare no expense on his journey to Avignon, but to go and return within eighteen days on pain of life and limb.[2] Perhaps they spoke the literal truth.

The story of Isabella's interference on behalf of Robert of Newington further suggests that politics might influence appointments in the household, even in the lower grades, where experience and capability would normally weight most. But against that possibility must be set the fact that the Ordainers' purge of the household made no drastic alteration in the messenger group. Of the ten messengers employed by Edward in 1312, eight were still in his service in 1316, the difference representing no more than normal wastage over four years.[3] The chroniclers, reporting popular rumours, and not in themselves in close touch with the household, were bound to exaggerate the changes actually made in personnel. Though the thirteenth and fourteenth centuries saw many disputes about the king's right to chose his own ministers, these hardly concerned the rank and file, except in so far as a man's contacts happened to be with members of one party rather than another. If appointments depended largely on personal recommendation, then politics became important to prospective messengers

[1] E.A. 308/10 and 363/25 No. 14.
[2] E.A. 312/4.
[3] E.A. 375/8 and 376/7 : See Tout, *Chapters* II, 238.

and their fellow servants because they were involved in their lord's political alliances, just as, in the last resort, they ranged themselves behind his banner on the battlefield. There may or may not have been a pro-Isabella factor inside Edward's household. Robert's story only shows that the king's servants still reserve their right to grumble.

4. *Social and Economic Background*

The place occupied by the messenger within the household was neither very high nor very low. It might therefore be anticipated that during this period, the men who entered the king's service as messengers would be drawn from a similar level of society, neither the knight nor the serf. Upton indeed said that messengers might become knights because of the dangers of their occupation, but he spoke of a subsequent generation and under the inspiration of an ideal. The real messengers of the fourteenth century, still less their predecessors of the thirteenth, were never dignified with knighthood. In this the messengers were typical of the great majority of men in the king's familiar household, and the level of society from which the messengers came was probably that which supplied all the lower clerical and higher domestic grades.

The most personal piece of evidence about the messenger's status outside court is provided by this story of Robert Newington the messenger and Saer Kayn the sub-bailiff of Newington. When Robert scandalized the country bailiff and his friends by his vehement disapproval of a king who degraded himself with manual labour, there speaks, I think, the authentic voice of the petty bourgeois. On that occasion bailiff and messenger were talking very much as equals, each being invested in a little brief authority, the advantage if any being on the side of the messenger. Robert, as he talked, may have been wondering whether a bailiff's job would suit him when he wanted to retire, as another Newington man, Robert Rideware, had done shortly before, on being made the king's bailiff for Dartford.[1] This was the sort of post to which a retiring messenger aspired, and such, presumably, his station in society, one comparable to that of the hundred bailiff or the estate steward. Though they might plead poverty when fined, bailiffs and stewards were generally landholders, occasionally clerks, always freemen.[2] A messenger might not need any clerical qualification, but personal and economic freedom were essential.

For the messenger was not a landless man, without ties. True, he could not farm himself while he travelled for the king. But messengers could and did own land and houses; and property was sometimes given to them by way of reward for good services. John of Barneby, for

---

[1] When Robert Rideware, as bailiff, was in trouble about this time over the wrongful seizure of a cow, one of the men by whom he was attached was this same Saer Kaym. (K.R. writs bundle 10).

[2] Cam, H. *Hundred and Hundred Rolls* p. 152.

instance, when in the middle of his career as a king's messenger, was engaged in a private law suit against men of Leicester in 1277.[1] When John Piacle fell ill at Huntingdon in 1296, he was able to pay his expenses there for seventy-seven days, together with the cost of a doctor and medicines (for which he was afterwards reimbursed), and on recovering from a second illness in 1299 could be sent *ad domum suam propriam* for convalescence.[2] This again argues a social background far above that of a labourer. Henry III gave a house at Bridport worth a mark a year to his messenger John Chubbe, who held it till 1257, when it escheated to the king because the ex-messenger 'had taken the religious dress'. The house was then regranted to the king's mason, also a skilled man with a responsible task, and both of them persons of sufficient standing to make such a gift appropriate, for Henry, though generous, understood the value of his gifts.[3] A Shrewsbury house, rented at 12*d.* a year from the bailiffs, was given by Henry to his messenger Robert Blund,[4] and another messuage in Stamford in the king's escheat was granted to the messenger Nicholas in 1253, with a virgate of land as well.[5]

This Nicholas may be the same man as Nicholas le Waleys the King's messenger who for his long service received from Henry III in 1261 a life interest in a messuage and virgate of land at Brockton in Munslow Hundred (Salop) which had escheated to the king on an outlawry for murder. In return, Nicholas was to find a bowman with lance to serve at Montgomery for fifteen days in time of war. It is not likely that the messenger actually occupied the house or performed the service himself. For the first ten years at least he paid no suit to the hundred court and until 1275 he had a daily pension to collect from the exchequer. But after the pension was commuted, he may have retired to Shropshire; his name at any rate suggests a Marcher origin, and though the feodary of 1284 shows that he had found a tenant Alexander le Cold for half the land and half the service, nothing is said about the rest. Certainly Nicholas enjoyed the proceeds for upwards of thirty years. When an investigation into the Crown's Shropshire rights was being held at the October assizes of 1292, the sheriff certified Nicholas to be dead; and though Hugh de Louther affirmed him still *in plena vita*, the sheriff's information must have been more up-to-date, for the serjeanty passed, through Robert Burnell bishop of Bath and Wells who died in 1292, to the Burnells of Langley.[6]

Grants of timber to several messengers suggest that they were building themselves houses. Two grants of Windsor oaks were made

[1]*C.C.R.* 1272–1279 p. 416.
[2]Add. MS. 7965 f. 10; E.A. 356/8 m. 12.
[3]*C.Ch.R.* 1257–1300 p. 5; *C.I.Misc.* I, No. 2045; *C.P.R.* 1266–1272 p. 402.
[4]*C.Ch.R.* 1226–1257 p. 134; *C.R.* 1227–1231 p. 519.
[5]*C.P.R.* 1247–1258 p. 179; *C.R.* 1253–1254 p. 19; and 1268–1272 p. 288.
[6]Eyton *Antiquities of Shropshire* II 95–6.

to the messenger Walter of Marden or Mawordyn, who, if not possessed of land himself, was certainly connected with the land-holding class.[1] Four of the best chestnut trees near the king's highway from Newington to Sittingbourne, a pair from each side of the street, were to be delivered to Robert Rideware (at that time messenger of the prince). The locality is of interest because other evidence shows Robert to have been a native of Newington, and chestnut wood, largely used for roof beams, would have been a useful gift to a man intending to build himself a house near his old home.[2] Later messengers were rewarded with other property, some in London, some in Essex and Northamptonshire. Though the evidence is scanty, it is enough to dispose of any picture of the king's messenger as a landless man, with no home but the peripatetic court.

A further confirmation of this may be found in occasional references to messengers' wives. These ladies did not accompany their husbands on their travels, nor was there any place for them at court.[3] Thus it is only by accident that wives and families are mentioned. Christiana the wife of John of Canterbury (Cantuaria) collected his allowance of 1*d.* a day from the sheriff of Essex during the messenger's protracted absence abroad in 1227.[4] William le Engleis had a daughter of age to be married in 1233, and the match which he made for her, with the son of a small tenant in chief, was not to be thought meanly of in an age which made marriage a matter of business.[5] Marsilia, widow of Henry the messenger, received a gift of clothing from the king in 1268, perhaps the equivalent of a widow's weeds.[6] Douce the wife of Thomas of Oxford collected the arrears of her husband's pension in 1275, and in 1295 Constance wife of Simon Lowys received his grant from the exchequer.[7] When Walter Cardinal's daily allowance was in arrears in 1374, his wife Cecilia was able to get an imprest of 66*s.* 8*d.* out of the exchequer officers.[8] Since wives' names occur in the accounts only by chance, it is unlikely that these were the only married messengers. Two points emerge, first that a messenger was in a position to support a wife if he wanted to (and this he could hardly have done on the surplus from his official travelling expenses); second, that he was free to marry if he wished, without the impediment of even minor orders. His wife was no doubt expected to remain at home to look after the property while her husband was at court, and in this capacity might be a great help to an ambitious man. The recurrence of surnames in household lists suggests that sons often succeeded fathers in the king's service.

[1]*C.R.* 1261–1264 p. 36 and 1264–1268 p. 279. See below p. 128.
[2]*C.C.R.* 1296–1302 p. 263.
[3]Household Ordinance 1318 (Tout *Place of Edward II* p. 280).
[4]*C.L.R.* 1226–1240 pp. 32, 34.
[5]*C.R.* 1231–1234 p. 276.   [7]*I.R.* 28, 91.
[6]*Ibid.* 1264–1268 p. 461.   [8]*I.R.* 451.

One other consideration supports the theory that the average messenger was not as much cut off from the world outside the court as the medieval civil servant described by Tout. 'When the public servant was attached to the court, he had . . . no salary or a very small one. But he made up for this by receiving lodging, clothing, food, drink, and firewood, at the king's expense. He had, therefore, as little need of money as a soldier in the trenches or a monk in a convent.'[1] Though the messenger received advance expenses when he set out on the king's errand, there were often incidental charges not provided for. Jacke Faukes was as much as £3 14s. 10d. out of pocket on his return from Avignon in 1343, and it might be months before such a debt could be recovered. The messenger was likely to be in difficulties if he had no private means to fall back on. Again, no official provision was made at the time for the comfort of the messenger in case of accident or illness. The expenses of a prolonged stay in lodgings after the court had moved on cannot have been light, and in the instance mentioned above, John Piacle may well have spent on lodging, doctor's fee and medicine, far more than the 26s. 8d. which he was later given out of the king's alms.[2] In any case, the messenger must be able to provide himself with a horse, perhaps more than one, as part of his equipment for the post; and no allowance at all was made towards this initial expenditure.

All these clues put together suggest that the king's messengers came of land-holding stock, probably from the smaller free tenants on the royal demesne, that they had means of their own with which they could finance themselves in need, maintain a family, and supplement an inadequate pension when they retired. It sometimes amounted to much more than this. Dagonet the Black Prince's messenger was so much of a capitalist that he was able to lend money to his master.[3] Others may have lent money outside court, for in 1324, John of Arches was a private creditor for £10 and Stephen of Hamslope for 6 marks, the latter assured on land and chattels in Lincolnshire.[4] The grants of wardship and custody of lands which some messengers received were lucrative; and in spite of periodic complaints that the king gave wardships and marriages of his tenants in chief to household servants of inferior rank, it is improbable that messengers would have been rewarded so often in this way unless they were of at least approximately equal standing with their intended wards.[5] There could be no case of political motive here and little occasion for personal favouritism.

[1]Tout 'The English Civil Service in the Fourteenth Century' *Bulletin of John Rylands Library* 1916 p. 21.
[2]Add. MS. 7965 f. 10.
[3]A matter of 60s. 'which he handed to the Prince to be offered to St. Augustine of Canterbury' and for which he was paid in underwood and charcoal out of the prince's stock. *Black Prince's Register* IV 481.
[4]*C.C.R.* 1323–7 pp. 185, 169.
[5]For examples of such wardships, see above p. 71.

The very fact that the household messenger was preceded by the messenger-serjeant adds to the probability of his being a landholder. In the thirteenth century, when the messenger service had only recently grown out of the messenger serjeanty, it would be most natural for the king to draw his household messengers from the families of former serjeanty tenants. This is difficult of proof, but there are two instances at least in which a connexion can be shown or suggested. The Herefordshire manor of Maworthin or Marden had been held under a messenger obligation, and from Marden came three at least of Henry III's messengers. The first of them was William le Engleis[1] whose name suggests the Marches of Wales. In 1233 he was given permission to marry his daughter to the son and heir of Jocelin de Maworthin, a small tenant in chief, but unfortunately the chancery clerk who recorded the licence was not interested in the christian name of the intended son-in-law. One may presume that William was by that date a valued and experienced messenger, since five years later he received the daily alms of 1*d*. from the issues of Herefordshire which he continued to draw until his death in 1244. Very soon after this, Walter of Marden or Mawordyn,[2] possibly the son-in-law, was in the king's service as messenger. He too received alms, this time from Surrey, when he retired in 1263 with a testimonial to his 'long and praiseworthy service'; and as he was given timber oaks from Windsor forest in 1261 and 1266, he may have settled down near Windsor for convenience in drawing his pension, leaving the Herefordshire lands to a brother or perhaps a son. But the link with Marden lasted one generation longer. The year after Walter received his pension, a new Herefordshire messenger, Simon of Mawordin,[3] appeared in the accounts, first as a courier and then as a mounted messenger. His career in the household may have begun while Walter was still at court, since at first his christian name was always given, though later he was called Mawardin without distinction. He remained in the service until 1284, and perhaps died in harness, for he received no pension. With his death, the connexion between the messenger service and this particular manor was broken at last after three generations. No messenger called Maworthin or Marden appeared in the accounts after 1284.

A similar link, though less well authenticated, can be plausibly suggested between the Gloucestershire serjeant Robert le Sauvage, whose duties were commuted in 1251, and the messenger Geoffrey Sauvage who was employed in the household in 1214 and retired in 1226 with a grant from the issues of Gloucestershire. Somewhat later,

[1] *C.R.* 1231–1234 p. 276; 1237–1242 p. 34; 1242–1247 p. 179. *cf.* the Herefordshire place-name 'England's Gate'.
[2] *Ibid.* 1261–1264 p. 233; p. 36; 1264–1268 p. 279.
[3] E.A. 308/2 and 3; 372/5.

a messenger known as Arnold Bon or Bon le Sauvage served Edward I and his son, and the second variant of his name may connect him also with this family of messenger-serjeants. These hints are enough to show that the thirteenth century messenger service was still linked in men's minds with land tenure, and that families of petty serjeants might provide the household with suitable recruits. This does not automatically define their social position, for serjeanty was promiscuous and 'impinged on many other classes' but it does imply personal freedom.[1]

Some further evidence is supplied by the messengers' surnames, which connect them more frequently with places than with occupations. Of all classes of surname in the messenger lists, those derived from places are most common; and, as might be expected, these are primarily places connected with the king's household by ownership, tradition, or strategic position on a main road. Messengers appear to have entered that household from royal hundreds such as Brehull (Bucks.), Tichfield (Hants.), Bradley (Lincs.) and Chelmsford (Essex); from favourite manors such as Woodstock and Langley; and from towns with important royal castles such as Windsor, Corfe, Colchester, Norwich, Nottingham, Shrewsbury, and Canterbury. The royal honour of Ludgershall supplied a messenger of that name. A succession of messengers came from London and its environs, either true Londoners like John, Peter, Robert, and Walter of London and John of Arches, or men from the immediate neighbourhood like Simon of Westminster. These names demonstrate the importance of towns, large or small, but with a royal castle or residence as the focal point of each, as recruiting grounds for the household. Old cathedral cities like Winchester, Canterbury, York, Norwich, Durham, and London itself; and growing mercantile communities like Leicester, Nottingham, Shrewsbury, Warwick, Bristol, Oxford and others, were represented among the king's servants, not because they were religious or trading centres, but in each case because of their close connexion with the crown. The expansion of all royal and baronial establishments in wartime must have opened the way to service for many would-be messengers. At every political crisis, the number of messengers was suddenly increased, and at the same time, men temporarily employed (like John of Waltham and Stephen of Hamslope) as archers or men-at-arms, had a chance to demonstrate their efficiency and put themselves into the way of a permanent post. The corporate sense of a garrison or a fighting force might be developed into the more solid loyalty of a household.[2]

[1]A. L. Poole *Obligations of Society in the Twelfth and Thirteenth Centuries* p. 7.

[2]Compare the fourteenth century baronial indentured retainers whose status and emoluments were not unlike those of a messenger. These seem to have been recruited primarily from the lord's tenantry but secondarily from men who were attracted to his banner in time of war.

N. B. Lewis 'The Organization of Indentured Retinues in Fourteenth Century England' *Trans. Royal Hist. Soc.* 4th Series (1945) pp. 29–39.

At the same time, the town may have proved a more favourable recruiting ground for the king's household than the countryside. Life there may have fostered independence and given it more scope than the life of a manor. A royal borough provided contacts when the court came on progress, and business connexions with the household a means of introduction to appropriate officials. In one respect, it was to the king's advantage to employ freemen of the cities of London, Canterbury, Norwich or Rochester. Men from those four places still enjoyed their freemen's privilege of paying no dues at Dover when leaving or returning on the king's business. John Faukes' account shows that there was one burgess at any rate among the Londoners in the messenger group, and if surnames are any guide, men from three of the four select places were at one time or another in the king's service.

But though the names of messengers often linked them with towns, they were rarely occupational surnames, or if occupational, then unconnected with trades or crafts. This is not surprising, for a man could not be called Butcher or Baker till he had served his apprenticeship, and a messenger also began his training young. John Taverner, Walter le Mariner, and perhaps Skippermyne, were the only exceptions in a hundred and eighty years.[1] On the other hand, there were some names, particularly in the fourteenth century, which seem to be derived from the guild plays performed in many towns at Corpus Christi. It was natural that after a man had taken his part several years running, he became known as Cardinal, Pope, Prior, Clerk, or Preacher. Adam Merlyn's name may also have come from a figure in a play. The actor's son may have adopted his father's name in jest or have inherited it when surnames began to be conventional, for it seems more likely that these were names passed on from father to son than freshly-coined descriptions given to messengers at court.

The only occupational surnames used by messengers were derived from domestic service in a large household, and in all there were about a dozen of these, mostly early. Walter and John le Ewer, Robert le Herberger, Roger Passavant (the Pursuivant), Page, Alexander and Walter le Norreys, Hugh le Serviens, Walter Scutard, William Hunt, Ralph le Keu, and John Cook. How natural that a man who had served in a baronial household should want to place his son in a similar but if possible a slightly better position, in the same or another household; and how much greater his chance of introducing his boy to someone's

[1]There is a note in the *Black Prince's Register* 'Be it remembered that on the same day, John de Donvill the younger did homage and fealty to the Prince at the inn of Dagenet at Redyng' .This extraordinary reference to an innkeeper's name suggests the possibility that John Dagonet the Prince's messenger was either himself owner of an inn or, more probably, son of an innkeeper at Reading whose house was sometimes visited by the Prince. (*Op. cit.* III, 455). If he were, the charcoal and wood sold to him out of the Prince's store may have been for domestic use. (*Ibid.* IV 481). At any rate, the note shows how contact between the prospective messenger and the court could be made.

notice. A campaign, a royal progress, a season at court, might provide
the link; and the smart young servant, already partly trained, might be
advanced from his lord's service to the king's. These names confirm
what has been said already about the importance of patronage to a man
seeking a career in the household.

The remaining surnames found in messenger lists were simple
patronymics, such as Auncell (son of Anselm) or Godbehere (son of
Godber) or more plainly in the early part of the period as Richard son
of Ralph; and some nicknames. Bongarsun (i.e. Goodfellow), Fox,
Blund, Little, Russel, Ramage (the Wild), and Carbonel (Firebrand)
all served as messengers; but there were fewer nicknames than might
have been expected. This again may indicate a certain social status,
which did not like to be laughed at and was more sensitive on the point
because its standing was modest.

One thing is certain, that neither messenger nor courier came from
the villeins on the manor or the labourer, skilled or unskilled, in the
town. The villein was tied to the land, both by his personal servitude
and obligations, and by his farming methods. He could not cultivate
his holding and pay his rents in money or services by himself. Small-
holding farming is always a family business in which the labour of
every member is needed for success; and children, as soon as they can
work, are an asset, not a liability. The thirteenth or fourteenth
century villein family owing labour services or rents in lieu of them
must have found its only chance of a reasonable livelihood in family
solidarity, especially during the economic depressions of the fourteenth
century. It is true that for a few years of Henry III's minority, his
chancery employed a small group of messengers, Brice Bongarsun,
William Cherl, William le Chareter, Gilbert Godswein, Adam and
Thomas Nevreman, Norman Nevregodman, William Nusquam,
John Pesewamb, Patrick Pluckhenn, Adam son of Pluckhenn, and
William le Vilein, who all sound like country cousins;[1] and thirty
years later one Bacon, originally perhaps a swineherd, was a royal
letter carrier. But there were no more such names in later messenger
lists, until Richard Swin, Henry le Veel, and John Wetherhird joined
the household. Pressure of custom, fear of fine or forfeiture, and
the needs of the farm, combined to keep the sons of smallholders at
home. But as soon as a tenant could afford to hire labour or had customary tenants of his own, the position was reversed. Then the desire
to preserve his eldest son's inheritance intact began to operate, and
younger sons, whose labour could be dispensed with, were encouraged
to find a living elsewhere. The younger sons of a small tenant in chief
could not share the estate; and the decision that a serjeanty-holder who
alienated part of his land must still perform the whole service due,
restricted the subdivision of property held by serjeanty. In less striking

[1]*C.L.R.* I.

fashion, the same principles were at work in the town. The small tradesman could not afford to hire labour and needed the help of all his sons to make ends meet; so did the journeyman who had no capital to set up on his own. When the craftsman became master enough to employ journeymen and apprentices, he might be willing to let an adventurous boy seek his fortune away from home. When his business became still more flourishing, and especially if it were mercantile rather than mechanical, he would be glad to see him do so. Younger sons might have their portion of his fortune to equip them and give them financial backing; but they could not expect a division of their father's business which would make them equal partners with their elder brother. Thus, both in town and country, the English law of inheritance helped to create a reserve of men from whom the king could draw for his household.

One more point brought out by messengers' surnames is the number of strangers in the household at the beginning of the thirteenth century. John chose for his messengers men like Robert and Henry of 'Alemannia', Ralph and Hugh of Cambray, Robert le Fleming, Roger of Roches, William of Vendôme; and others with names like Hamelin, Alberic, Hispannia (probably from Espagne in Gascony), and Garland (a Breton name), who probably came from abroad. The still existing connexion between England and Normandy would explain place names from the north of France, and John's alliance with the emperor might account for Germans entering his household. But even so, the proportion of foreign names remains high, unless these messengers were trained men who came to form a nucleus for the new household messenger service just developing from the serjeant messenger and the kitchen knave. It is interesting to see that in spite of Henry III's supposed predilection for foreign favourites, he employed few among his messengers. John of Lyons, John of Brabant, William le Burgillun, Philip of Schoccevill (probably from Escoville in Normandy), and Butevilein (another Norman) may have come from France, but not one of his messengers was from Germany or Flanders. Edward I was served by John (or Janinus) le Burguillon, Philip of Salines, and Normann; and Edward III had his John of Paris; but with these few exceptions, recruitment from abroad ceased as soon as the household service was well established and under wardrobe control.

Examined geographically, all the names show a tendency to group themselves into areas, though not sharply defined. The Thames valley, an obvious royal route, and the southern counties from Dorset to Kent, supplied many names. Thus messengers can be traced to their homes in Windsor, Hamslope (Bucks.), Malmesbury and Ludgershall (probably Wilts.), Bayworth and Wallingford (Berks.), Spelbury, Oxford and Woodstock (Oxon.). There was a marked gap over the Surrey heaths and Sussex downs and weald, but except for these areas,

names were scattered freely over Wessex and Kent, from Canford and
Cerne (Dorset.), Winchester and Dogmersfield (Hants.) and
Cheriton (Hants. or Kent), to Canterbury, Newington, Faversham
and Alkham (Kent). In the West Midlands, Warwickshire was particularly well represented, and at different times messengers from
Banbury, Cosford, Kinwarton, Itchington and Warwick itself were in
the king's service. Another strong Midland contingent came from
Nottinghamshire, including men of Nottingham, Wirsop, Retford
and Manfield, while there were others from Chebsey (Staffs.) Leicester and Rothby (Leics.). Probably all these places had some direct
contact with the court as it travelled. In contrast, only a few men from
East Anglia were attracted into the king's service and those chiefly
from the areas most accessible to London, such as Colchester, Chelmsford (Essex) and Burstall (Suffolk). During the whole period, one
messenger only from Lindsey and one from Norwich represented the
wide stretch of country from Lincoln south to Essex, for the fens and
broads, and the difficulty of skirting the Wash with its quicksands and
marshes, kept the court away from much of eastern England. Greater
freedom of tenure in some areas of East Anglia and greater agricultural
prosperity generally may be other contributing causes, which it is
difficult to assess.

The western and northern groups illustrate well the importance of
direct contact between the prospective messenger and the court.
Apart from the Marden group, which disappeared in 1284, Ledbury
(Hereford), Shrewsbury (Salop), Elmbridge and Powick (Worcs.)
are all Marcher names and there were several le Waleys in the household of Henry III. Gloucestershire, the county of the Clares, and
Somerset were outside the orbit of royal influence, but there were
men from further west at court, for one Deveneys and one Cornwalleis
at least served Henry, and already in 1202, Roger le Tort another
west-countryman was receiving a pension. But after Edward I's con-
quest of Wales, when Welsh campaigns no longer drew the court to
the Marches so frequently, the name 'Waleys' disappeared from the
messenger accounts. Cornish and Devon men found other outlets for
their energies, though one Odo of Cornwall was still attached to the
exchequer in 1318. Instead, the court began to move more often to the
Scottish border, and with the fourteenth century, the king's service was
enriched by north countrymen from Athol and Galloway, as well as
Carlisle (Cumberland), Kendal and Lonsdale (Westmoreland),
Durham (co. Durham), Knousley and Meol (Lancs.), Dacre, Guis-
borough, Whitby, York, and Calder (Yorks.). John of Bolton
(whichever Bolton he came from) and John Tailfer (a Northumberland surname) were also from the north. The majority of these were in
Edward III's household, and there must have been noticeable cock-
ney and north country accents among his messengers, in contrast

to the south, midland and west country voices of Henry III's and Edward I's men. Yet another type of accent was no doubt provided by John le Iryssh, also called Lyrissh or Lirroys, who was once described as John Lirreys of Windsor, and may therefore have been an Irishman domiciled on a royal manor, or perhaps the English-born son of an Irish man-at-arms attached to the castle guard. This introduction of men from the north into the lower household during the fourteenth century is parallel to the introduction of north country clerks into the higher administrative service, which began during the chancellorship of Robert Burnell, and continued throughout the fourteenth century, a result of personal contacts with the church of York.[1] No doubt the geographical affinities of their immediate superior was a powerful factor in the selection of all grades of household personnel.[2]

[1]Hamilton Thompson *The Medieval Chapter* (York Minster Hist. Tracts), pp. 12–15; *Register of Archbishop Greenfield* (Surtees Soc. I, xviii.)
[2]In this connexion, attention may be drawn to the importance now attributed to geography as determining the political loyalty of Edward II's bishops, many of them former civil servants. (K. Edwards *E.H.R.* LIX p. 346).

CHAPTER VIII

CONCLUSION

I N my summing up of the little that can be known about the social
background of the household, I have been obliged to speak as
though the period and its life were static. But clearly this was not so.
The messenger's social standing was not quite the same under Edward
III as it had been under John. The fourteenth century belonged in part
to the Middle Ages and in part to that post-medieval age which linked
the fourteenth and the seventeenth centuries. In 1234 wardrobe
administration was just beginning, by 1343 it was in decay and a
rejuvenated exchequer had taken over all its non-domestic functions
long before 1377. The seventeenth century title 'messenger of the
chamber' was just beginning to appear on the rolls during the last years
of Edward III. Administrative and constitutional development during
the period of this study had made an efficient messenger service far
more important than in 1199. By 1377, it was essential to any government. As the work of the messengers, mounted or unmounted, increased, their official position improved; and with this improvement,
their social background changed also. Under Edward I, the running
messengers were casual labourers, only a stage removed from kitchen
knaves. Under Edward III they were indispensable and beginning to
qualify for sick benefits and pensions. By the reign of Henry V, a
writer on chivalry was ready to include them in his scheme. The
mounted messenger's status also rose. He had always been respected
as a member of the household and as one often connected with landholders; but under Edward III he received a higher rate of pay and
more privileges than hitherto; and in another generation it would not
seem fantastic to declare a messenger eligible for knighthood on
account of the risks he ran in serving the king. That this was not
entirely vain talk is demonstrated by one small clue from the fifteenth
century. In a list of the 'men of courte' slain at the Battle of St. Albans
in 1455, after all the noble and knightly names, someone found it
worth while to mention 'Rogere Mercroft, the Kynges Messanger.'[1]

It only remains to compare the position of the messenger with that
of other household groups. The slow but definite improvement in the
messengers' status throughout these centuries was not necessarily
paralleled in other grades. The king's huntsmen, and falconers, carters
and cooks, were no more and no less necessary to the administration

[1] *Paston Letters* ed. Gairdner, I, 350.

in 1377 than in 1200. If the messengers' status rose, it was because their functional importance increased as more letters were sent out each year. On the other hand, conditions of service which they shared in common with all the household were already fixed by custom and were being set out in household ordinances. These could not change. In these particulars and in the general picture they give of household organization, the king's relations with his servants and theirs with him, their work at court and their social standing outside it, the messenger group was from the time of John to Edward III as typical as any below the highest and above the lowest ranks.

This would not be true much longer. Up to the fourteenth century, the household was still the administrative centre, and new departments grew out of it. Before the end of the century, its powers had been curtailed, its weakness exposed, and its growth checked. Financial initiative and control now lay outside, and not long after the death of Edward III, the messengers in their turn went out of court (as exchequer and chancery had done previously) because their work no longer came from the wardrobe. They left behind four household messengers to show that all had once shared in the privileges of membership and been proud of their status in the king's *familia*.

SOURCES AND ABBREVIATIONS

I. ORIGINAL AUTHORITIES

1. *Wardrobe Accounts, original and enrolled*

E.A.—Exchequer king's remembrancer various accounts, (P.R.O. list XXXV Wardrobe and Household' and '*Nuncii*'), E.A. 350/5—398/14, and 308/1—317/40.

Misc. bks. E.T.R.—Exchequer treasury of receipt miscellaneous books, E. 36/201–205.

Chanc. misc.—Chancery miscellanea bundles 3 and 4.

Brit. Mus. Cotton MSS. Nero C VIII, Galba E III and XIV, Harl. MS. 152, Stowe MS. 553, Add. MSS. 36762, 35294, 7965, 7966, 35282, 8835, 37655, 37656, 22923, 35093, 17362, 9931, 38006, 35181; Egerton MS. 2814.

John Rylands Library Latin MSS. 229–237.

Society of Antiquaries MSS. 120–121.

L.Q.G.—*Liber Quotidianus Contrarotulatoris Garderobae anno regni regis Edwardi primi vicesimo octavo*, ed. Lort, Gough, Topham, and Brand, for the Society of Antiquaries, 1787.

'The Wardrobe and Household of Henry, son of Edward I, 1273–4', ed. H. Johnstone, *Bulletin of John Rylands Library* 1923.

'Roll of expenses of Edward I in Wales, 1281–2', ed. Lysons, *Archaeologia*, 1812, XVI 32–79.

'Extracts from the *Rotulus Familiae* for 18 Edward I', ed. Lysons, *ibid*. 1806, XV 350–362.

'A brief Summary of the Wardrobe Accounts of the 10th., 11th., and 14th. years of King Edward II', ed. Stapleton, *ibid*., 1846, XXVI 318–345.

'Account of expenses of the Great Wardrobe of Edward III, 1344–1349', ed. Nicholas, *ibid*., XXXI 5–103.

'A Wardrobe account of 16–17 Richard II, 1393–4', ed. Baildon, *ibid*., 1911, LXII pt ii 497–514.

'Particulars of account of Langton's embassy in 1296–7, (E.A. 308/19)', ed. G. P. Cuttino, *Studies in British History, Essays in Honour of H. G. Plum*, 1941, pp. 147–183.

Enrolled account 1224–1227, ed. Tout, *Chapters*, I 233–238.

Enrolled account, 1282–1285, in *Chronica Johannis de Oxenedes* ed. Ellis (Rolls Series) 1859, pp. 326–336.

Enr. Accts. (W. & H.)—Lord Treasurer's remembrancer enrolled accounts (Wardrobe and Household) Nos. 1–5.

Enrolled wardrobe accounts on pipe rolls 79, 80, 81, 88, 95, 99, 113, 114, 115, 116, 119, 121, 123, 124, 128, 129, 136, 138, 139, 144, 166, 168; and on chancellor's rolls 45, 125.

2. Exchequer Accounts

I.R.—Issue rolls E. 403/18–462.

Issue Roll of Thomas de Brantingham, Bishop of Exeter, 1370 trans. Devon, 1835.

Issues of the Exchequer, Henry III—Henry VI (extracts) trans. Devon, 1837.

P.R.—Pipe rolls 62–78, 82, 84, 86, 87.

Great Roll of the Pipe, 1199–1207, volumes edited for the Pipe Roll Society 1934–1946.

Great Roll of the Pipe, 1241 ed. H. L. Cannon, Yale Historical Publications, 1918.

R.R.—Receipt rolls 3b–8 and 10b.

Rolls of Writs for issues 1200 a and b, 1201, 1202, 1307.

Exchequer *liberate* rolls E. 403/1202, 1203; and E.401/11.

Warrants for issues file 1, nos 28, 30, 38.

L.T.R.M.R.—Memoranda rolls, lord treasurer's remembrancer 1–5 (P.R.O. transcript); 13–28 (P.R.O. abstract); 48, 49, 50, 78, 79, 102–9.

K.R.M.R.—king's remembrancer 1–5 (P.R.O. transcript), 108–9.

Chancellor's roll 1201–2, ed. Record Commission 1833.

Memoranda Roll, King's Remembrancer, 1230, ed. Chalfont-Robinson for the P.R.S., 1933.

Red Book of the Exchequer, ed. Hall (Rolls Series) 1896.

3. Chancery Enrolments

R. L. Pat.—*Rotuli Litterarum Patentium 1201–1216,* ed. T. D. Hardy for the Record Commission, 1835.

Pat. R.—*Patent Rolls,* 1216–1232.

C.P.R.—*Calendars of Patent Rolls,* 1232–1377.

R.L.Cl.—*Rotuli Litterarum Clausarum 1204–1227,* ed. T. D. Hardy for the Record Commission, 1833.

C.R.—*Close Rolls,* 1227–1272.

C.C.R.—*Calendars of Close Rolls,* 1272–1377.

Ch.R.—*Charter Rolls,* 1199–1216.

C.Ch.R.—*Calendars of Charter Rolls,* 1227–1377.

R. de Lib.—*Rotuli de Liberate ac de Misis et Praestitis regnante Johanne,* ed. T. D. Hardy, 1844.

Cole's *Records—Rotulus Misae Anni Regni Johannis Quarti Decimi,* ed. Cole, *Documents Illustrative of English History in the Thirteenth and Fourteenth Centuries,* 1844, pp. 231–268.

C.L.R.—*Calendars of Liberate Rolls,* 1226–1251.

Ch. C.W.—*Calendar of Chancery Warrants,* 1244–1326.

C.I.P.M.—*Calendars of Inquisitions Post Mortem* I—VII, 1216–1377.

C.I.Misc.—*Calendars of Inquisitions Miscellaneous* I.

4. Household Ordinances

The household ordinance of 1279, ed. Tout, *Chapters,* II 158–163.

The household ordinances of 1318 and 1323, ed. Tout, *The Place of Edward II,* 2nd ed. pp. 241–284.

A Collection of Ordinances and Regulations for the Government of the Royal Household, ed. Lort, Gough, Topham, and Brand, for the Society of Antiquaries, 1790. Cited as *Collection of Ordinances.*

5. The Black Prince's Register

Vols I–IV

II. SECONDARY AUTHORITIES

FOWLER, G. H.   Introduction to *Rolls from the Office of the Sheriff of Bed-fordshire and Buckinghamshire* (Bedfordshire Hist. Record Soc. III, 1929).

HILL. M. C.   'Jack Faukes, King's Messenger, and his journey to Avignon in 1343' *E.H.R.* LVII, 19–30 (1942). 'King's Messengers and Administrative Developments in the thirteenth and fourteenth centuries' *E.H.R.* LXI, 315–328 (1946).

HOUSDEN, J. A. J.   'Early Posts in England' *E.H.R.* XVIII, 713–718 (1903).

JOHNSON, C.   'The System of Account in the Wardrobe of Edward I' *Trans. Royal Hist. Soc.* 4th series VI, 50–72 (1923).

JOHNSON, J. H.   'The System of Account in the Wardrobe of Edward II' *Ibid.* 4th series XII, 75–104 (1924).

JOHNSTONE, H.   'The Eccentricities of Edward II' *E.H.R.* XLVIII, 264–267 (1933). 'Poor Relief in the Royal Households of Thirteenth Century England' *Speculum* IV, 149–167 (1929). 'A Year in the Life of King Henry III' *Church Quarterly Review* XCVII No. CXCIV (1924).

JUSSERAND, J.   *English Wayfaring Life in the Middle Ages* (trans. Smith, 1920).

KIMBALL, E.   *Serjeanty Tenure in Medieval England* (1936).

LARSON, A.   'The Payment of Fourteenth Century English Envoys' *E.H.R.* LIV, 403–414 (1939).

MADOX, T.   *History and Antiquities of the Exchequer* (2nd ed. 1769).

RENOUARD, Y.   'Comment les Papes d'Avignon expédiaient leur Courrier' *Revue Historique* CLXXX, 1–22 (1937).

RODOCANACHI, E.   'Les Courriers Pontificaux de xive au xviie Siècle' *Revue d'Histoire Diplomatique* XXVI, 392–428 (1912).

TOUT, T. F.   *The Place of Edward II in English History* (2nd ed. H. Johnstone 1936). *Chapters in the Administrative History of Medieval England* (1920–3). 'The English Civil Service in the Fourteenth Century' *Bulletin of the John Rylands Library* 1916. 'Some conflicting tendencies in English Administrative History during the fourteenth century' *Ibid.* 1924. 'The Household of Chancery and its Disintegration' *Essays Presented to R. L. Poole* (1927).

STENTON, F. M.   'The Road System of Medieval England' *Economic Hist. Review* VII, 1–21 (1936–7).

STRETTON, G.   'Some Aspects of Medieval Travel' *Trans. Royal Hist. Soc.* 4th series VII, 77–97. 'The Travelling Household of the Middle Ages', *Journal British Arch. Ass.* new series XL, 75–103 (1935).

UPTON, N.   *Nicholai Upton de Studio Militari libri quatuor Edoardus Bissaeus e Codicibus MSS. primus publici fecit* (1654).

WHEELER-HOLOHAN, V. *History of the King's Messengers* (1935).

VAILLÉ, E.   *Histoire Générale des Postes Françaises* (Paris 1947).

WILKINSON, B.   'The Household Ordinance of 1279' *History* XII, 46–7 (1927–8).

WILLARD, F.   'The Dating and Delivery of Letters Patent and Writs in the 14th Century' *Bulletin of the Institute of Historical Research* X, I–II (1932–3).

APPENDIX I
THE NUMBERS OF MESSENGERS EMPLOYED

	Date	Nuncii regis	Cokini or Cursores	Chancery or Exchequer Messengers	Sources
JOHN	1209–10	15	0		Rot de Liberate ac de Misis
	1212–13	16	0		Misae Roll. Cole's Records
HENRY III	1220–1	11	0		Rot Lit. Cl. I, 444
		12	0		Receipt roll 4
	1221–2	11	0		Rot Lit. Cl. I, 484
	1222–3	9	0		Ibid. I, 527
	1223–4	13	0		Ibid. I, 580
	1236–7	18	0		Pipe roll 81 Enrolled wardrobe account
	1237–8	17	0		Ibid.
	1252–3	4	15		E.A. 308/1
	1259–61	9			Cl.R. (1259–1261)
	1264–5	18	19		E.A. 308/2
EDWARD I	1277–8	13	15	Exch. 2 Nuncii	E.A. 308/4 Add. MS. 36762
	1284–6	10	27		E.A. 351/17; 308/8
	1288–9	14	33	Chanc. 1 Nuncius 1 C.	E.A. 308/10
	1289–91	13	27	Exch. 1 Nuncius Chanc. 1 Nuncius, 2 C.	E.A. 352/24; I.R. 66
	1296–7	14	41	Exch. 3 Nuncii, 3 C.	Add. MS. 7965
	1299–1300	14	29	Exch. 2 Nuncii	Lib. Quot. Gard. E.A. 357/21
	1303–4	17	28	Exch. 1 Nuncius, 4 C.	Add. MS. 8835
EDWARD II	1307–8	6	30	Exch. 1 C.	E.A. 373/15
	1310–11	12	24	Exch. 2 C.	E.A. 374/2, 7, 8; 373/30; Nero C VIII f. 30 v; I.R. 155
	1315–6	9	16	Exch. 7 C.	E.A. 376/7; I.R. 176, 178, 180
	1319–20	8	28		Add. MS. 17362; E.A. 378/4; I.R. 189, 191
	1323–4	10	30	Exch. 3 C.	E.A. 379/19; I.R. 205, 207
	1325–6	12	37	Exch. 2 C.	E.A. 381/14, 11; I.R. 217, 218

Date	Nuncii regis	Cokini or Cursores	Chancery or Exchequer Messengers	Sources
EDWARD III 1330–2	10	22	Exch. 10 C.	E.A. 385/2, 4; 385/16; I.R. 252, 255, 256
1334–6	11	52	Exch. 8 C.	E.A. 387/9; Nero C VIII f. 285–293 v; I.R. 276, 281, 284
1340–2	21	46	Exch. 3 C.	E.A. 389/8; I.R. 313, 317, 320
1350–4	21	30	Exch. 1 C.	E.A. 392/12, 326/2; I.R. 353, 355, 358, 359, 364, 368
1359–61	19	17		E.A. 393/11; 309/11; I.R. 395, 396, 400, 401
1361–2	14	13		I.R. 409, 410
1365–7	8	15		E.A. 315/1, 396/2; I.R. 421, 422, 425, 427
1368–70	7	18	'divers' messengers Chanc. Nuncii & C.	E.A. 315/25, 33; I.R. 433, 434, 437, 438
1375–7	7	14	Exch. 2 C.	E.A. 316/40; 317/13, 40; 398/9; I.R. 456, 457, 459, 460

APPENDIX II

EXPENDITURE ON THE MESSENGER SERVICE

I. Wardrobe Expenditure on Messengers

*Includes expenses of solemn envoys as well as *nuncii*.
†Added by me.

Date	Amount £ s. d.			Source
HENRY III				
19 May 1234–28 Oct. 1234	16	3	4	Pipe roll No. 79
28 Oct. 1234–28 Oct. 1235	58	13	1	
28 Oct. 1235–3 May 1236	24	14	8½	
3 May 1236–27 Oct. 1236	67	12	10	Pipe roll No. 80
28 Oct. 1236–27 Oct. 1237	119	18	3½*	Pipe roll No. 81
28 Oct. 1237–6 Feb. 1238	9	16	9½	
6 Feb. 1238–27 Oct. 1238	183	9	2*	Pipe roll No. 83
28 Oct. 1238–27 Oct. 1239	152	17	3*	
28 Oct. 1239–4 Feb. 1240	82	18	8½*	

No accounts for Feb. 1240–Oct. 1241

28 Oct. 1241–28 Oct. 1242	140	4	5½*	Pipe roll No. 88
28 Oct. 1242–28 Oct. 1243	256	13	2*	
28 Oct. 1243–28 Oct. 1244	397	2	7½*	
28 Oct. 1244–14 Feb. 1245	97	5	9½*	
14 Feb. 1245–30 Sept. 1249 and				
30 Sept. 1249–14 Feb. 1252	811	3	7½	Pipe roll No. 95
17 Feb. 1252–28 Oct. 1252	49	7	0½	Chancellor's roll No. 45
24 June 1252–24 June 1253	65	16	1	E.A. 308/1

No accounts for June 1253–Jan. 1255

10 Jan. 1255–30 April 1256	209	14	0½*	Pipe roll No. 99

No accounts for 30 April 1256–28 Oct. 1257

28 Oct. 1257–25 July 1261	763	4	0½*	Enrolled account (W. and H.) No. 1
25 July 1261–31 Dec. 1264	571	0	5*	Pipe roll No. 113
1 Jan. 1265–6 Aug. 1265	13	5	10	Pipe roll No. 114 E.A. 308/2
6 Aug. 1265–3 March 1268	790	2	5*	Pipe roll No. 115
4 March 1268–4 Nov. 1272	469	8	7½*	Pipe roll No. 116

EDWARD I				
4 Nov. 1272–18 Oct. 1274	295	16	6*	Pipe roll No. 121 m22
18 Nov. 1274–20 Nov. 1275	44	8	7	Pipe roll No. 119 m22
20 Nov. 1275–20 Nov. 1276	58	14	8	Pipe roll No. 123 m23
20 Nov. 1276–20 Nov. 1277	46	10	9	*Ibid.* and E.A. 308/3 m23 d
20 Nov. 1277–20 Nov. 1278	44	0	1½	*Ibid.* and E.A. 308/4
20 Nov. 1278–20 Nov. 1279	68	15	1½	Pipe roll No. 124 m24

Date	Amount £ s. d.	Source
20 Nov. 1279–20 Nov. 1280	84 13 0½	*Ibid.* m30 d
Expenses in Wales 1281–5	70 14 9	Pipe roll No. 136 m31
	70 19 10	E.A. 308/5
20 Nov. 1283–20 Nov. 1284	67 4 7	E.A. 308/7
20 Nov. 1284–20 Nov. 1285	73 14 0	Pipe roll No. 136 m31
		E.A. 308/8
20 Nov. 1285–20 Nov. 1286	70 17 11	Pipe roll No. 136 m31
20 Nov. 1286–20 Nov. 1287	52 8 2	*Ibid.* m31 d
20 Nov. 1287–20 Nov. 1288	38 12 2	*Ibid.* m31 d
20 Nov. 1288–20 Nov. 1289	26 10 9½	Pipe roll No. 138 m26
	26 10 10½	E.A. 308/10
20 Nov. 1289–20 Nov. 1290	22 17 6½	Pipe roll No. 138 m26
		E.A. 308/12
20 Nov. 1290–20 Nov. 1291	82 11 2	Pipe roll No. 138 m25
20 Nov. 1291–20 Nov. 1292	41 2 7	Pipe roll No. 138 m26
20 Nov. 1292–20 Nov. 1293	46 17 1	Pipe roll No. 139 m6
20 Nov. 1293–20 Nov. 1294	79 3 5	Pipe roll No. 144 m20
20 Nov. 1294–20 Nov. 1295	84 3 7	Pipe roll No. 144 m20 d
20 Nov. 1295–20 Nov. 1296	102 16 7	*Ibid.* m22 and Chancellor's roll No. 92 m13
20 Nov. 1296–20 Nov. 1297	120 15 9½	Chancellor's roll No. 92 m13. Add. MS. 7965
20 Nov. 1297–20 Nov. 1298	116 14 0	Pipe roll No. 144 m22
No account for 1298–1299		
20 Nov. 1299–20 Nov. 1300	87 11 1	*Lib. Quot. Gard* p. 303
20 Nov. 1300–20 Nov. 1301	83 8 6	Add. MS. 7966. f. 128 v. E.A. 360/25 m1.
No account for 1301–1303		
20 Nov. 1303–20 Nov. 1304	87 6 0	Add. MS. 8835.
No account for 1304–1305		
20 Nov. 1305–20 Nov. 1306	103 8 10	E.A. 369/11
No account for 20 Nov. 1306–8 July 1307		

EDWARD II

Date	Amount	Source
8 July 1307–7 July 1308	120 10 11	Pipe roll No. 168
No accounts for July 1308–July 1310		
8 July 1310–14 Feb. 1311 and 14 Feb. 1311–7 July 1311	62 18 5†	Journals E.A. 374/7 and 373/30
No accounts for July 1311–Sept. 1313		
29 Sept. 1313–30 July 1314	303 14 0*	Enrolled account (W. and H.) No. 2 m4.
31 July 1313–4 July 1314	13 8 7	E.A. 375/9
No accounts for August 1314–Nov. 1314		
1 Dec. 1314–7 July 1315	26 13 2	Pipe roll No. 166
8 July 1315–31 Jan. 1316	47 7 1	E.A. 376/7
1 Feb. 1316–7 July 1316	23 2 1	Enrolled account (W. and H.) No. 2 m. 1 d and 17 d.
7 July 1316–7 July 1317	85 19 3	*Ibid.* m. 18 and 1 d
7 July 1317–7 July 1318	85 17 11	*Ibid.* m. 1 d. and 18
7 July 1318–7 July 1319	63 2 0	*Ibid.* m. 1 d. and 18

Date	Amount £ s. d.	Source
7 July 1319–7 July 1320	63 2 9	*Ibid*. m. 2 and 18 Add. MS. 17362
7 July 1320–7 July 1321	55 19 4	Enrolled account (W. and H.) No. 2 m. 2 and 18 Add. MS. 9931
7 July 1321–7 July 1322	104 8 11	Enrolled account (W. and H.) No. 2 m. 2 and 18
1 May 1321–8 July 1323 and 8 July 1323–19 Oct. 1323	176 1 11	*Ibid*. m. 20
8 July 1323–17 Oct. 1323	18 12 7	Stowe 553
20 Oct. 1323–7 July 1324	17 17 2	Enrolled account (W. and H.) No. 2 m. 22
8 July 1324–7 July 1325	48 4 11	*Ibid*. m. 24 E.A. 381/4
8 July 1325–7 July 1326	79 14 11	Enrolled accounts (W. and H.) No. 2 m. 26
	69 14 8	E.A. 381/14
8 July 1326–1 Nov. 1326	18 9 0	Enrolled accounts (W. and H.) No. 2 m. 26 E.A. 382/6
1 Nov. 1326–16 Jan. 1328	56 19 8	E.A. 382/9

EDWARD III

Date	Amount £ s. d.	Source
1 Nov. 1326–20 Aug. 1328	74 9 2	Enrolled account (W. and H.) No. 2 m. 27
25 Jan. 1328–19 Aug. 1328	19 7 2	E.A. 383/15 and 20
21 Aug. 1328–23 Sept. 1329	18 16 6	Enrolled account (W. and H.) No. 2 m. 30
24 Sept. 1329–26 Oct. 1331 (24 Sept.–25 Jan. 1330 £12 14s. 3d. 25 Jan.–25 Jan. 1331 £40 17s. 11d. 25 Jan.–26 Oct. 1331 £44 16s. 9d.)	98 9 9	*Ibid*. m. 32
16 Oct. 1331–29 Sept. 1332	4 11 0	Chancellor's roll No. 125 m. 41 d
29 Sept. 1332–29 Sept. 1333	28 11 1	Chancellor's roll No. 125 m. 41 d Enrolled account (W. and H.) No. 2 m. 34 d
29 Sept. 1333–30 July 1334	53 0 1	*Ibid*. No. 2 m. 35
31 July 1334–31 Aug. 1337	147 8 4	*Ibid*. m. 36
6 Oct. 1334–29 July 1335	53 0 1	E.A. 387/9 (Foreign exp.)
31 Aug. 1337–11 July 1338	62 7 3	E.A. 388/5 and Enrolled account (W. and H.) No. 2 m. 37
12 July 1338–27 May 1340 (1338–9 £61 12s. 6d. 1339–1340 £118 7s. 2d. 1340 £44 16s. 11d.)	306 1 7	*Ibid*. m. 38 and Misc. Bks. Exch. T.R. 203
27 May 1340–25 Nov. 1341	146 4 10	Enrolled account (W. and H.) No. 2 m. 40
25 Nov. 1341–11 April 1344 (15 Nov. 1341–Nov. 1342 £50 15s. 3d. Nov. 1342–Nov. 1343 £13 8s. 8d. Nov. 1343–April 1344 £5 11s. 7d.†)	69 15 6	*Ibid*. m. 40 d. and Misc. bks. E.T.R. 204

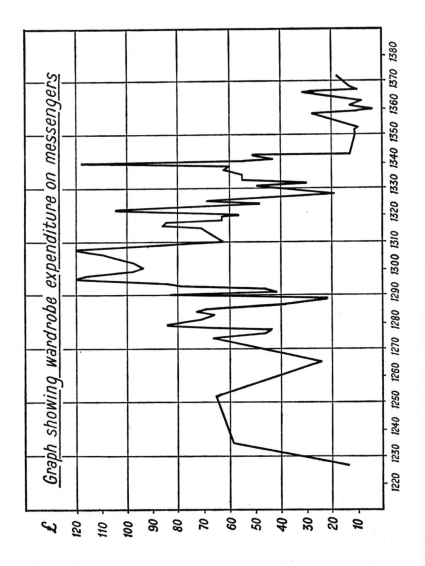

Graph showing wardrobe expenditure on messengers

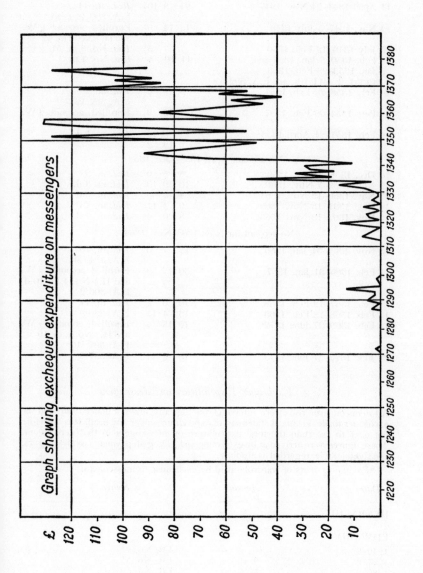

Date	Amount £ s. d.	Source
11 April 1344–24 Nov. 1347	94 8 10½	*Ibid.*. m. 41
		E.A. 390/12 f. 45
24 Nov. 1347–5 July 1349	13 14 6	Enrolled account (W. and H.) No. 2 m. 42
5 July 1349–13 Feb. 1350	7 7 5	*Ibid.* No. 3 m. 51
14 Feb. 1350–5 Jan. 1353 and	11 10 4	*Ibid.* No. 4 m. 1
5 Jan. 1353–23 Feb. 1353		
(1351–2 £11 10s. 4d. E.A. 392/5)		
23 Feb. 1353–22 Feb. 1354	9 19 6	*Ibid.* m. 2
		E.A. 392/12
23 Feb. 1354–26 Feb. 1357	127 15 9	Enrolled account (W. and H.) No. 4 m. 2
6 Feb. 1357–21 April 1358	13 9 10	*Ibid.* m. 1 d.
	8 18 2	

No account April 1358–Dec. 1358

Date	Amount £ s. d.	Source
16 Dec. 1358–3 Nov. 1359	28 5 0	*Ibid.* m. 3
3 Nov. 1359–7 Nov. 1360	10 9 10	*Ibid.* m. 3 d.
7 Nov. 1360–13 Nov. 1361	4 3 0	*Ibid.* m. 5 d
14 Nov. 1361–13 Nov. 1362	9 4 11	*Ibid.* m. 7 d
13 Nov. 1362–13 Nov. 1363	8 0 4	*Ibid.* m. 7 d

No account for Nov. 1363–Nov. 1364

Date	Amount £ s. d.	Source
13 Nov. 1364–31 Jan. 1366	17 7 0	*Ibid.* m. 10
		E.A. 394/20
1 Feb. 1366–31 Jan. 1367	30 17 3	Enrolled accounts (W. and H.) No. 4 m. 10 d
		E.A. 396/2
1 Feb. 1367–12 Feb. 1368	10 0 4	*Ibid.* m. 11
13 Feb. 1368–12 Feb. 1369	13 4 11	E.A. 396/9
13 Feb. 1369–27 June 1372	10 18 4	Enrolled account (W. and H.) No. 4. m. 19
		E.A. 396 /10
27 June 1372–27 June 1373	18 2 4	E.A. 397/5

2. *Exchequer Expenditure on Messengers*

All items on issue rolls were entered chronologically, and not under *tituli*; and the exchequer made no annual statement of expenditure under any head. It is therefore not easy to ascertain the total expenditure on messengers in that department. These figures were arrived at by extracting and adding all payments to messengers, and should not be regarded as absolute.

*Excluding debts of wardrobe paid by exchequer to messengers.

Date	Amount £ s. d.	Source
HENRY III		
EDWARD I		
1272–3	5 0	I.R. No. 21
1287–8	2 13 4	I.R. No. 57
1288–9	1 0 0	I.R. No. 59
1290–1	4 19 3	I.R. Nos. 66, 67, 70, 71
1292–3	2 5 0	I.R. Nos. 76, 79
1293–4	2 4 6	I.R. No 85
1294–5	13 7 11	I.R. Nos. 91, 95, 96, 99
1298–9	13 6	I.R. No. 105

Date	Amount £ s. d.			Source

EDWARD II

Date	£	s.	d.	Source
1314–5	7	17	2	I.R. Nos. 172, 175
1315–6	5	2	6	I.R. Nos. 176, 178, 180
1317–8		1	0	I.R. No. 183
1318–9	4	18	4	I.R. Nos. 186, 187
1319–20	16	5	6	I.R. Nos. 189, 191
1320–1		1	5	I.R. No. 195
1321–2	4	3	3	I.R. Nos. 197, 198, 199.
1322–3	5	5	11	I.R. Nos. 200, 202, 203
1324–5		15	0	I.R. Nos. 211, 213
1325–6	6	13	3	I.R. Nos. 217, 218

EDWARD III

Date	£	s.	d.	Source
1326–7	3	17	10	I.R. Nos. 226, 231
1327–8	2	5	1	I.R. Nos. 232, 239
1328–9	1	8	8	I.R. Nos. 241, 243
1329–30		15	2	I.R. Nos. 247, 252
1330–1	3	0	4	I.R. Nos. 255, 256
1331–2	8	4	8	I.R. Nos. 261, 262
1332–3	16	8	10	I.R. Nos. 266, 269
1333–4	5	11	7	I.R. Nos. 274, 276
1334–5	52	2	11	I.R. Nos. 281, 284
1335–6	19	4	4	I.R. Nos. 287, 290
1336–7	32	8	7	I.R. Nos. 293, 295
1337–8	18	3	9	I.R. Nos. 297, 301
1338–9	27	9	0	I.R. Nos. 304, 306
1339–40	29	15	5	I.R. Nos. 307, 313
1340–1	11	17	7	I.R. Nos. 317, 320
1341–2	24	5	1	I.R. Nos. 321, 326
1342–3	66	6	$5\frac{1}{2}$	I.R. Nos. 327, 328
1343–4	82	13	5	I.R. Nos. 331, 334
1344–5	25	11	$11\frac{1}{2}$	I.R. No. 335 (Michaelmas term only)
1345–6	59	10	3	I.R. No. 336 (Michaelmas term only)
1346–7	52	18	$3\frac{1}{2}$	I.R. No. 339 (Michaelmas term only)
1347–8	91	5	$7\frac{1}{2}$	I.R. Nos. 340, 341
1348–9	48	2	5	I.R. Nos, 344. 348
1349–50	92	6	4	I.R. Nos. 350, 353*
1350–1	128	11	2	I.R. Nos. 355, 358
1351–2	110	15	9	I.R. Nos. 359, 364
1352–3	52	11	2	I.R. Nos. 365, 368
1353–4	79	11	$1\frac{1}{2}$	I.R. Nos. 373, 374
1354–5	118	4	3	I.R. Nos. 376, 377
1355–6	131	18	$8\frac{1}{2}$	I.R. Nos. 378, 380
1356–7	131	14	$0\frac{1}{2}$	I.R. Nos. 382, 386, 387
1357–8	55	16	$5\frac{1}{2}$	I.R. Nos. 390, 393
1358–9	72	13	$5\frac{1}{2}$	I.R. Nos. 395, 396
1359–60	85	4	$10\frac{1}{2}$	I.R. Nos. 400, 401
1360–1	67	19	7	I.R. Nos. 406, 407, 408
1361–2	64	8	$9\frac{1}{2}$	I.R. Nos. 409, 410
1362–3	54	2	10	I.R. Nos. 412, 415
1363–4	45	15	3	I.R. Nos. 417, 419
1364–5	57	17	6	I.R. Nos. 421, 422
1365–6	38	0	8	I.R. Nos. 425, 427
1366–7	62	7	10	I.R. Nos. 429, 431
1367–8	52	3	3	I.R. Nos. 433, 434

Date	Amount £ s. d.	Source
1368–9	117 12 5	I.R. Nos. 436, 438
1369–70	183 9 9	*I.R. of Thomas de Brantingham*
1370–1	85 11 7	I.R. Nos. 441, 443
1371–2	103 3 5	I.R. Nos. 444, 446
1372–3	89 13 8	I.R. Nos. 447, 449
1373–4	104 3 7	I.R. Nos. 451, 455
1374–5	110 9 2	I.R. Nos. 456, 457
1375–6	128 7 8	I.R. Nos. 459, 460
1376–7	91 19 10	I.R. Nos. 460, 462

APPENDIX III

LONDON MESSENGERS

THE king's *nuncii* and *cursores* were not the only men who could call themselves professional messengers. There were besides the common messengers of London and some other large towns, who hired out their services. Some of these may once have been feudal messengers holding land by the service of summoning suitors to the manor court, or taking four message carryings in Lent, or similar petty duties.[1] Others may have been landless villeins eager for work, men who had acquired their freedom by living in the city for the customary year and a day; or, like the king's messengers, they may have come from younger sons of more substantial householders. A similar type of professional messenger was found abroad in places like Avignon where innkeepers or messenger masters engaged couriers, and hired out their services to clients.[2] University cities such as Paris had common messengers[3], sometimes semi-official ones nominated by the rector but depending for a living on the fees paid by students who wanted to send home the sort of letters quoted by Miss Waddell in *The Wandering Scholars*. Mercantile communities such as the Flemish towns preferred to appoint permanent town messengers, a practice which may have cost more, but was probably more reliable. When Edward III was in Flanders and Zealand in 1351[4], he hired one Arnald, *nuncius de Middelburgh* and two others from the same town, who were probably the official letter carriers for that thriving community, so well known to Chaucer's shipman.

By the fourteenth century, there were a number of these common messengers in the service of the City of London. It is not clear from references in the issue rolls whether they were partially in the pay of the City, like the Flemish messengers, or independent of control. They seem to have worked for private citizens, but were occasionally hired by the government from 1309 onwards. The issue roll for 1309–10 names twelve London couriers, nine of whom were again taking official letters in the following year.[5] During the king's absence in

[1]H. S. Bennett *Life in the English Manor* p. 70. An example of this villein messenger service is given in an assignment of dower in 1316 (*C.C.R.* 1313–1318 p. 349); and the prevalence of the practice in England is shown by the frequent appearance of the surname 'messenger' in chancery enrolments.

[2]Yves Renouard *Revue Historique* CLXXX, 1–22.

[3]Georges D'Avenel *L'Evolution des Moyens de Transport* pp. 70, 145–6.

[4]I.R. 358.

[5]I.R. 152; E.A. 374/2.

April 1310, Richard le Mercer, courier of London, was sent to Berwick by the Council: incidentally his surname gives an indication of the class he came from.[1] In the next decade, London messengers were mentioned more frequently. Eight were hired in 1313–14, seven took out commissions of the peace and business letters in 1314–15; two were employed in 1315–16 and nine in 1319–20.[2] Writs for parliament were sent out 'by the hands of divers London messengers' in 1321, and two messengers 'de la Charing' were paid in 1324.[3] Whenever such men were hired, they were carefully distinguished in the accounts from the ordinary royal messengers; and were not paid by the wardrobe but by the exchequer, even during the period of wardrobe supremacy.Edward II's messenger service was not reduced by the Ordainers but it had no chance to expand, though the number of writs and letters sent out was increasing yearly. This probably explains the use of outside men to deal with rush jobs, such as the summoning of a parliament. It is noteworthy that under Edward III the number of king's messengers increased considerably, and the payment of outside messengers ceased until the very end of the reign, when once again the regular service was cut, and money for 'divers messengers and couriers and others of the towns of Westminster and London' had to be accounted for on the issue rolls. In August 1369 they took out writs for a levy, and in December 1369 summoned the barons of England to the queen's funeral.[4]

A few casual references to messengers from other towns may be cited. Adam and Ralph, couriers of York, were employed in 1317 and 1323–4, while Thomas Hamond, courier of York, figured in the roll for 1373.[5] William of Bristol was messenger of the town of Chichester about the same time, William Sparewe messenger of Lincoln came into a file of miscellaneous messenger payments, and William Stanley was mentioned as a courier to Westminster, in addition to the unnamed men working there in 1369.[6]

A little more light is thrown on the London messengers by the entries, in the appendix to Archbishop Sudbury's register, relating to the excommunication of John of Stratton, 'corsour of the City of London.'[7] The aid of the secular authorities was prayed against John in May 1374, and he was confined for the next six days in Newgate

[1]I.R. 158.
[2]I.R. 170; 172; 175; 176; 180; 191.
[3]Add. MS. 9951 f. 36 v; I.R. 207.
[4]I.R. 438 m. 36; *Issue Roll of Thomas de Brantingham* p. 408.
[5]Society of Antiquaries MS. 121 p. 96; Stowe MS. 553 f. 129 v and I.R. 200; I.R. 449.
[6]I.R. 456 (1374–5); E.A. 317/40 (1377–8).
[7]*Registrum Simonis de Sudbiria* (Canterbury and York Society) II, 140 Appendix III (Acts not entered in the register). There are unfortunately no Gaol Delivery rolls for this year in which John's imprisonment might have been noticed. I am indebted to Professor H. Johnstone for this reference to a London courier outside the accounts of exchequer and wardrobe.

prison until he submitted and took an oath to stand to the commands of the church. He was then absolved. His fate is unknown, and even his original offence is not stated; it is impossible to tell whether he had fallen foul of the ecclesiastical authorities for expressing his opinions too freely and entertaining Lollard views, or merely for neglecting to pay his tithes and duties to his parish priest. His profession at least was accepted as commonplace; and there seems little doubt that several English towns already possessed a rudimentary postal service in the fourteenth century. The services offered were at the command of any citizen who could pay the messenger's fee; they were uncontrolled by either king or commune. Such messengers were a convenience to the expanding trade of the city, and occasionally useful to the government, but of no real administrative importance. When all the evidence has been put together, it amounts to very little; and no outside messenger agency infringed in any serious degree the monopoly of the king's messengers.

INDEX OF PERSONS

INDEX OF PLACES